SOCIAL COST-BENEFIT ANALYSIS IN AUSTRALIA AND NEW ZEALAND

THE STATE OF CURRENT PRACTICE AND WHAT NEEDS TO BE DONE

SOCIAL COST-BENEFIT ANALYSIS IN AUSTRALIA AND NEW ZEALAND

THE STATE OF CURRENT PRACTICE AND WHAT NEEDS TO BE DONE

Leo Dobes, Joanne Leung and George Argyrous

Australian National University

PRESS

ANU PRESS

the Australia and New Zealand
School of Government

Published by ANU Press
The Australian National University
Acton ACT 2601, Australia
Email: anupress@anu.edu.au
This title is also available online at press.anu.edu.au

National Library of Australia Cataloguing-in-Publication entry

Creator: Dobes, Leo, author.

Title: Social cost-benefit analysis in Australia and New Zealand :
                    the state of current practice and what
                    needs to be done / Leo Dobes, Joanne
                    Leung, George Argyrous.

ISBN: 9781760460198 (paperback) 9781760460204 (ebook)

Series: ANZSOG series.

Subjects: Cost effectiveness--Social aspects.
                    Public administration--Australia.
                    Public administration--New Zealand.

Other Creators/Contributors:
                    Leung, Joanne, author.
                    Argyrous, George, 1963- author.

Dewey Number: 352.439

Cover design and layout by ANU Press. Cover photographs adapted from:
150124-construction-area-work-site by r. nial bradshaw, www.flickr.com/photos/
zionfiction/16173386649/ and *2010_1310 - Coins_3* by Ben Hosking, www.flickr.
com/photos/benhosking/5077118332/.

Contents

Foreword

As towns and cities grow, pressure on infrastructure increases, from schools and hospitals to utilities and transport. As always, resources available to governments are limited. Prudent choices are therefore essential.

Interviews with government officials and surveys of members of the New Zealand Government Economics Network and the Economic Society of Australia revealed some not inconsiderable disquiet about the use — and non-use — of cost-benefit analysis (CBA) in government decision-making.

Like any analytical tool, CBA can be misused, but it remains the most rigorous method available to assist decision-makers. It is the central tenet of this monograph — supported by survey results — that one practical means of improving quality is to harmonise the framework that is used for CBA in the various Australian and New Zealand jurisdictions. Greater transparency — through publication of all CBA studies commissioned by governments — is an important complement to harmonisation, albeit one requiring a degree of political courage.

Discount rates are typically the focus of those promoting analytical consistency in CBA. But results can also be sensitive to input variables such as travel time, the depressive effect of taxes or loans used to fund infrastructure, and the application of risk analysis. Recognising this, the following pages argue for a comprehensive systematisation of the framework used for CBA.

Dr Leo Dobes (Crawford School of Public Policy, The Australian National University) is the primary author of the publication. Dr George Argyrous (Australia and New Zealand School of Government and University of New South Wales) was the principal author of Chapter 2 (with econometric analysis contributed by Dr Patrick Doupe, Crawford

School) and Appendix 7. Ms Joanne Leung (New Zealand Ministry of Transport) authored appendices 4 and 5, and provided input to other chapters.

Professor John Wanna
Sir John Bunting Chair of Public Administration
The Australian National University

Acknowledgements

The authors wish to acknowledge the government officials in Australia and New Zealand who generously made time for the interviews on which many of the conclusions in this volume are based. Many of them declined acknowledgement or requested anonymity, so none have been identified individually. The authors are nevertheless grateful to them all.

A large measure of thanks is also due to the Economic Society of Australia (ESA) and the New Zealand Government Economics Network for their assistance in the conduct of the survey of their members. Dr Matthew Butlin (ESA President), Dr Richard Tooth (President, ESA NSW) and Ms Diane Litherland (Administrator, ESA) assisted generously with their time in the process of conducting the survey. Sara Rahman (Australia and New Zealand School of Government) helpfully compiled the survey data.

Particular thanks are due to the Australia and New Zealand School of Government for its grant of research funding as part of its priority research theme of 'cross-jurisdictional policymaking'.

Professor Andrew Podger (Honorary Professor of Public Policy, College of Arts and Social Sciences, The Australian National University) and Dr Richard Tooth provided invaluable comment on a pre-publication manuscript. Sam Vincent helped read and steer the manuscript through the publication process.

While the authors accept responsibility for the contents of this monograph, they are most grateful for the very useful respective contributions of all those involved.

Leo Dobes
Joanne Leung
George Argyrous

.

Acronyms and abbreviations

ABS	Australian Bureau of Statistics
ANZSOG	Australia and New Zealand School of Government
ATC	Australian Transport Council
AWE	average weekly earnings
BCA	benefit-cost analysis (US usage; see also CBA)
BCR	benefit-cost ratio
BITRE	Bureau of Infrastructure, Transport and Regional Economics
CAPM	capital asset pricing model
CBA	cost-benefit analysis (Australia, NZ and UK usage; see also BCA)
CEA	cost-effectiveness analysis
CGE	computable general equilibrium
CM	choice modelling
CO_2	carbon dioxide
$CO_2(e)$	carbon dioxide equivalent (greenhouse gas)
CVM	contingent valuation method
DALY	disability adjusted life years
DTF	Department of Treasury and Finance
EAV	equivalent annual value
EEM	*Economic Evaluation Manual*
EJD	effective job density
ESA	Economic Society of Australia
EVRI	Environmental Valuation Reference Inventory
GAM	goals-achievement matrix
GDP	gross domestic product

GEN	Government Economics Network (New Zealand)
GVA	gross value added
IAM	integrated assessment model
LUTI	land use transport interaction
MCA	multi-criteria analysis
METB	marginal excess tax burden (deadweight loss)
NBIR	net benefit investment ratio
NBN	National Broadband Network
NGOs	non-government organisations
NPV	net present value
OBPR	Office of Best Practice Regulation
OC	opportunity cost
OECD	Organisation for Economic Cooperation and Development
QALY	quality adusted life years
RFT	request for tender
RIA	regulatory impact assessment
RIS	regulatory impact statement
SLA	statistical local area
SOC	social opportunity cost
SRTP	social rate of time preference
TGV	train a grand vitesse
TTB	travel time budget
VLY	value of a life year
VOSL	value of statistical life
WEB	wider economic benefit
WEI	wider economic impact
WTA	willingness to accept
WTP	willingness to pay

Tables and figures

1

Introduction

Economics is about choice. The resources available to society — from people, machines and materials to environment goods — are limited. Scarcity means that using a specific resource for one project or policy will preclude its availability for alternative uses.

Project funding should thus be considered against the context of missed opportunities. At the most confronting level, a decision-maker may need to ask how many people will die because the government spent money to reduce bushfire hazards (e.g. Ashe et al., 2012), for example, rather than providing more diagnostic equipment in hospitals. As Gittins (2015) observes, 'the moral of opportunity cost is: since you can't have everything, choose carefully'.

It is a primary role of governments to direct social resources to where they will most benefit the community as a whole. Cost-benefit analysis (CBA) can be used to assist governments in making relevant decisions. While it should not be seen as replacing common sense, or political judgement, it is an important tool in ensuring that government is informed of the costs and benefits to society of proposed actions.

Although it is difficult to formulate a concise, non-technical definition of CBA, however, its objective can be summarised as the assessment of proposed public projects, policies or regulations to determine whether their social benefits exceed their social costs. Chapter 4 describes the technique of CBA as a series of sequential steps.

The basic decision rule in CBA is that the additional social benefits should exceed the additional social costs, even if some members of society may be adversely affected by a project. Social cost-benefit analysis is the most systematic and rigorous tool for informing decision-makers of the likely net benefits of a policy, program or project.

In principle, CBA can be applied to virtually any project or policy. Examples include reducing blood alcohol limits for drivers (Leung, 2013), addressing gambling addiction (Productivity Commission, 1999), including health warnings on tobacco products (Abelson, 2003a), phasing out lightweight plastic bags (Allen Consulting, 2006), pursuing water fluoridation (Doessel, 1979), climate change mitigation (Garnaut, 2008), and preservation of river red gum forests through improved environmental water flows (Bennett, 2008). In practice, it is generally easier to estimate the costs and benefits of infrastructure projects, such as a dam (Saddler et al., 1980) or a transport improvement (Tsolakis et al., 1991), than less tangible elements, such as the effect on national pride or esprit de corps of a country that proposes to host the Olympic or Commonwealth games (Moore et al., 2010). It is for this reason that pedagogic presentations of CBA tend to use infrastructure projects as examples.

The terms 'economic analysis', 'economic appraisal' and 'economic evaluation' are sometimes used as substitutes for 'cost-benefit analysis'. The term cost-benefit analysis itself is a shortened form of the more descriptive 'social cost-benefit analysis', which indicates that conventional CBA automatically includes all social elements of a proposal — financial, environmental and social — from the perspective of all the actors in a society. While these alternative terms may have specialised meanings in some bureaucracies or disciplines, they are generally used interchangeably in the literature, and have been treated as being equivalent in this monograph. A slight difference in the United States is usage of the term 'benefit-cost analysis' (BCA) or 'social benefit-cost analysis'.

North American textbooks typically ascribe the emergence of the official use of CBA to the 1936 US *Flood Control Act*, although it has been argued that the antecedents of CBA in America extend back further in time (e.g. Reuss, 1992). The 1936 legislation contained the now-famous phrase that flood-control projects should proceed 'if the benefits to whomsoever they may accrue are in excess of the estimated cost, and if the lives and social security of people are otherwise adversely affected'. Several presidential executive orders in the last three decades have extended and strengthened requirements for Federal US agencies to undertake economic appraisals for projects and regulatory proposals.

1.1 Economic evaluation in Australia

Economic appraisal of projects has firm roots in Australia. In evidence to a committee of the Victorian Parliament discussing railways legislation in 1871, the responsible engineer provided a detailed exposition of the application of discounted cash flow methodology (*Evidence Taken at the Bar of the Legislative Council* ..., 1871, appendices K & L). His example demonstrated that it would be cheaper to build a wooden viaduct that would last for only 10 years and rebuild it every decade thereafter, than to build a stone structure with steel girders that would last for 100 years.

In examining proposals for gauge unification prior to Federation, the colonial railways commissioners drew on rudimentary economic appraisals (Dobes, 2008). Studies were published by academics (e.g. Webb & McMaster, 1975) and on behalf of government (see Sinden & Thampapillai, 1995, app. 1) intermittently during the latter part of the 20th century (mainly for a couple of decades from the 1960s), which was the heyday of CBA in Australia.

Australian governments, including at the federal level, however, have been diffident at best in requiring economic appraisals of projects and regulatory measures. There is no statutory equivalent in Australia to the 1936 US *Flood Control Act* to require analysis of social costs and benefits of policy or project proposals. The Commonwealth Treasury (1966) published an information bulletin supplement that outlined the essentials of CBA and, in 1988, New South Wales became the first government in Australia to require all proposals by all agencies for new capital projects to be supported by an economic appraisal (pers. comm. NSW Treasury, 20 August 2015).

Upon taking office, new governments have on occasion announced that Cabinet would only consider expenditure proposals supported by an economic appraisal. These good intentions have been wont to fall into abeyance, particularly as senior or politically influential ministers have often been able to gain prime ministerial approval to have their submissions considered 'under the table' in Cabinet, thus circumventing any prescribed evaluation processes.

Further, projects are necessarily submitted by ministers to Cabinet at different times during the life of a government. They cannot, therefore, be compared at the same time, with only the best ones being chosen. Clearly, standards of some sort are required to ensure a degree of intertemporal comparability. One commonplace standard is that net present value (NPV) exceed zero, or the benefit-cost ratio (BCR) should exceed one. In the absence of a harmonised approach, however, the calculation of the components of NPVs and BCRs can be manipulated in different ways, limiting their utility as decision rules (see also Chapter 5). It is therefore something of a mystery how the Cabinets of state and national governments can validly compare the relative merits of different proposals.

A potential source of public cynicism about government appraisal of major projects is the avoidance of CBA entirely, even for major projects that generate negative externalities. One means of avoiding undertaking a CBA that captures the effect of a project on the whole affected community is to establish so-called community consultation groups.

In 2011, for example, the Australian Government established such groups (Department of Infrastructure and Transport, 2011) to ostensibly allow 'Australians to have a bigger say in the planning and operation of ... airports'. Australian airports are able to seek approval for major changes of use through the development of 20-year master plans, without CBA. The private sector lessees of Canberra Airport, for example, obtained approval (Truss, 2015) to introduce international flights in a curfew-free situation. Given the obvious potential for large aircraft to increase noise disturbance for residents of Canberra and Queanbeyan, it is disconcerting that, in this case, social costs have been ignored in policy formulation.

1.2 Regulatory impact statements

Australian Government processes that are intended to ensure rigorous evaluation of proposals for regulatory measures have fared little better than general economic appraisal. The Office of Regulation Review was established in 1986 and succeeded by the Office of Best Practice Regulation (OBPR), which issued detailed guidelines on conducting a CBA. Harrison (2009, pp. 44–45) pinpointed the reasons for the flawed nature of the processes involved:

> Many regulations (such as delegated legislation) do not go to Cabinet, and can be passed without OBPR approval. Whether a Department that does so is declared non-compliant depends on OBPR staff detecting regulations that should have been subject to an RIA [regulatory impact assessment] process. There is not much incentive to declare regulations that have already been passed as non-compliant, as this could upset the Department and Minister, and potentially embarrass the government. Not only is it easier (and less work) to declare a regulation compliant with (or exempt from) the RIA process, it is difficult for the conscientious to see any positive results from declaring a passed regulation non-compliant. The only sanction is an increased non-compliant proportion of the Department's regulations in the OBPR Annual Report (a fact which may even be seen to reflect badly on the OBPR and the RIA process if it is in fact noticed by anyone) … Likewise, life is more difficult for an OBPR officer if an RIS [regulatory impact statement] is declared inadequate. Rejections are scrutinised closely; acceptances are not. Pressure on the junior staff can include irate telephone calls to their supervisor from a Departmental Secretary or Minister. The result is the so-called tick-and-flick mentality.

Detailed CBA guidelines were removed from the OBPR website soon after the transfer of the OBPR from the Department of Finance to the Department of Prime Minister and Cabinet following the September 2013 election. The guidelines were replaced by the *Australian Government Guide to Regulation* (Commonwealth of Australia, 2014), which is focused specifically on the regulatory impact statement (RIS) process.

The current *Guide to Regulation* presents a general framework template for appraising proposed regulations. Although it requires an evaluation of the net benefit of the proposed regulation, it adopts triple bottom line language and an approach that recommends assessing impacts such as 'lower prices ... improved productivity or the creation of new jobs' to 'achieve some form of desirable social outcome'. Quantification of benefits and costs is specified in terms of 'business, community organisations and individuals to a level of detail commensurate with the impact of the policy proposal'. It therefore bears little relationship to a rigorous, conventional CBA.

The scope for CBA to be used in decision-making has recently been expanded by a number of jurisdictions. Queensland Government (2014), New South Wales Government (2013) and the Western Australian Program Evaluation Unit (2015) are examples of whole of government evaluation frameworks that refer explicitly to both cost-effectiveness and CBA as relevant types of summative evaluation approaches. These frameworks tie funding for a program to the adoption of explicit plans for how the program will be assessed in terms of effectiveness and efficiency. Such evaluation plans are increasingly including CBAs to address the issue of allocative efficiency.

1.3 Economic evaluation in New Zealand

Like Australia, New Zealand has a long history of economic appraisal of projects, and all regulatory and legislative proposals require completion and publication of a RIS. Initially used for major highway improvements, the use of CBA was extended in the 1980s to all road projects. The New Zealand Transport Agency (2013) *Economic Evaluation Manual (EEM)* provides a set of detailed input variable values for use in transport analysis, with update factors published regularly.

The New Zealand Treasury has developed expertise in CBA over the years. It provides evaluation and assessment guidelines to government departments on how to complete CBAs and regulation impact statements. It updated its 2005 *Guide to Social Cost Benefit Analysis* (the *Guide*) in July 2015 (New Zealand Treasury, 2015). The *Guide* (pp. 48–49) covers the principal aspects of CBA, specifies values for discount rates and the value of statistical life, as well as specifying a factor of 20 per cent of project costs to allow for the deadweight loss of taxes where a project is funded by general taxation.

However, the *Guide* (p. 45) also outlines a living standards framework that is intended to complement a CBA, if not already taken into account in the CBA. The living standards framework promoted by the Treasury has the following five elements:

- economic growth (intended as a proxy for increases in overall economic welfare, which is what CBA tries to measure)
- sustainability for the future (usually taken to refer to impacts on climate change, biodiversity and loss of natural habitat, but can also refer to fiscal sustainability)
- increasing equity (usually taken to refer to ensuring there is a safety net, to reducing income inequality and to achieving procedural fairness)
- social infrastructure (refers to institutional structures and customs that underpin the way society works. They reduce the transaction costs of doing business, of securing one's income and property, and of social interactions)
- managing risks.

It is not clear from the *Guide*, however, how these principles are practically implemented during Cabinet consideration of project proposals, or why the underlying principles would not have already been taken into account in a social cost-benefit analysis.

1.4 Confusion and opaqueness in the area of economic evaluation

An instructive comment made by an agency in one Australian jurisdiction during background research for this volume was that politicians often call for a CBA, but few, if any, actually understand what a CBA is. The same appears to be true of many public servants.

This raises the broader question of whether politicians can rely on the advice of public servants, or even on their advice regarding studies commissioned from specialist consultants. At the extreme, it raises the fundamental question of whether a minister who presents what is purported to be a CBA in support of legislation is guilty of misleading parliament if the analysis is not based firmly on established economic principles.

Clarke's (1995) examination of the abortive introduction of the Australia Card scheme illustrates the lack of even basic levels of expertise in the Australian Public Service. An excerpt is worth quoting at length:

> The over-enthusiasm of the Department [of Social Security] for the program is of historical interest. Of ongoing concern, however, was the Department's failure to apply conventional cost/benefit analysis principles to the exercise. Indeed, there was evidence of failure to even understand the concepts involved. In the 1992 [Annual] Report, for example, net present value techniques were not applied, hardware and maintenance costs were overlooked, no costs were imputed for the efforts of other agencies and clients (which in the case of a program of such wide scope is essential), and the bases on which savings were projected into the future were not stated. The most glaring error was the complete omission of the staff costs involved in 137,000 manual examinations of files, 18,000 actual reviews, 10,000 actions against clients, 1,300 queries by clients, 150 formal appeals, 1,500 debt recovery actions (of which 700 involved negotiations with the debtor), and 100 briefings of the Director of Public Prosecutions. This omission was despite statements that 'the real cost has been in the time and effort of staff administering the program' and 'the reporting requirements are stringent and a lot of time and effort is needed to comply with them' ...
>
> The Privacy Commissioner expressed similar concerns, albeit more gently ... An external audit [by the Australian National Audit Office] of the Parallel Data Matching Program also criticised the quality of cost/benefit analysis undertaken, and pointed out that the Act 'requires the tabling of a comprehensive report in both House of Parliament ... Sufficiently comprehensive cost/benefit information had not been included in either Report ... '

Clarke's example highlights the importance of requiring a rigorous and comprehensive analysis of social costs and benefits. More importantly, it demonstrates that mandating the use of rigorous cost-benefit (or other) analysis will not be effective unless the bureaucracy understands the underlying principles, and applies them of its own volition. Cultural factors are more important, therefore, than formal guidelines and rules.

In recent years, the term cost-benefit analysis has been appropriated by the financial sector, where it is now frequently used to refer to additional costs and revenues — in terms of cash flows alone — that are generated by a private sector (i.e. commercial) project. Such studies are based on financial, rather than economic values. Compounding the problem is the fact that media commentators rarely, if ever, explain their terminology. Confusion about the meaning of CBA is, therefore, understandable.

A further source of potential confusion is the fact that public projects and programs can validly be analysed from a number of different perspectives: government budgets, social CBA, a 'business case', off-budget financial analysis of a public–private partnership, or impact analysis. Any or all of these approaches may constitute valid analytical or presentational perspectives, depending on the purpose at hand. It is not always clear to non-technical audiences, however, which is being presented or why. The lack of technical understanding, compounded by a lack of clarity in usage, can spark debate that flows at cross-purposes because protagonists do not make sufficiently clear which perspective or technique is being discussed.

Possibly due to the complexity of social CBA, or simply in reaction to its perceived focus on economic efficiency alone, policymakers in many countries, including Australia, began to use multi-criteria analysis (MCA) from about the 1980s. Appendix 2 uses a road-widening example to illustrate why 'composite index' approaches like MCA are subjective and arbitrary (see also, Ergas, 2009; and Dobes & Bennett, 2009). Nevertheless, some government agencies present MCA as an alternative to CBA when it is felt that not all costs or benefits can be quantified (e.g. Government of Victoria, 2014, p. 14), or as a complementary approach that supplements perceived gaps in CBA. It is therefore not surprising that some public servants and politicians may be confused about the appropriateness of different methods of undertaking a project or policy appraisal.

1.5 What can be done to improve the use of economic evaluation?

Handbooks of CBA have been produced by a number of state agencies, as well as by the Commonwealth (Department of Finance and Administration, 2006). While these handbooks are useful, and help raise general awareness about the technique, they can provide only a summary of the theory and techniques available in more detailed textbooks and journal articles. Moreover, they generally tend to outline what *should* be done, but often neglect to address the issue of what should *not* be done.

Despite the existence of government manuals and handbooks that provide the basics of CBA, all does not seem to be well in terms of the application of CBA in the various jurisdictions. Chapter 2 reports the results of a survey of academics, public servants, non-government organisations and private sector (including consultants) individuals in Australia and New Zealand. Their responses indicate that CBA is not conducted independently and objectively, is used to 'justify rather than inform' and is not always undertaken on important decisions.

Almost two-thirds of survey respondents supported, with qualification, greater harmonisation of variable values and methodologies in CBA as a means of increasing consistency in analysis. A third or so supported the approach without qualification. Interviews with government officials in the various jurisdictions confirmed that there was some degree of underlying support for increased harmonisation, either to achieve better quality or to facilitate the use of CBA by agencies with limited expertise. Chapter 3, therefore, examines different possible approaches to harmonisation, but concludes that harmonising variable and parameter values or methodologies at a national or state level would require a level of effort that would be impracticable.

Chapter 4 proposes harmonisation of only the framework to be used for CBA. While such frameworks already exist in textbooks and many government manuals and handbooks, Chapter 4 proposes a framework that requires an increased level of consistency and transparency. For example, in the first step of specifying the objective of a project, a list of alternative means of achieving the objective is required, *as well as* the reasons for not including any of them in the CBA analysis. Similarly, where standard features like risk analysis are not used, an explicit explanation for the omission is required.

A 'belts and braces' approach is advocated in Chapter 5. Government handbooks are invariably authored by an official or consultant who is familiar with CBA and the emphasis tends to be on what ought to be done in carrying out an economic evaluation. True, warnings and caveats are typically included about issues like double counting or the limitations of benefit-cost ratios, but it is rare, for example, to see a comprehensive discussion on why the number of jobs created by a project should *not* be included in the CBA. At best, a handbook will indicate that issues such as job creation should be discussed separately to the CBA. While such advice is not incorrect, a non-expert may not fully appreciate the reason for it. To reduce the scope for potential error, an explicit explanation of erroneous approaches would assist in harmonising the quality of CBA studies.

Finally, a number of appendices have been included to assist readers who may wish to further explore some of the points made in the main chapters.

2

Professional perspectives on harmonisation and cost-benefit analysis in Australia and New Zealand

Following interviews with government agencies in the various jurisdictions over the period October to December 2014, it was apparent that there was only patchy use of cost-benefit analysis (CBA) in Australia and New Zealand.

At one extreme, transport agencies were generally well equipped with expert analysts and modelling capability to carry out conventional CBA studies of proposed projects. Some, but not all, central agencies possessed in-house expertise in CBA but were generally engaged only in reviewing studies prepared by line agencies or their consultants as part of budgetary processes. Health and environment agencies, which generally lacked CBA expertise, tended to favour the introduction of harmonised values to facilitate utilisation of CBA in their portfolio areas.

Available resources did not permit more extensive face-to-face canvassing of views with portfolios other than the central agencies: transport, health and environment. In order to access a wider range of views among those familiar with CBA, a survey of professionals was conducted under the auspices of the Economic Society of Australia (ESA) and the Government Economics Network in New Zealand.

The objective of the survey was to identify the views of respondents about the use of CBA in public sector decision-making and the potential for greater harmonisation of parameters and variable values.

2.1 General survey responses

The web-based survey questionnaire (see Annex to this chapter) was distributed to 1,068 members of the ESA and the participants in a CBA Forum hosted by the NSW Branch of the ESA and NSW Trade and Investment in Sydney on 18 July 2014. An identical questionnaire was distributed to 774 members of the Government Economics Network in New Zealand. In total, 360 responses out of 1842 were received, although not all questions were answered by all respondents.

Table 2.1: Responses by area of employment and education

Respondent characteristics	Per cent
Employment sector (n=229)	
Australian Public Service	22%
New Zealand Public Service	24%
Private sector	32%
Academics	14%
Other	7%
Highest level of education (n = 357)	
Undergraduate degree — economics	29%
Postgraduate degree — economics	36%
Postgraduate degree — business, finance, or public administration	11%
Undergraduate degree — other discipline	15%
Postgraduate degree — other discipline	10%

Source: George Argyrous with Sara Rahman

Table 2.1 indicates that respondents were spread across the public, private, and academic sectors, with 55 per cent of respondents having worked in their current position for 10 years or more. Fewer than 14 per cent had held their current position for less than two years. Further, respondents came from a wide range of policy fields, including transport, environment, health, and urban planning, with only 14 per cent listing their work field as 'economics'. Respondents were also highly qualified, with over half having a postgraduate degree, and high economic literacy, with over two-thirds having a degree in economics.

In terms of experience with CBAs, respondents showed a reasonable level of familiarity with various aspects of the use of CBAs in decision-making, as shown in Table 2.2.

Table 2.2: Responses by degree of experience with CBA

Level of experience	Per cent
Preparing CBAs (n = 310)	
Not at all experienced	22%
Some experience	44%
High level of experience	34%
Arranging for CBAs to be prepared (n = 299)	
Not at all experienced	34%
Some experience	41%
High level of experience	25%
Reviewing CBAs (n = 309)	
Not at all experienced	17%
Some experience	46%
High level of experience	37%
Using the results of CBAs (n = 307)	
Not at all experienced	12%
Some experience	48%
High level of experience	39%

Source: George Argyrous with Sara Rahman

Prior to seeking the views of respondents on the specific issue of harmonisation of CBA values and methodologies, information was sought on their views regarding some of the broader issues faced by those using CBA in policy formulation and decision-making. Respondents were asked to rate and rank the importance of a range of issues relevant to CBA on a five-point Likert scale with a range from 0 to 4. Table 2.3 presents the main results.

Table 2.3: Importance of issues associated with the use of CBAs

CBA issue	Mean rating score	Per cent rating this as the most important issue
CBAs are undertaken at the wrong time	2.2	2.0%
The wrong options for CBAs are being considered	2.6	4.3%
The results of CBAs are not effectively communicated	2.8	5.5%
Variables used in CBAs (e.g. discount rates, value of time) are not consistent	2.7	5.9%
CBAs are not generally published	2.8	6.7%
Policies and programs are not evaluated using ex post CBA	3.2	7.1%
CBAs are ignored in decision-making	2.8	11.1%
CBAs are not being conducted independently and objectively	2.9	12.3%
CBAs are being used to justify rather than inform	3.1	22.1%
CBAs are not undertaken on important decisions	3.1	22.9%

Source: George Argyrous with Sara Rahman

There was variation among different groups of respondents regarding the relative importance of the issues listed in Table 2.3. In general, respondents from outside of the public sectors in Australia and New Zealand were less concerned about the issues listed in Table 2.3. Most notably, public sector respondents did not feel as strongly that CBAs are not undertaken for important decisions, or that they are not being conducted independently or objectively, or ignored in decision-making. A smaller proportion of New Zealand public sector respondents indicated that the fact that CBAs are not generally published was an important issue compared with their Australian counterparts, which possibly reflects a different culture of transparency. Table 2.5 below provides more detail.

As might be expected, there were differences between groups of respondents regarding the issue that was considered to be the most important. One quarter of Australian respondents placed emphasis on the issue that 'CBAs are not undertaken on important decisions', but other groups rated as most important the view that 'CBAs are used to justify rather than inform'. No group considered that 'variables used in CBAs (e.g. discount rates, value of time) are not consistent' as a major issue, with less than 10 per cent rating this issue as the most important across any cross-classification of respondents.

Support for harmonisation predominated, although Table 2.4 indicates that it was not unqualified. Support for trans-Tasman harmonisation of CBA, however, was not as effusive as support for within-country and within-jurisdiction harmonisation.

Table 2.4: Responses regarding support for differing degrees of harmonisation

Level of support for harmonisation	Within each jurisdiction (n = 227)	Across similar agencies within a country (n = 229)	Across jurisdictions within a country (n = 224)	Between Australia and New Zealand (n = 198)
Do not support	5.3%	4.8%	7.6%	25.8%
Support with qualifications	63.0%	62.0%	66.1%	63.6%
Support without qualifications	31.7%	33.2%	26.3%	10.6%

Source: George Argyrous with Sara Rahman

More respondents from the public sector supported harmonisation, mainly for consistency purposes and cross-departmental comparisons to be made possible. A significant group, however, also supported the alternative of greater transparency through publication. This was largely based on the need to accommodate and justify different variables for sector-specific areas.

Private sector respondents were evenly split between harmonisation and transparency — with support for harmonisation based on much the same reasons as those given by public sector counterparts. Transparency was considered to be the best way to improve the overall quality of CBAs.

Academics also tended to favour harmonisation, but most had reservations regarding how values were to be set; they were sceptical about the ability of a centralised body to set good standards for variables.

2.2 Quantitative analysis of survey results

To investigate the strength of the survey results in greater detail, the data were interrogated econometrically to check for insights about relationships between the characteristics of respondents and the answers that they provided to survey questions. The key details of the survey are reproduced below as an annex to this chapter.

The survey questions were grouped around four broad themes:

- application and usage of CBA studies
- support for greater harmonisation in CBA across agencies and jurisdictions
- principles and preferences for increased harmonisation
- potential areas for greater harmonisation in CBAs.

Results in tables 2.5 to 2.8 are presented in blocks based on these four themes. Various questions were asked within each theme and overall there were 30 questions posed in questions 2, 4, 5 and 7 of the survey (which were used as dependent variables) and, therefore, 30 (ordinal logistic) regressions. Due to the large number of regressions and covariates involved, only those relationships that were statistically significant at the 10 per cent level are presented in the tables, but with actual p-values shown in brackets. The tables provide information about which sectors, jurisdictions or experience levels favoured survey question propositions more (or less) than others.

The survey questions were posed on 3- or 5-point Likert scales, so that numerical values from 0 to 2 or 0 to 4 were assigned to them in order to estimate relationships. A higher value means the respondent agrees more with, or assigns a higher importance to, the survey question. Although a ranking of 2 is 'higher' than a ranking of 1, it is not 'twice as large'. There is no numerical measure of distance between the scores. The numerical values represent an ordinal scale rather than a cardinal measure.

An important assumption in the model is, therefore, that the relationship between each pair of outcome rankings is homogenous; for example, the estimate of moving from, 'do not support' to 'support with qualifications' is the same distance as moving from 'support with qualifications' to 'support without qualifications'.

Because the survey questions have an ordinal structure, ordinal logistic regression was used to analyse the data. Estimated regression coefficients were converted to proportional odds ratios. A proportional odds ratio of 2 can be interpreted as a characteristic having twice the odds (twice as likely) of being associated with a higher ranking response to the survey question. A proportional odds ratio of 0.5 means that those with the characteristics are half as likely to rate a given issue as being important.

Based on questions 1, 8, 9 and 10 of the survey, four broad classes of characteristics were used — CBA experience, education, employment sector and job experience — and their component categories formed the independent variables in the 30 logistic regressions.

'CBA experience' refers to four sub-categories in descending order of extent of experience:

- preparing CBAs
- arranging for CBAs to be prepared
- reviewing CBAs
- using CBA results

Survey question 1 asked respondents to indicate their level of experience against each of these four sub-categories on a 5-point scale. Responses stating 'Not applicable' or 'Can't say' were eliminated, leaving only three levels of experience for each of the four categories:

- high level of experience (assigned value of 2)
- some experience (assigned value of 1)
- not at all experienced (assigned value of 0).

Response values were averaged across the four sub-categories. The independent variable 'CBA experience' was then defined by combining those with a high level and some level of experience, relative to the base case of 'not at all experienced'.

Sub-categories for education included the following variables:

- undergraduate: economics
- undergraduate: other discipline
- postgraduate: economics
- postgraduate: business, finance, public administration
- postgraduate: other.

In tables 2.5 to 2.7, 'Economics qualification' includes both undergraduate and postgraduate economics qualifications (i.e. excluding business, finance, or associated disciplines). Results for the economics qualification dummy variable (value 1) are expressed relative to the base case (value 0) of undergraduate and postgraduate qualifications in all other disciplines.

A dummy variable of value 1 was used for 'Postgraduate qualification', which included all postgraduate qualifications, irrespective of discipline. The base case was therefore 'no postgraduate qualification', irrespective of discipline.

The following sectoral employment variables were used on the basis of survey information collected:

- academic
- public sector: Australian state government
- public sector: Australian (Commonwealth) Government
- public sector: New Zealand
- 'other' sector: student, retiree, non-government organisation
- private sector: the base case dummy variable; all other sector results are expressed relative to the private sector.

'Job experience' refers to the number of years of experience in the area of current employment. Possible responses ranged from 0 (less than one year) to 10, as well as a category for 'more than 10'. The number of years in the job was compared to a base case of 0 (less than one year). Regression coefficients in the tables are interpreted as the increase in the odds for a one-year increase in experience.

Survey respondents' views were sought regarding the importance of issues to do with the way that CBAs are used or not used. Table 2.5 presents results that were significant at least at the 10 per cent level, with p-levels shown in brackets below the logit coefficients. Respondents with economics qualifications were roughly twice as likely as non-economists to consider that 'CBAs not being published', or 'CBAs being undertaken at the wrong time', were important issues. Respondents classified as part of 'other' sector (students, retirees, NGOs) were between 2.8 and 7.6 times more likely than those in the private sector to rate the following issues as more important: CBAs used as justification for projects; CBAs not being consistent, evaluated, published, or the results being ignored.

Table 2.5: Application and usage of CBA studies

Estimated proportional odds ratios	CBA experience	Economics qualification	Job experience	Sector other	Sector public NZ
CBAs are being used to justify rather than inform	0.675 (0.068)			3.354 (0.06)	0.357 (0.005)
CBAs are being ignored in decision-making				3.108 (0.062)	
Variables used in CBAs are not consistent				7.556 (0.011)	
Policies and programs are not evaluated using ex post CBA				2.755 (0.076)	
CBAs are not generally published		1.937 (0.075)		3.245 (0.09)	
CBAs are not undertaken on important decisions					0.515 (0.096)
CBAs are undertaken at the wrong time		2.013 (0.052)	0.891 (0.008)		0.383 (0.008)

Note: p-values are shown in brackets below the logit values (logarithms of the odds ratios) recorded in the body of the table. See text for interpretation of logit values.

Source: Patrick Doupe

Respondents from the NZ public sector were two to three times less likely to find some issues more important relative to the private sector. These issues were that CBAs are being used to justify rather than inform; not being undertaken; or, when undertaken, being undertaken at the wrong time. Respondents with more experience in CBAs, however, were less likely than their less experienced peers to think that CBAs 'being used to justify rather than inform' is an important issue.

Table 2.6: Support for greater harmonisation in CBA across agencies and jurisdictions

Estimated proportional odds ratios	Economics qualification	Postgraduate qualification	Job experience	Sector public AU state	Sector public NZ
Across similar agencies within a country	2.151 (0.074)			0.468 (0.098)	2.123 (0.059)
Between Australia and New Zealand		2.619 (0.025)	0.838 (0.001)		

Note: p-values are shown in brackets below the logit values (logarithms of the odds ratios) recorded in the body of the table. See text for interpretation of logit values.

Source: Patrick Doupe

Survey question 4 asked respondents about the desired degree of harmonisation of input variables used in CBAs. Opinions differed across the Tasman (Table 2.6). Amongst public sector employees, those from New Zealand were two times more likely than their private sector counterparts to believe that harmonisation across agencies was important. State-level public sector employees from Australia were two times less likely than private sector respondents to hold such a view. Australian Commonwealth public sector employees did not differ significantly from private sector respondents in their views.

Those with an economics qualification were 2.2 times more likely than non-economists to be associated with a higher preference for CBA harmonisation across similar agencies in a country. Postgraduates (all disciplines) were 2.6 times more likely than those without a higher degree to be associated with a preference for harmonisation between Australia and New Zealand. Those with more job experience were less likely to be associated with a preference for trans-Tasman harmonisation.

Table 2.7 analyses responses to survey question 5, which asked respondents for their preferences surrounding harmonisation based on different approaches and principles.

Table 2.7: Principles and preferences for increased harmonisation

Estimated proportional odds ratios	CBA experience	Economics qualification	Sector academic	Sector other	Sector public AU state
Agreement on how values are to be updated	1.453 (0.078)				
Variable capable of clear definition		0.402 (0.022)			
Full disclosure of estimation method used			3.468 (0.026)	3.191 (0.095)	0.515 (0.093)
Probability distribution of variable values made available				5.815 (0.002)	
Variable values and underlying data to be made publicly available				2.886 (0.072)	

Note: p-values are shown in brackets below the logit values (logarithms of the odds ratios) recorded in the body of the table. See text for interpretation of logit values.

Source: Patrick Doupe

NGO workers, students and retirees ('Sector other') exhibited a higher propensity relative to the private sector to designate disclosure of estimation methods as more important in fostering harmonisation. This includes making the results and probability distributions or variable values publicly available. Academic economists were three times more likely than the private sector to believe that full disclosure of the estimation method was more important. On the other hand, Australian state public employees were two times less likely than the private sector to consider disclosure to be important.

Surprisingly, those with an economics qualification were only half as likely as non-economists to consider the clear definition of variables used in CBA to be important. Respondents with greater CBA experience were more likely than those without CBA experience to think that agreement about how variables will be updated in the future is important.

Table 2.8: Potential areas of greater harmonisation

Estimated proportional odds ratios	CBA experience	Job experience	Sector academic	Sector other
Deadweight loss due to tax-funded project		0.919 (0.065)		0.324 (0.079)
Flora and fauna values	1.763 (0.027)			
Period of the analysis		0.893 (0.017)		
Social discount rate	1.696 (0.02)			
Value of statistical life	1.461 (0.098)		0.348 (0.035)	0.182 (0.01)

Note: p-values are shown in brackets below the logit values (logarithms of the odds ratios) recorded in the body of the table. See text for interpretation of logit values.

Source: Patrick Doupe

Question seven asked survey respondents about potential areas of harmonisation of values in CBA (results shown in Table 2.8). Greater CBA experience was associated with a higher weight on the importance of harmonisation for flora and fauna values, the social discount rate and the value of a statistical life. Greater job experience had an opposing relationship with harmonisation of deadweight loss and specification of the period under analysis. Relative to the private sector, academic respondents were less likely to consider that harmonisation of the value of a statistical life was important.

2.3 General qualitative feedback

Some qualitative feedback reinforced points already made above, but other, more nuanced points were also made. Some of the more notable issues raised were as follows:

- When ex ante CBA is employed to support a particular policy instead of informing decision-making, ex post CBA is not undertaken.
- CBAs do not necessarily mean that a project is rejected or approved solely based on the CBA, rather CBA is used as a tool for decision-makers to make informed decisions, especially since some factors cannot be easily monetised or there are mandatory restrictions on programs and their outcomes (e.g. targets/standards).

- Where only an ex post CBA is undertaken, viable options that should have been considered in an ex ante CBA are not examined at all.

- Due to the subjective nature of CBAs, a wide range of calibrations to the analysis can be justified. Monetary considerations, coupled with the view of CBAs as subjective, leads to pressure on practitioners to manipulate variables to support a client's position, effectively resulting in an 'opinion for hire' market for CBAs.

- Discount rates were a specific concern, with several respondents citing instances of discount rates being manipulated to 'spectacularly high' levels in order to dismiss a particular policy. Non-market values were also cited to be commonly and easily manipulated to achieve 'desirable' results.

- Although some respondents thought that publication would be enough to solve the problems faced by CBA, a smaller group was concerned that, without proper communication and explanation of CBAs, the general public would remain uninformed about their content and how to assess their validity. If the public is to influence debate using the CBAs, then they must be able to access the full assumptions, model and calculations involved in CBAs as well as have enough knowledge to understand how to interpret them.

- Having clear definitions would make a big difference to how CBAs are understood and applied in decision-making and would ease comparisons and external validation of different CBAs.

- Harmonisation was thought to be best implemented as default values or ranges and included for comparison purposes across different analyses, with alternative values allowed with justifications for scenario-testing purposes. This approach was thought to reconcile the need for reducing manipulation while allowing for practitioners to use their expertise in employing different approaches. Significant disagreement persists, however, over how harmonisation should be carried out and whether it is a superior solution to greater transparency in the CBA process.

2.4 Qualitative responses reflecting concerns about harmonisation

Qualitative responses reflecting concerns about the concept of harmonisation were equally illuminating and instructive. The following is a paraphrased selection of comments made:

- The most common concern that respondents expressed regarding harmonisation related to differences in parameters and situations across different jurisdictions, countries, and agencies, which would make harmonisation difficult.

- Additionally, some were concerned that standardisation across sectors could result in certain types of projects being favoured more than others. Examples given of possible difficulties in harmonisation were interest rates across different countries, laws in different jurisdictions and different non-market valuations across different sectors.

- Another concern regarding possible harmonisation of CBA standards is the degree to which standards can be ignored. Harmonisation and rules must prevent tinkering for political purposes, but allow enough flexibility to allow practitioners to conduct accurate or more robust analyses for their projects and to account for difficulties in collecting data.

- Harmonisation was also thought to possibly restrict debate and prevent innovation in how CBAs are conducted, with some respondents saying that CBAs should be a 'brain on' and not a 'brain off' process. The innovation and debate process was thought to be important, especially with some doubting the ability of a centralised body to create good standards.

- Creativity can be encouraged, because, over time, external scrutiny of transparent CBA processes may lead to a convergence around key variable values, without that having to be a formal process.

- Disagreement was also widespread over which variables should be standardised. One way that respondents approached this was to harmonise variables that they classified as stable across jurisdictions and areas. There was no real agreement, however, on what these variables were, with disagreements even over key variables, such as the period of analysis and discount rates.

- Some respondents supported harmonisation of variables which the average practitioner could not estimate better than standardised values — basically those that may be difficult to estimate.
- There was more agreement about variables that should not be standardised than those that should — travel time, flora and fauna, and analysis periods were the major variables that were thought to not be suitable for harmonisation whereas harmonisation of the value of statistical life and the cost of emissions was supported.

Annex to Chapter 2: Survey questionnaire[1]

1. How would you rate your experience with each of the following CBA activities?

	Not at all experienced	Some experience	High level of experience	Not applicable	Can't say
Using the results of CBAs					
Preparing CBAs					
Arranging for CBAs to be prepared					
Reviewing CBAs					

2. In your view, how important are each of the following issues in the use of CBAs as part of public sector decision-making?

	0 — Not at all an issue	1	2	3	4 — Extremely important issue	Don't know	No opinion
CBAs are ignored in decision-making							
CBAs are not generally published							

1   The survey questionnaire was compiled by Leo Dobes, George Argyrous and Joanne Leung with input by Richard Tooth. The questionnaire was administered by Diane Litherland on behalf of the Economic Society of Australia which sponsored the survey. Initial results were compiled by Sara Rahman and George Argyrous. Econometric analysis was carried out by Patrick Doupe.

	0 — Not at all an issue	1	2	3	4 — Extremely important issue	Don't know	No opinion
The wrong options for CBAs are being considered							
CBAs are undertaken at the wrong time							
The results of CBAs are not effectively communicated							
CBAs are not being conducted independently and objectively							
Policies and programs are not evaluated using ex post CBA							
CBAs are being used to justify rather than inform							
CBAs are not undertaken on important decisions							
Variables used in CBAs (e.g. discount rates, value of time) are not consistent							

3. Which of these issues do you consider to be the MOST IMPORTANT in the use of CBAs as part of public sector decision-making?

☐ CBAs are not undertaken on important decisions

☐ The wrong options for CBAs are being considered

☐ CBAs are undertaken at the wrong time

☐ CBAs are being used to justify rather than inform

☐ CBAs are not being conducted independently and objectively

☐ CBAs are ignored in decision-making

☐ CBAs are not effectively communicated

☐ CBAs are not generally published

☐ Variables used in CBAs (e.g. discount rates, value of time) are not consistent

The following questions relate to the degree of harmonisation that public sector agencies across Australia and New Zealand should adopt. In this case harmonisation means the extent to which agencies should use agreed values, or ranges of values, for major elements of public sector CBAs, including consistency in the approaches to determining those values. Harmonisation does not mean uniformity or standardisation. It refers to guideline values that can be ignored if specific, local estimates can be justified as being better.

4. To what extent do you support greater harmonisation of input variables used in CBA undertaken by government agencies, or consultants commissioned by these agencies?

Do not support	Support with qualifications	Support without qualifications	Don't know	No opinion
Within each jurisdiction				
Across similar agencies within a country				
Across jurisdictions within a country				
Between Australia and New Zealand				

Can you provide the reasons for your opinion?

5. If a policy of harmonisation were to be adopted for public sector CBAs, please rate each of the following principles in terms of their importance to help guide the specification of input variables.

	0 – Not at all important	1	2	3	4 – Extremely important	Don't know	No opinion
Variable capable of clear definition							
Ease of collection of data required							
Variable value and underlying data to be made publicly available							
Probability distribution of variable values made available							

	0 — Not at all important	1	2	3	4 — Extremely important	Don't know	No opinion
Full disclosure of estimation method used							
Harmonised variable values used as default only Alternative estimates permitted if demonstrably better							
Harmonise only variables that have significant influence on net present values							
Agreement on how values are to be updated in future							

6. Which of these principles do you regard as the MOST IMPORTANT?

☐ Variable capable of clear definition

☐ Ease of collection of data required

☐ Variable value and underlying data to be made publicly available

☐ Probability distribution of variable values made available

☐ Full disclosure of estimation method used

☐ Harmonised variable values used as default only

☐ Harmonise only variables that have significant influence on net present values

☐ Agreement on how values are to be updated in future

7. Do you generally support, within each jurisdiction, harmonisation of the values, or range of values or consistency in the approaches to determining those values, for each of the following CBA input variables?

	Do not support	Support with qualifications	Support without qualifications	Don't know	No opinion
Period of the analysis (by type of project or regulation)					

	Do not support	Support with qualifications	Support without qualifications	Don't know	No opinion
Noise (by source of noise; e.g. cars, aircraft)					
Travel time					
Social discount rate					
Damage cost of greenhouse gas emissions					
Value of statistical life					
Flora and fauna values					
Deadweight loss due to tax-funded project					

Can you provide the reasons for your opinion?

These final questions will provide some background to our survey respondents. Your responses will remain confidential and anonymous

8. Which of the following best describes your current or more recent position?

☐ Public sector — Australian Commonwealth
☐ Public sector — NSW
☐ Public sector — Victoria
☐ Public sector — Queensland
☐ Public sector — South Australia
☐ Public sector — Western Australia
☐ Public sector — Tasmania
☐ Public sector — Territories
☐ Public sector — New Zealand
☐ Private sector — Consultant
☐ Private sector — Other
☐ Academic
☐ Student
☐ NGO
☐ Retired

9. For how many years have you worked in this area?

- [ ] Less than 1 year
- [ ] 1
- [ ] 2
- [ ] 3
- [ ] 4
- [ ] 5
- [ ] 6
- [ ] 7
- [ ] 8
- [ ] 9
- [ ] 10 or more years

10. What are your qualifications (select all that apply)?

- [ ] Undergraduate degree — economics
- [ ] Undergraduate degree — other discipline
- [ ] Postgraduate degree — economics
- [ ] Postgraduate degree — business, finance, or public administration
- [ ] Postgraduate degree — other discipline

3

Potential approaches to harmonisation

Pressure for structural change in the Australian economy increased during the 1970s (e.g. Treasury, 1978; Rattigan, 1986), with significant micro-economic reform taking place over the following two decades in areas ranging from floating the exchange rate, reducing import tariffs and liberalising financial markets, as well as corporatising government business enterprises, particularly in transport and telecommunications, and exposing them to competition (Willis, 1989; Banks, 2014). Much of the policy debate was underpinned by economic analyses undertaken by the Productivity Commission and its predecessor institutions.

Almost from its historical beginnings, economic thought has been subjected to a variety of criticisms (Pearce & Nash, 1981; Coleman & Hagger, 2001; Coleman, 2002). Perhaps due to 'reform fatigue', and growing attacks by anti-economists on cost-benefit analysis (CBA) (e.g. Self, 1975) and its 'econocrat' proponents, the 1990s presaged a reduced political appetite for economic reform and economic appraisal of policy proposals. Attacks on so called 'economic rationalism' (e.g. Pusey, 1991) and derogatory references to 'econorats' by opponents to continued reform coincided with the reduced influence of economic analysis, in Canberra at least.

Notwithstanding the publication by the Department of Finance (1991; revised 2006) of a *Handbook of Cost-Benefit Analysis*, subsequent decades saw a concomitant increase within the Australian Public

Service of managerialist methodologies like triple bottom line reporting (e.g. Department of the Environment and Heritage, 2003), and multi-criteria analysis (MCA) (e.g. Resource Assessment Commission, 1992). MCA is examined in Appendix 2.

Despite the projections of the then Federal Department of Employment, Education and Training, which considered at the time that economists were the third-ranking growth profession, Millmow (1995) drew attention to the decline in availability of academic positions for economists. Riley (1994) detected a corresponding fall in the number of secondary students studying economics. Despite the optimism of Maxwell (2003) of a possible renaissance over the next 50 years in numbers taking tertiary-level economics degrees, Lewis et al. (2004) noted a continued decline in numbers. Reviewing an Economic Society of Australia (ESA) survey of heads of economics departments, Abelson (2005) concluded that student standards had also declined, due to lower entry standards, high student–staff ratios, and a declining culture of study. A decade later, Lodewijks & Stokes (2014) reported on the inevitable consequence, noting the closure of economics departments across Australia, with many being subsumed within business schools and other faculties.

A desktop survey of 39 Australian university websites in February 2015 revealed that only five offered undergraduate or postgraduate courses devoted to CBA, with a further four offering courses that partially covered CBA. This may be an underestimate because details were not always fully available of the specific content of postgraduate programs and because online search facilities did not always provide comprehensive information. Although seven out of eight New Zealand universities appear to offer CBA in their undergraduate or postgraduate courses, it is uncertain what proportion of students take up those courses.

On the other hand, the Government Economics Network in New Zealand has found a high level of demand for CBA courses by members, indicating a general lack of sufficient training in this area. In Australia, executive courses presented by the Australia and New Zealand School of Government (ANZSOG) in various cities in Australia and New Zealand, and by the Crawford School of Public Policy at The Australian National University in Canberra, continue to attract healthy numbers of participants. CBA forums organised in 2014 and

2015 by the NSW branch of the ESA and NSW Trade & Investment attracted in the order of 200 participants from a range of government departments, universities and the private sector.

Although direct evidence is not available, it is likely that the fall in the number of economics graduates and the relatively low number of CBA courses offered at universities is reflected in the ostensibly diminished extent of CBA expertise in government agencies across Australia. A NSW central agency pointed out that the paucity of economic positions within the NSW public service that are focused specifically on economic evaluation is an important factor in the loss of expertise. Any expertise that existed was not harnessed appropriately. A Centre for Program Evaluation has recently been established in the NSW Treasury in order to concentrate evaluation expertise.

During face-to-face interviews with staff from government agencies from October to December 2014, those responsible for portfolios such as health and environment reported that they tended, out of necessity, to resort to assistance from their colleagues in other specialised agencies when they were required to produce or commission an economic appraisal. Transport agencies were seen as repositories of expertise and one interviewee related that a contact in the (since abolished) Queensland Office of Best Practice Regulation was considered to be especially helpful to agencies in that state.

A number of those interviewed indicated that their strong preference to use CBA was stymied by the lack of resources and expertise. Interlocutors regularly stated that the provision of harmonised 'plug-in' values endorsed by a central agency or recognised authority such as the Productivity Commission would encourage their use of CBA.

3.1 Harmonisation versus standardisation

Standardisation implies the inflexible, procrustean imposition of pre-specified variable values or methodologies. In other words, standardisation would insist on strict uniformity in an economic appraisal, with little or no scope for variation, irrespective of circumstances. The less rigid approach of harmonisation is based primarily on the use of default values or 'yardsticks', or even ranges of recommended values.

In the case of recommended default 'plug-in' values, the onus would be on the consultant or the government agency concerned to justify use of a different value. Justification might be offered on the basis of differences in local conditions and greater relevance, or use, for example, of more up-to-date information or estimates. To ensure transparency, results of CBA studies that use harmonised values could be presented in two separate analyses: one using the set 'plug-in' value and one using values preferred by the analyst.

Inter- or intra-jurisdictional harmonisation would necessarily require agreement not only about the values of the variables themselves, but also about the underlying methodology. For example, values used for the value of statistical life (VOSL) are generally estimated using either the human capital approach or some form of stated preference that reflects a change in risk of mortality or morbidity. At present, jurisdictions differ in the methodological approach that is used to derive a value for this variable, so there can be significant differences in values.

Lack of harmonisation is not a new issue. An example regarding its effect was provided several decades ago by McKnight (1982), who concluded from a survey of travel time values in Australia that:

> the results of the survey indicate a reluctance on the part of most agencies to make independent estimates of value of time for use in analysis. In general, they lack the appropriate resources or technical skills. Consequently these agencies seek some standard, 'off the shelf' set of values. Most agencies are willing to carry out simple analysis to update such standard values to current price levels, but there was no uniformity among respondents in the method of update adopted, with both consumer price and average wage rate indices being popular.

Nevertheless, harmonisation would also require care to ensure internal analytical consistency. Suppose an agency is using the value of a life year (VLY) based on a 40-year annuity of an estimate of the VOSL, using a specific discount rate. Disregarding the reason and appropriateness of choosing between VLY and VOSL, to ensure consistency it is necessary to make sure that the overall discount rate used for the CBA and for the annuity is the same.

The Australian Bureau of Transport Economics (BTE, 2000, p. 29) used a central 4 per cent per annum (consumption) discount rate to obtain the value of labour lost to society's production levels due to road crashes, while an updated report (Bureau of Infrastructure, Transport and Regional Economics, 2009, p. 90) uses a 3 per cent rate. However, Austroads (Rockliffe et al., 2012, p. 7) recommends an annual discount rate of 7 per cent for public transport infrastructure projects, which is the same rate that is used by a number of Australian jurisdictions. A search for any discussion of the potential effects of such inconsistencies proved fruitless.

3.2 Potential approaches to developing harmonised values

Various methods for estimating economic costs and benefits are presented in standard texts such as Boardman et al. (2011), Perkins (1994), Mishan & Quah (2007), Campbell & Brown (2003), Pearce & Nash (1981) and Pearce et al. (2006). They include revealed preference methods, such as direct econometric estimation, hedonic pricing, damage costs avoided, travel cost methods and market analogies, as well as two stated preference methods: the contingent valuation method (CVM) and choice modelling (CM).

Each of the standard estimation methods has advantages and weaknesses, depending on the context, data availability and rigour of application. Although not explored specifically here, it is important to be aware that the choice and application of a particular estimation method will affect downstream development of 'plug-in' values. For example, a meta-analysis or expert elicitation of values for noise externalities may be influenced by a hedonic comparison of differences in house prices near an airport and further away that may not have taken into account other factors, such as the size of houses or the quality of their construction. An alternative estimation method, such as CVM, may have been better in such circumstances, but it too is likely to suffer from particular weaknesses.

The objective of developing harmonised values is to allow their use as 'off-the-shelf' variables. That is, readily available 'plug-in' values that can be used without the need for separate estimation on each occasion that a CBA is carried out. This approach comes within the broad rubric of 'benefit transfer', which is itself subject to a range of qualifications (see below).

3.2.1 Publication of CBA guidelines and manuals

Publication of CBA guidelines and manuals is a common practice worldwide, particularly in the transport sector, but central agencies also issue such publications from time to time. For the transport sector, publications usually also include unit values for benefit variables or parameters, as well as the method for updating such values to current dollars. One limitation, however, is that many benefit values, for example in the NZ context, are based on outdated studies and may, therefore, not be accurate reflections of the current values of the benefits.

3.2.2 Access to completed CBA studies

Access to CBA studies undertaken by others can assist public servants, academics and the general public through an educative process. Information about methodological approaches used can be particularly helpful in assisting those tackling analogous issues. Over time, the availability of completed studies can also assist in setting standards or establishing canonical values for variables and parameters that are included in the analysis.

The New South Wales Government Department of Premier and Cabinet (2013) has instructed government agencies to make 'Evaluation findings ... publicly available, unless there is an overriding public interest against disclosure, in line with the *Government Information (Public Access) Act 2009*': arp.nsw.gov.au/c2013-08-program-evaluation-and-review. Although a welcome development, this policy does not guarantee the use of CBA or evidence-based methods. An example, albeit one that predates the 2013 instruction, is a review of the use of tablet and iPad technology in school classrooms which appears to have been based primarily on opinions expressed by teachers and parents as well as the researcher's personal observations (Goodwin, 2012).

The Commonwealth Government, on the other hand, has restricted public access to economic analyses under the *Freedom of Information Act 1982*. The Act generally exempts from release any material developed as part of a 'deliberative process' which 'involves the exercise of judgement in developing and making a selection from different options', although section 47C(3)(a) excludes reports of scientific or technical experts.

Somewhat incongruously, the social sciences, including economics, are not considered to be scientific or technical for the purposes of section 47 (Office of the Australian Information Commissioner, 2014, ss 6.74–6.76). As it is inherently the task of a CBA to 'deliberate' among a set of options, a CBA can evidently be precluded from release to the public. At the Commonwealth level, therefore, the scope for sharing information and improving the standards of CBAs through greater transparency is severely constrained.

3.2.3 Establishment of databases of variables and parameters

In 1995, the NSW Environment Protection Authority released its Envalue online database of environmental valuation studies (www.environment.nsw.gov.au/envalueapp/). The database was intended to facilitate the incorporation of environmental values into CBA studies and environment impact statements.

Due to the cost of maintaining the Envalue database, it was later subsumed into the Environmental Valuation Reference Inventory (EVRI) online database (www.evri.ca/Global/Splash.aspx), which is sponsored jointly by Australian (NSW), Canadian, French, British and American environmental agencies. Access to EVRI is free to nationals of the sponsoring countries. Environmental databases are also maintained separately by other countries, including the NZ Non-Market Valuation Database, which is maintained by Lincoln University (www2.lincoln. ac.nz/nonmarketvaluation/QuerySearch.asp).

An advantage of compilations of valuation studies, especially those with free access like Envalue and EVRI, is that they reduce search costs for analysts. Nevertheless, as the number of studies accumulated in a database grows, search costs may no longer be negligible. Specialist skills — not generally available within government agencies — may also be required to apply database information that has been based on sophisticated choice modelling techniques. It may also not be clear how values extracted from older studies should be updated over time.

In sum, databases are useful for specialist practitioners of CBA, but their utility to generalist public servants, who are often subject to time pressure to provide advice to government, is probably limited (Pearce et al., 2006, ch. 17). It is instructive that none of the officials interviewed in 2014 in the various jurisdictions proposed greater use of databases, but a number did raise the desirability of provision of officially sanctioned 'plug-in', 'off-the-shelf' values. While databases themselves are not necessarily useful in practice, they do provide the necessary basis for more specific approaches, like benefit transfer.

3.2.4 Canonical values

Inertia, lack of information, or reluctance to break with tradition may lead over time to the de facto establishment of canonical 'plug-in' values. An example is the use of different discount rates for road projects. In the past, it has invariably been recommended by Austroads that road projects be discounted at an annual real rate of 7 per cent (e.g. Austroads, 1996; Rockliffe et al., 2012, part 2), and this rate is generally used by road transport agencies.

Appraisal of rail projects, on the other hand, is less definitive in its use of specific discount rates. The Bureau of Transport Economics (1976) used a 7 per cent real per annum rate for an analysis of a Victorian rail line, and real annual rates of 4 per cent, 7 per cent, and 10 per cent for an evaluation of standard gauge links to selected ports (Starr et al., 1984), but applied three annual rates of 7 per cent, 10 per cent and 15 per cent in a study of the Tasmanian rail system (Tsolakis et al., 1991). Luskin et al. (1996) used an annual 11 per cent real rate in an analysis by the bureau of the proposed Melbourne–Brisbane inland rail route, but a later bureau analysis of the same route by Reynolds et al. (2000) applied a real discount rate of only 4 per cent per annum. Referring to a recommendation by Luskin & Dobes (1999) for the use of risk-free discount rates based on the long-term government bond rate, the Australian Transport Council (ATC, 2006, vol. 5) endorsed the approach for transport projects.

Another example of a canonical value in Australian transport practice is the designation of the value of travel time. McKnight (1982) presents separate tables of travel time values that are used by various Australian state road authorities, urban transport agencies and planning agencies, showing a wide range of values due to differences in updating methods and treatment of modes and passenger types. Unfortunately, McKnight's tables do not reveal the precise method of calculation of the values by the various agencies, or their identities. In recent years, travel time values have been based on wage rates in Australia, presumably because they are officially recorded by the Australian Bureau of Statistics (ABS) and hence easily discovered.

Austroads has invariably recommended (e.g. Tan et al., 2012) that the value of travel time should be based on average weekly earnings (AWE), as estimated by the ABS. Travel time values for private car travel to and from work, travel time for pensioners, tourists, bicycle travel, public transit passengers, pedestrians and waiting time, for example, for public transport, are set at 40 per cent of seasonally adjusted full-time AWE by Tan et al. (2012). It is not clear why a production-oriented approach should be used, rather than a stated preference valuation from the perspective of both employers and/or those travelling, but the Austroads methodology has gained general acceptance among analysts.

The Australian Transport Council (ATC, 2006) guidelines specify default values for a range of environmental effects, and they emphasise the desirability of maintaining consistency of values used in analysing transport projects:

> If a growth rate for the VTTS [Value of Travel Time Savings] is assumed over the life of an initiative, index all labour costs throughout the BCA … In Australian BCAs, it is more usual not to increase the VTTS, the costs of labour, crashes and externalities in line with forecast growth in real income. Yet increasing these attributes is the correct approach. The difficulty is that if proponents choose their own growth rates for parameters, there could be a loss of comparability between appraisal results, and proponents may use over-optimistic growth forecasts to achieve more favourable BCA results … If Austroads specifies growth rates for road initiatives, jurisdictions should develop a consistent set of growth rates for rail initiatives. (vol. 5, p. 51)

As of early 2015, the Australian Transport Council and Austroads are in the process of combining their transport system evaluation methodologies and parameters.

Canonical values may also develop organically if the producer of the data is well respected. For example, forecasts of Australian population levels published by the ABS are used by most researchers because of the reputation of the ABS for quality statistical research. Although population forecasts depend heavily on contestable assumptions about parameters such as longevity, net immigration and reproduction ratios, the ABS projections are generally accepted in both the commercial and the public sectors.

3.2.5 Meta-analysis

Meta-analysis summarises findings from previous studies. Its objective is to identify representative values, or an associated range, that can be used as a 'plug-in' to a current study. Apart from saving resources, the technique is sometimes justified on the basis that a value derived from a combination of different studies, and hence more observations, offers greater statistical power-efficiency than one derived from a single study. Values can be obtained either qualitatively or by using statistical techniques, typically regression analysis.

On occasion, lack of local data necessitates use of data from other countries. Abelson (2003b) found that there was no general VOSL in Australia based on willingness to pay. He therefore reviewed European estimates of VOSL on the basis of the broad similarity of European and Australian incomes. Based on European values, he recommended a VOSL of about $A2.5 million for a healthy prime-age individual for Australian policy purposes. Australian road agencies at that time were using a VOSL of about $1.3 million that was based on the human capital approach and which did not, therefore, reflect willingness to pay.

An essential first step in a credible meta-analysis is a systematic review of the available literature. Ideally, the review should be 'reproducible for others to prevent author-induced selective bias in the inclusion of studies' (van Wely, 2014). Nevertheless, the technique can suffer from a number of problems:

- so-called 'publication bias' — sometimes called 'the file drawer problem' — is a major potential problem. Studies that report definitive results, or surprising ones, are more likely to be published in learned journals than ones that offer an equivocal result or a less dramatic narrative. Rothstein et al. (2005) note that suppression of studies may also occur due to language bias (e.g. preference for studies published in English), or familiarity bias (e.g. inclusion only of studies from a familiar discipline). There are no obvious ways of overcoming such fundamental data problems

- the analysis can only be as good as the quality of the underlying studies. But any attempt to weed out poor quality studies itself runs the risk of selectivity bias

- two separate studies may yield similar results indicating a particular effect. When combined, however, they may indicate the opposite effect, sometimes termed 'Simpson's paradox'. This is illustrated in Figure 3.1 below, which shows regression lines for two separate data sets having a positive slope, but the combined data set showing a negative slope. Similarly, Bickel et al. (1975) present an intriguing study of apparent sex discrimination in university admissions when analysed at an aggregated level, but no apparent discrimination when data are pooled into disaggregated sets.

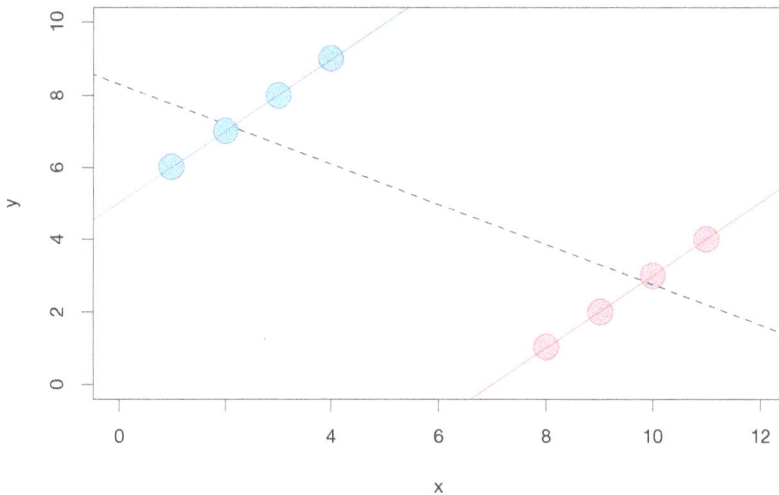

Figure 3.1: Simpson's paradox
Source: en.wikipedia.org/wiki/Simpson%27s_paradox

It would be difficult to unreservedly recommend the use of meta-analysis for determining 'plug-in' values. The principal reason is that cost-benefit studies suffer from the invariable reluctance of governments to publish them. Estimates of costs and benefits used in such studies, therefore, seldom see the light of day either. The extent of the publication bias is not known, but is likely to be not inconsiderable.

3.2.6 Expert elicitation

In a paper on 'rapid cost-benefit evaluation' of measures to manage effects of climate change, such as floods, Oldfield (2012) advocates the use of 'subjective judgement obtained using expert elicitation techniques' in a 'structured workshop environment'. Experts' opinions about costs and benefits are garnered using a unitary rating scale from 1 to 7 and then translated to monetary units using 'an equivalent monetary scale'. Oldfield gives as an example a rating of 2 being valued at $100 and a rating of 3 at $1,000. The term 'evaluation' is used rather than 'analysis' in order to recognise the associated loss of accuracy.

Whether the use of expert elicitation is a credible method of developing harmonised 'plug-in' values is an open question. Defining, identifying and selecting experts poses a key problem in methodological approach. Definitional issues aside, the identification and recruitment of knowledgeable persons is potentially subject to subjectivity and the sort of biases that afflict meta-analysis.

For example, *The Economist* (3 January 2015) published a table ranking economists by their publication record, compared to their ranking according to media prominence. Some, like Paul Krugman, scored well on both measures, but a large proportion of the socially more prominent economists did not score well in terms of academic performance, and vice versa. Choosing an expert panel on the basis of prominence may thus fail to satisfy the criterion of academic expertise or specialist knowledge.

In a review of the literature on biosecurity risk assessment, Burgman et al. (2006) found that experts tend to be overconfident compared to the accuracy of their estimates, are subject to value-induced biases, and influenced by the framing of issues. Elicitation techniques range from general opinion surveys to numerical (e.g. 'standard gamble') and language-based (e.g. expressed as 'highly likely', to avoid the 'false precision' of numerical probabilities) tools, but few of them have been tested for accuracy or reliability in the area of biosecurity.

Arnell et al. (2005) sought unsuccessfully to garner expert views on the likelihood of rapid climate change due to the collapse of the North Atlantic Thermohaline Circulation. They concluded that a problem with expert elicitation is 'that it does not factor in the process of judgment making; it focuses simply on the outcome of the judgment process', and therefore prefer not to aggregate the significantly divergent results. To ensure consensus, a commonly used approach is the structured Delphi method where a facilitator provides feedback iteratively on the responses of all expert participants until they arrive at a consistent view. A key risk of deliberately seeking consensus is agenda-driven bias, as is the risk of papering over differences that reflect genuine uncertainty, ambiguity or bimodalism.

It is at least arguable that expert elicitation is likely to be more reliable in issues relevant to the physical sciences than for social sciences like economics. Physical effects or dose-response relationships are often governed by the laws of physics or chemistry, and so provide some bounds to likely outcomes.

Economics and other social sciences tend to involve multiple possible interrelationships, which are often influenced by unpredictable human behaviour and 'unknown unknowns'. Benefits, in particular, should preferably be based on the community's willingness to pay, rather than an estimate of physical damage avoided and its financial cost. Reliance on expert elicitation of economic costs and benefits therefore does not seem to be a particularly sound approach to establishing harmonised values.

3.2.7 Benefit transfer using stated preference methods

A low-cost, back-of-the-envelope estimate of benefit values is often feasible where even only limited amounts of market data are available. For example, where few or no resources have been made available, it might be possible to carry out hedonic pricing of noise costs by asking a sample of real estate agents about differences of prices of houses near an airport and further away.

When no market data are available, revealed preference methods like hedonic pricing cannot be used and stated preference methods like Contingent Valuation Methods (CVM) or Choice Modelling (CM) need to be used instead. Both methods, however, are expensive and time-consuming because of the need to undertake detailed surveys. Analysts, therefore, welcome opportunities to use results from stated preference studies that have been carried out by others, so that they can transfer them to their own work. The process of extrapolating results from one study to another is termed 'benefit transfer'.

CVM studies yield unique values for a specific good or service because of the way that questions about willingness to pay (WTP) or willingness to accept (WTA) are put to survey respondents. For example, a CVM study by Imber et al. (1991) sought to estimate the value of the Kakadu Conservation Zone by asking: 'Would you be willing to have your income reduced by $X for the next ten years to add [a particular] area to Kakadu National Park, rather than use it for mining?'. Because responses specifically addressed a particular area in Kakadu, the resulting valuation cannot realistically be applied elsewhere.

CM, on the other hand, establishes separate values for the constituent characteristics of a good or service, rather than a single holistic value. Had a CM study been conducted of Kakadu, it might have defined its characteristics by the number of bird species, the quality of rivers, and the range of native food types. By presenting survey respondents with different combinations of the number of bird species and native food types, varying river water quality, and the (different) cost to the respondent of preserving each combination, it is possible to estimate the relative value of each characteristic. For example, it is possible to estimate how much more value is placed by respondents on bird species, compared to river water quality. More importantly, it is possible to estimate the value placed on an increase or decrease of each separate characteristic (called a 'part worth'), so that the values can be applied to a larger area of Kakadu, or a similar ecological area. By capturing the socio-economic characteristics and site characteristics, benefit transfer can be extended to sites with different characteristics.

Because stated preference studies are expensive and time-consuming, they are not always an option for CBA studies commissioned by government. Even if funds are available, agencies often fail to budget for such studies. Ministers often require advice at short notice, thus precluding a time-consuming survey. Although databases such as Envalue and EVRI do contain a range of studies to draw on, they may not always be relevant, and specialist expertise in stated preference techniques is necessary to make proper use of them.

Table 3.1: Types of 'benefit transfer' methods for stated preference techniques

Transfer method	Example	Valuation technique
Single point value transfer	A rainforest protection value of $50 per person per year is transferred from Case Study A to Site B	Generally CVM
Marginal point value transfer	A rainforest protection value of $2 per hectare/person per year is transferred from Case Study A to Site B. The values are adjusted for the size of the area protected	Part-worths of CM. CVM can also be used, but values may not be rigorous unless multiple CVM studies are available.
Benefit function transfer	A rainforest valuation function that involves several attributes (i.e. characteristics) is transferred from Case Study A to Site B.	Model from CM study. Allows automatic adjustment for variations in attribute levels.
Meta value analysis	Results from studies A, X, Y, Z are pooled to estimate a value for Site B.	Either CVM or CM

Source: adapted from Rolfe (2006, Table 2.2)

Given that this problem faces all Australian and New Zealand jurisdictions, one solution might be to carry out large-scale CM studies of commonly appraised projects (e.g. protection of wetlands) in a manner designed to maximise the potential for benefit transfer across jurisdictions, including ease of deriving 'plug-in' values. The cost could be shared between jurisdictions in some agreed proportion, with provision for regular updating of values, perhaps through readily available price indexes.

3.3 Points in favour of making available harmonised variable values

A feature of CBA that is not shared by techniques like cost-effectiveness analysis (CEA) or Multicriteria Analysis (MCA) is that results can be expressed fully in a common numeraire of money values. Use of a monetary metric allows valid comparisons of projects as different as a road upgrade and the construction of a hospital. From a conceptual perspective, commensurate estimates allow decision-makers to compare and choose between demands on limited resources in a way that best enhances the community's overall well-being.

3.3.1 Consistency in decision-making

Implicit in the literature is the perspective that the purpose of CBA is to provide decision-makers with adequate information to determine whether social costs are exceeded by social benefits, or vice versa. If the present value of the social benefits exceeds the present value of the social costs, then net present value (NPV) is positive, and the project or policy is typically deemed to be worthwhile and should proceed.

Subject to some of the qualifications canvassed in Chapter 5, if more than one project or policy is available for implementation, it is generally presumed that decision-makers should give precedence to the one with the highest NPV. Projects or policies that have positive but lower NPVs should also proceed progressively to the extent of available (budgetary) resources.

In order to be able to make judgements about the allocation of scarce community resources, however, decision-makers need to be confident that the NPV for each project or policy has been calculated in a comparable manner. Inappropriate methodology, or the use of different values for key input variables will preclude valid comparisons between the relative merits of potential projects and policies. Harmonisation of key variables and associated methodologies would help engender a degree of consistency that does not exist today.

3.3.2 Reduction in transaction and search costs

CBA is expensive when estimates of social benefits or costs are not readily available, especially so in the case of non-marketed goods and services, because collection of appropriate data, administration of surveys and recording and analysis of findings requires considerable financial resources. Arriving at estimates dedicated to a specific project or proposal may also not be possible within a tight timeframe set by decision-makers if a stated preference survey is required. In those situations, the benefit of conducting a dedicated analysis may be outweighed by the costs.

The availability of harmonised 'plug-in' values based on techniques such as CM offers a workable solution because 'part-worth' values can be applied in different contexts. Their disadvantage is the expense of establishing a database that provides values for a comprehensive range of different situations and variables. On the other hand, a CBA may not be carried out at all in the absence of 'plug-in' values, resulting in a less than socially optimal selection of projects.

3.3.3 Procurement practice and commissioning of CBA studies

Harmonised values are likely to be beneficial to both consultants and to the government agencies that commission CBA studies.

Preparation of request for tender (RFT) documentation can be time-consuming. It is also a difficult process from the perspective of a government agency because lack of uniformity can make assessment of bids more difficult. One consultant may nominate a higher fee because they intend to estimate the value of travel time using an expensive survey, while a competitor may propose the use of a 'plug-in' value that is not entirely accurate but is sufficiently 'fit for purpose'. The difference between the technical responses of the two tenders requires a degree of expertise to interpret the proposals and this is not always available within government agencies. The use of ad hoc survey results for different CBAs also raises issues around consistency and comparability between projects, interventions and decisions.

A list of harmonised values specified in an RFT would allow consultants to quote rates on a common basis, enabling better comparisons between competitors. This would not preclude consultants from providing separate estimates for more resource-intensive work, such as estimation of local travel time values, where more specific estimates are considered to be justified. Lower resource costs incurred by consultants would be likely to be reflected in lower costs to government, and hence taxpayers.

3.3.4 Use of 'rapid CBA' (back of the envelope)

Government agencies faced with the task of evaluating projects at short notice at the request of a minister would find it easier to perform the analysis using readily available, harmonised values. As ministers and their office staff became more familiar with the use of harmonised values, the likelihood of their acceptance of 'back of the envelope' analyses would increase and hence assist in fostering more rigorous decision-making processes.

3.3.5 Reduced public confusion about the nature of cost-benefit analysis

Public understanding of CBA is limited and there appears to be a widespread misconception that the process only estimates financial costs and revenues. This may be because of the increasing commercial use of the same term to mean a financial analysis. Because money is used as the standard numeraire in social CBA, any confusion in the public mind is understandable.

Harmonisation cannot in itself dispel misconceptions about CBA, but it may assist in clarifying its nature by publishing values, and methodologies for determining non-market goods and services such as congestion or the value of statistical life. Public presentation of the various non-market values would help reassure the public that non-financial impacts are also taken into account in an economic appraisal. In particular, it would help counter inappropriate use of MCA or triple bottom line approaches.

3.3.6 Pliant consultants may bring government projects into disrepute

Exaggerated CBA studies or those that use unrealistic values will ultimately lead to a loss of confidence in such analyses on the part of the public, and even by decision-makers. In some circumstances, even socially desirable projects may be derailed for the wrong reason.

Lack of harmonisation provides ample scope for massaging results to suit a client government agency. Discussion of draft reports between consultants and clients, for example, can afford an opportunity to signal a desired outcome. Even if an agency does not explicitly or implicitly indicate what result is desired, consultants, who rely on continuing business, may prefer to provide a result that will not displease a client.

Peer review and publication of CBA studies are important tools for ensuring credible analysis, but even credible analyses can differ considerably if values of key variables, such as the value of travel time can be chosen without constraint by a consultant. The proliferation of values generated in various studies, whether based on appropriate methodologies or not, leaves open the possibility of a consultant being able to 'justify' the use of any preferred value simply on the basis that it has been used by others.

3.3.7 Common evidence base

Apart from the valuation of benefits, CBA also requires realistic projections of future impacts. Projections generally rely on a range of inputs and assumptions (e.g. about population growth or economic outlook). Whether or not input values and assumptions are modified to deliberately influence results, experience has shown that optimism bias (below) is an ever-present risk. Even in the absence of optimism bias, inappropriate use of input values or assumptions can result in misguided intervention decisions. Greater collaboration between agencies to share common evidence bases and key assumptions would help to reduce search costs as well as improving consistency in assessments across projects.

3.3.8 Reduction of optimism bias

Optimism bias is a problem worldwide, particularly with regard to transport infrastructure projects (Flyvbjerg, 2009). In some cases, the reason may be innocent, but bias is more likely to occur in cases where a project proponent carries out the CBA, or where special interest groups are able to influence the way in which a study is carried out.

Optimism bias typically arises in projects where projected demand for infrastructure or services is overestimated compared to the final outcome. The Productivity Commission (2014, p. 685) suggests that optimism bias can be countered through:

- the use of sensitivity analysis to test the robustness of outcomes to changes in variables or assumptions
- ensuring a clear statement of the assumptions underpinning the analysis to ensure transparency
- identification of the results of comparable projects carried out elsewhere.

The latter approach, called 'reference class forecasting' (Flyvbjerg, 2009), involves the identification of a relevant reference class of comparable past projects, establishing a probability distribution of a parameter being forecasted for the reference class, and comparing the current project proposal with the reference class distribution. It is therefore not much different in concept — except that it is focused on outcomes — from a quantitative meta-analysis that might be used to establish harmonised variable values.

Harmonisation can further assist in ameliorating optimism bias. For example, projected road traffic may primarily be a function of population growth projections. Specification of estimated population growth, or at least that of a credible source of estimates of population growth, can help limit any overestimate of future traffic. Similarly, any associated estimate of the social cost of car crashes can be constrained by specifying default values for the value of statistical life.

3.4 Drawbacks of using harmonised variables

It is at least arguable that harmonisation of input variable values would impose inappropriate constraints, and potential bias in terms of specific or localised analyses. Analysts and consultants, however, would be free to use their own values, so long as they were able to justify them. Ways of ensuring credible justifications might include some or all of the following:

- the results of the CBA pass a 'commonsense', 'pub', or 'sniff' test
- the study and underlying analysis and data are published
- the study is subjected to independent expert peer review
- if variable values other than those recommended in a harmonised system are to be used, the justification for their use should be published <u>before</u> the analysis is started.

3.4.1 Cost considerations

Considerable cost in resources would be incurred in selecting and harmonising values of variables to be used, as well as ensuring updating in the future. On the other hand, this cost would be partly offset through resources saved in search costs for 'plug-in' values. But it is not immediately apparent that the social benefits of doing so would exceed the social costs.

3.4.2 Inappropriate application and use of plug-in values

Use of harmonised 'plug-in' values runs the risk of their inappropriate use, particularly where a CBA envisages large changes in the use of resources or production of goods and services.

Take as an example the construction of a public housing estate. A CBA of a relatively small project could validly use a 'plug-in' value for the cost of concrete because the national price of concrete would not change much, if at all, due to the construction of several houses. A large project, by contrast, would be likely to see an increase in the price of concrete, making the use of the recommended 'plug-in' value unrealistic. Boardman et al. (2011, ch. 4) illustrate the effect of price changes of resources on both existing users of those resources (who lose consumer surplus due to higher costs) and on the project itself.

Automatic application of fixed harmonised values cannot be a substitute for rigorous economic analysis. Estimation of harmonised values covering all potential situations of supply and demand is, however, unlikely to be a realistic proposition.

3.4.3 Potential ossification

Harmonisation risks ossification in the absence of an institutional mechanism that ensures regular updating of methodologies and variable values. Federal systems with several stakeholders would be particularly prone to this problem in the absence of a collegiate approach. Arrow's impossibility theorem reinforces the likelihood of difficulty in reaching agreement on all issues. In Australia, the Council of Australian Governments (COAG) is an existing institution that could be used to establish at least an umbrella framework.

Harmonising a variable may not be practicable if different agencies or jurisdictions require the variable for significantly different purposes and cannot agree on a common definition. An alternative to harmonisation is to link related databases, perhaps with input of additional information, to allow interrogation of different combinations of data. For example, police data on road crashes involving location and vehicle types could be integrated with hospital clinical data on type and severity of injury or period of treatment. But linking databases may raise sensitive privacy issues.

In New Zealand, for example, matching of police, hospital admissions data and the NZ Accident Compensation Corporation's new claims data is carried out periodically to assist estimation of the total social cost of road crashes and injuries. For privacy and commercial sensitivity reasons, however, such linkages have not been extended to include private insurance claims data.

3.4.4 Incomplete harmonisation

In cases like climate change analyses, a national perspective may not be sufficient for adequate harmonisation. Unless harmonisation of values, such as the national externality cost of carbon emissions, is also consistent with values used in other countries, national projects or policies may result in less than optimal results.

On the other hand, reliance on foreign databases can also be problematic. Austroads research underpinning its standardised environmental externalities unit values, for example, draws heavily on European methodology and data, including the calculation of air pollution costs due to exhaust emissions. Austroads issued a review notice on 7 October 2015 foreshadowing an examination of whether Volkswagen's reported emissions violations would affect standardised unit values.

3.5 Alternatives to harmonisation

If consensus cannot be achieved, the Commonwealth could develop a set of protocols and recommended values, perhaps in cooperation with only some of the states. Other states would be able to accede to the agreement or memorandum of understanding in the future, or to make use of the values without any formal commitment. Despite the potential for some free-riding, the long-term national efficiency gains elicited from better project selection may outweigh the costs.

Other, longer term approaches might include:

- publication of results of all CBAs, so that others can copy key variables, with some values ultimately becoming dominant in usage. The US Government in 2013 reportedly required federal agencies that spend more than US$100 million per annum on research to publish the results in locations where they can be accessed for free (*The Economist*, 2014, p. 80). A similar requirement in Australia — provided it passed a cost-benefit test — could increase transparency in government, as well as reducing the transaction costs of carrying out economic appraisals

- establishment of government research or evaluation units to provide leadership and expertise in analysis. Examples include the Centre for Program Evaluation in the NSW Treasury, the Program Evaluation Unit in the WA Treasury, and Superu in New Zealand. In a budget-constrained environment, peak workloads could be covered by seconding commercial analysts temporarily to a bureau, both to carry out work and to pass on skills

- establishment of a Government Economics Network on the NZ model (www.gen.org.nz/tiki-index.php), so that economists and other policy officers can exchange views and information on a regular basis

- establishment of a Government Economic Service on the UK model (www.gov.uk/government/organisations/civil-service-government-economic-service/about), with specialist economists outsourced to line agencies to transfer analytical skills.

3.6 The Pew-MacArthur Results First Initiative in the United States

Although its antecedents go back much further, the US 'federal government first mandated the general use of cost-benefit analysis in Executive Order 12291 in early 1981' (Boardman et al., 2011, ch. 1), requiring a regulatory impact statement (RIA) for all proposed federal regulations. Similar executive orders have been issued by presidents William Clinton (no. 12866) in 1993 and Barak Obama (no. 13563) in 2011. However, Shapiro (2013) considers that studies of RIAs have concluded that their quality 'has been uneven at best'.

A 'first-of-its-kind' survey by Pew-MacArthur Results First Initiative (2013), sponsored by The Pew Charitable Trusts and the John D. and Catherine T. MacArthur Foundation, from 2008 to 2011 of the 50 US states and the District of Columbia found that 10 states systematically evaluated costs and benefits of program alternatives and used them to inform policy and budget decisions. Practice in other states varied, but use of CBAs increased significantly over the study period, spurred on by budgetary pressures.

The Pew-MacArthur study found that key constraints on the use of CBA were:

- resource limitations in terms of cost and available expertise
- data limitations because 'state accounting systems often do not track expenditures by program or activity, making it difficult to compute the marginal and total costs. States also frequently lack robust systems to monitor program outcomes ...'
- tension between the length of time required to produce a CBA and shorter legislative timeframes and hence the need to inform decision-makers at short notice.

Distrust of CBA studies by policymakers and ineffective communication of results by analysts also constrained its acceptance. The study also found that 252 statutes mandated CBA in 48 states and the District of Columbia, but a July 2011 California law directed that 'the state oil-spill-response administrator "shall not use a cost-benefit or cost-effectiveness analysis or any particular method of analysis in determining which measures provide the best achievable protection"'.

Washington state was considered to be the national leader in the use of CBA. Established in 1983, the Washington State Institute for Public Policy (WSIPP) has developed a high-quality cost-benefit model. WSIPP is often called upon to provide advice to the legislature, partly because of the trust engendered by the rigour of its work, and its development of working relationships with various agencies over time.

The peer-reviewed WSIPP (2014) model is based on a rigorous and selective meta-analysis of available data and research literature to establish the costs and benefits of public policy initiatives in the following areas:

- criminal and juvenile justice
- K–12 and early education
- child welfare
- substance abuse
- mental and public health
- public assistance
- employment and workforce development
- health care.

A particular advantage of the model is considered to be the ready availability of cost and benefit data. Consistency and replicability are complemented by the ability to provide a relatively quick analysis of proposed programs.

Costs include any externalities and the deadweight loss of taxation, and are available in both average and marginal form, as well as equivalent annual values. Although data, such as earnings, are taken from the US Census Bureau, state-specific adjustments are made where considered appropriate.

Benefits, however, are generally estimated in the form of a 'costs avoided' approach (see also s. 5.6 for issues associated with this method). For example, crime-reduction programs are assessed on the basis of costs avoided by both the state and the victims of seven major types of crime. Costs to the state are primarily budgetary, while tangible costs to victims include property damage, medical and mental health care, and intangible costs such as pain and suffering are based on jury awards.

The Results First Initiative has extended the use of the WSIPP model to 14 other states in the United States. The initiative hosts annual meetings with the states involved in the program and provides technical expertise to assist users of the model. Pew-MacArthur representatives at a workshop connected to the March 2015 Society for Benefit-Cost Analysis conference in Washington DC reported that an important aspect of assistance to the states has been the identification and categorisation of relevant program costs.

3.7 Views and practice in the various jurisdictions regarding harmonisation in the period October to December 2014

Research for this volume involved the holding of semi-structured face-to-face interviews in all the Australian (except for the Northern Territory) and New Zealand jurisdictions over the period October to December 2014. Resource constraints dictated the selection of agencies consulted and, where possible, transport, health and environment departments, as well as central agencies, were included. In several jurisdictions, requests for interviews were declined by some departments (Appendix 1).

Because interviews were held in late 2014, some of the information and views garnered then may now be outdated. For example, line agencies in Queensland drew attention to the fact that all policy was aligned with the then government's 'four pillars' policies (www.thepremier. qld.gov.au/plans-and-progress/plans/6-months-july-dec-12/four-pillar-economy.aspx (viewed 31 October 2014)). The four pillars were:

- tourism
- agricultural development
- mining
- construction.

The then Queensland Government's policy focus was on streamlining and reforming legislation to meet business needs, including cutting red tape. Policy proposals were not examined in terms of social benefit, but rather how they would contribute to economic growth. Conventional CBA was not relevant in this context. An election in January 2015, however, saw a change in government, and the 'four pillars' webpage cited above was no longer available in July 2015. In April 2015, the Queensland Productivity Commission was established, subsuming the Queensland Office of Best Practice Regulation. Victoria also saw a not entirely expected change of government following the election on 29 November 2014, although interviews had been held there a month earlier. Despite significant changes such as these, the reported perspectives of jurisdictions on harmonisation issues are necessarily those recorded over the October to December 2014 period.

A significant constraint on reporting the outcomes of the interviews is the request for anonymity that was made by a number of officials. The problem was partially overcome by drawing on handbooks and appraisal guidelines issued in some of the jurisdictions. It should also be borne in mind that, in many instances, the views expressed were those of a single official speaking informally. In some circumstances a group of officials participated, but views recorded may have been those of a dominant discussant.

The New Zealand Treasury was in the process of revising its previous CBA guidelines in November 2014, and revised guidelines were published in July 2015 (New Zealand Treasury, 2015). Support among line agencies for harmonisation of CBA variables was less effusive than in some of the Australian jurisdictions, possibly because of a non-federated political structure and greater use of consultants to carry out CBAs. However, the transport portfolio collaborates closely with Austroads and, like its Australian counterparts, maintains in-house analytical expertise.

This section and relevant parts of Chapter 4 should, therefore, be taken as indicative, rather than as fully considered positions of the government agencies that were consulted.

3.7.1 New Zealand

New Zealand has a long history of economic appraisal of projects, particularly in the transport sector. In July 2015, New Zealand Treasury released its *Guide to Social Cost Benefit Analysis* to replace the previous version that had been in circulation since 2005. It reduced the recommended annual discount rate from 8 per cent to 7 per cent for infrastructure and special purpose buildings, with default annual discount rates unchanged at 8 per cent for projects that are difficult to categorise, including regulatory proposals.

The New Zealand Treasury (2015, pp. 43–44) *Guide* notes that there are a range of common criticisms of CBA that might have contributed to its low level of usage.

- 'CBAs produce false accuracy': It is not unusual to see CBAs that state that the benefit cost ratio is '1.17'. This is most likely to be spurious accuracy. The problem of false accuracy is overcome with the use of ranges.

- 'CBAs can't measure everything': We acknowledge that there are some intangible benefits that the analyst won't be aware of or that are too hard to measure. As this guide explains, there are more benefits that can be measured than people think. As for those that can genuinely not be measured, this guide recommends that they should be drawn to decision-makers' attention along-side the results of the CBA of those benefits and costs that can be measured.

- 'CBA can be misused to produce self-serving analysis': CBA is a tool, and like all tools it can be misused. This is not a reason to dismiss CBA in favour of some other tool.

- 'CBA is too complex': ... [it is] not recommended that inexperienced policy analysts should carry out CBAs of complex or large projects themselves. Either a 'rough' CBA can be carried out, or the job should be contracted out to specialists. However, it is important for those carrying out CBAs to produce an accessible report that heeds the recommendations of this guide.

- 'Information requirements are often too onerous': CBAs can be carried out with whatever information is available. If the information is poor, then the confidence intervals will be larger. There are no other project evaluation methodologies that can produce better results from the same information base.

- 'CBAs overlook equity considerations': It is recommended that equity implications of a project be discussed and drawn to decision-makers' attention along-side the results of the CBA.

- 'The CBA is not likely to support our Minister's objectives': This comment ignores the fact that public servants have two distinct roles. The first is to give ministers free and frank advice on what the likely consequences of their decisions are. A CBA is necessary for this role. The second is to implement the Minister's decisions, whether or not those decisions are consistent with the advice given.

Economic appraisal for transport projects has evolved over the last 35 years. In the early 1980s, CBA was compulsory only for major state highway improvements. Around the mid-1980s, an economic appraisal procedure for road improvement projects was developed. This was later updated and expanded to form the *Project Evaluation Manual*. Due to the demand for guidance on approaches to assessing alternatives to road construction (e.g. public transport investment), a separate guide was developed in the mid-1990s. The value of non-work travel time was later updated as a result. In the mid-2000s, the *Project Evaluation Manual* was combined with other new guidelines (including health benefits from walking and cycling) to form the *Economic Evaluation Manual* (*EEM*). Since its initial release in 2005, the *EEM* has been updated and improved annually with uplift factors for updating benefit parameter values published at the same time to ensure road controlling authorities use the same unit valuations in their assessments.

3.7.2 Victoria

As with other jurisdictions, Victorian transport agencies were well advanced in harmonising a range of variable values, in cooperation with Austroads and the Australian Transport Council. Nevertheless transport, like other portfolios, was subject to overarching Department of Treasury and Finance Guidelines on economic appraisals.

General line agency comments included:

- the desirability of consultants providing transparent lists of assumptions made, even if harmonisation of variables were instituted
- harmonisation would require a consensual top-down approach, with the Commonwealth 'putting money on the table'
- publication of CBAs should be avoided because of their commercial-in-confidence nature as part of tendering processes.

3.7.3 New South Wales

It was pointed out by several interlocutors that New South Wales, together with Victoria, was an early developer and adopter of guidelines for undertaking economic appraisal. Material developed by the former Roads and Traffic Authority, for example, provided a basis for the 2006 National Transport Council guidelines. There was a relative preference in some agencies for consistency in approach, rather than harmonisation of variable values, although it was also recognised that default values might be useful in the case of agencies that lack CBA expertise. However, the NSW Treasury (2007, p. 2) states that 'in order to ensure that a consistent approach is used by all public sector agencies, Treasury sets certain key parameters to be used in appraisals, such as the discount rate and the rate of real earnings growth'.

3.7.4 Queensland

Several interlocutor agencies in Queensland commented on the lack of CBA expertise in the state, with the provision of detailed guidelines and harmonised default values being seen as a desirable initiative. It is likely that these views reflected the rather minimalist and non-prescriptive nature of the project analysis guidelines issued by the Queensland Treasury at the time. One suggestion was that the Commonwealth's Productivity Commission could issue guidelines that incorporate a list of 'best practice' variable values in the same way that the Australian Government Office of Best Practice Regulation does. Transport was again the standout portfolio, drawing on its own modelling capabilities and Austroads parameters.

3.7.5 South Australia

Like the NZ Treasury, the SA Department of Treasury and Finance was in the process of revising its evaluation guidelines (Department of Treasury and Finance, 2014) in late 2014. In the past it has not recommended 'plug-in' values to agencies, but has considered that ensuring the accuracy of underlying data used in analysis was an issue of particular importance. One line agency considered that a set of 'plug-in values' that could be adjusted for different circumstances and situations would be a good start to encouraging more CBA. It would be important, however, to have transparency in the derivation of such values, including the assumptions made.

3.7.6 Western Australia

Discussion at central agency level in Western Australia indicated some predilection for the use of authoritative harmonised values. Unsolicited reference was made to the usefulness of the Environmental Value Reference Inventory (EVRI) database as a source for environmental variable values. One line agency, however, cautioned against the unqualified application of nationally harmonised variable values, especially because there were obvious differences in conditions and circumstances in Western Australia compared to other parts of Australia.

3.7.7 Tasmania

Analytical CBA expertise in Tasmania resides primarily in the Department of Treasury and Finance, although one agency referred to a proposal to establish an Infrastructure Tasmania organisation (in fact established mid-2015) to improve coordination of infrastructure appraisals. Specialist consultants are relied on to perform CBA. Austroads material was used in the absence of an internal manual for economic evaluation. The principle of harmonisation was regarded positively in principle, subject to the caveat of addressing local conditions and needs.

3.7.8 Australian Capital Territory

As in Tasmania, analytical expertise in the Australian Capital Territory resides primarily in the Treasury, but internal evaluation manuals are also provided to line agencies for the preparation of project proposals. Informal discussion indicated support in principle for a greater degree of harmonisation in terms of both default variable values and methodology. One view was that the benefit of harmonisation within the ACT government would probably be even more beneficial than inter-jurisdictional harmonisation.

3.7.9 Commonwealth Government

The leadership role exhibited in the past by the Department of Finance (1991) with its publication of the *Handbook of Cost-Benefit Analysis*, and the revised version in 2006, has not been maintained. While some officials have expertise in the area of CBA, Finance's previous role has dissipated. Further, its administrative responsibility for the Commonwealth's Office of Best Practice Regulation (OBPR) was transferred to the Department of the Prime Minister and Cabinet in September 2013. The Commonwealth Treasury Department has internal expertise in CBA, but its role is simply that of a 'consumer' of studies produced or commissioned by line departments when briefing the Treasurer on new proposals.

The Productivity Commission and Infrastructure Australia possess significant analytical capabilities. The Productivity Commission undertakes inquiries on topics referred to it by the Australian Government. It also undertakes internal research on productivity and regulatory issues, but does not have a coordination role with respect to inter-jurisdictional evaluation practices.

On 6 November 2014, the Minister for Infrastructure and Regional Development issued a statement of expectations (Truss, 2014) to the board of Infrastructure Australia, requiring it, inter alia, to produce a rolling 15-year plan of infrastructure priorities at the national and state levels on the basis of rigorous cost-benefit analysis. Infrastructure proposals to be considered include transport, water, communications, energy, and social infrastructure in the education and health areas. Given the broad range of areas to be covered, it is unsurprising that Infrastructure Australia officials informally favour a greater degree of harmonisation in the evaluation of projects.

3.8 Conclusion

With the exception of the transport sector, there is a surprising dearth of economic appraisal expertise in the line agencies of most jurisdictions. Whether due to deliberate outsourcing or not, relevant expertise is now primarily the domain of commercial consultants.

In principle, it should not matter whether appropriate expertise is held within the public service or outside it, because it is always possible to commission external experts to undertake any required studies. In practice, however, the current situation is less than ideal, partly because of the operational characteristics of the public service.

To the extent that new policy proposals are not predictable at the time of setting budgets, public service agencies generally do not set aside budgeted funds to undertake CBA studies. Even where funds may be available, procurement principles and processes mean that there may be insufficient time to commission an external CBA if a new policy proposal requires a quick response from a minister or the government. Where outside experts are commissioned, the paucity of internal expertise can mean that a request for tender may not be expressed with sufficient clarity. If the quality of the final product cannot be adequately assessed internally, even peer review processes may not obviate issues such as the optimism bias that afflicted some recent Australian urban tunnel projects. Given that ministers typically seek policy advice from their portfolios rather than external consultants, a general lack of expertise in CBA may also affect the quality of policy advice provided.

Harmonisation of variable values and methodologies offers some solutions in principle, but it is likely to require Sisyphean effort in practice. There are too many jurisdictions and competing interests within each one to establish a workable arrangement. The lack of in-house expertise itself would complicate any negotiations.

An alternative might be for an agency to adopt a de facto leadership role. Perhaps building on existing databases, like that provided by Austroads and Infrastructure Australia requirements, additional roles could be added over time. A central agency in one of the jurisdictions, a university, or a body like the (Australian) Productivity Commission or the Office of Best Practice Regulation could undertake this task, given an appropriate level of resources and collaboration with other jurisdictions.

A more practicable approach may be to begin a step further back, by harmonising the processes involved in economic appraisal. Harmonising the framework adopted for CBA studies would not only increase the transparency of results, it would also make them more accessible to readers. It could also accommodate the future establishment of any desirable harmonisation of variable values or methodologies.

4

A framework approach
to harmonisation

It is clear from discussions with government agencies in the Australian and New Zealand jurisdictions (except the Northern Territory) that all is not well in the area of economic evaluation. A survey of members of the Economic Society of Australia and the New Zealand Government Economics Network (Chapter 2) confirmed this impression. It is equally clear (Chapter 3) that any attempt to harmonise variable or parameter values to promote consistency and credibility in cost-benefit analysis (CBA) studies would be fraught with methodological and perhaps political difficulties.

Most academic texts implicitly also recognise that uniformity in approach is neither desirable nor practicable. They proceed instead on the basis of a general step-wise framework for conducting a CBA study. The 10 steps presented below are a typical presentational approach, although the number of steps, names and descriptions differ between texts.

1. specify the objective of the analysis
2. define 'standing' and scope
3. establish the base case: establishing a reference point
4. predict the effects of the policy or project over its life cycle
5. estimate the economic value of the costs and benefits
6. adjust costs and benefits for risk

7. calculate the net present value (NPV) of the costs and benefits

8. conduct sensitivity analysis

9. determine distributional consequences and distributional weighting of costs and benefits

10. arrive at a conclusion or recommendations for the CBA.

The framework is composed of a series of sequential processes. For example, clear specification of the objective of the proposed policy or project as the first step ensures that subsequent steps are executed with reference to it, so that the study remains internally consistent. The second step establishes the perspective from which costs and benefits are estimated. It ensures that a local government study, for example, does not include costs or benefits that are incurred or reaped only at a national level. The final steps are contingent on the results determined in the intervening analysis and provide the information that is typically required by decision-makers.

One advantage of systematising a CBA study in this way is that it helps clarify where different parts of the analysis fit within the overall picture. Complex studies may include detailed, and hence lengthy, sections that estimate components of variables, so it may not always be clear why or how a particular part relates to other sections of the study, or to the final result.

Because consultants and other analysts tend to approach CBA studies from unique perspectives — depending on the key estimation issues involved — reports can be idiosyncratic, following no particular order, and perhaps devoting considerable space to esoteric issues of particular interest to the problem at hand. Reading such reports, even if they are technically rigorous, is time-consuming, even for experienced users of CBA analyses, because it is necessary to identify the key components and to check for internal consistency.

Preparation, presentation and comprehension of CBA studies could be facilitated if a harmonised framework such as the one above were adopted by the various jurisdictions. Consistency in the order of the presentation of the steps would need to be maintained in order to maximise transparency for readers searching for specific information about a study.

Implementation of a harmonised framework need not require a formal agreement between all of the jurisdictions. Adoption of a framework — along the lines of that outlined in this chapter — by a central agency in one of the larger jurisdictions, the Office of Best Practice Regulation, or the Productivity Commission, would encourage others to follow over time.

Improved access to completed CBA studies undertaken by the Commonwealth Government would also assist in fostering increased harmonisation of approach. In this regard, amendment of section 47C(3)(a) of the *Freedom of Information Act 1982* to specifically include the social sciences would be an important first step.

Recommendations

- A common approach be adopted by the various jurisdictions in presenting the results of CBA studies, using a harmonised framework, such as proposed in the 10 steps outlined above.
- In the absence of a formal inter-jurisdictional agreement, consideration should be given by one of the central agencies to an informal leadership role by adopting a framework along the lines outlined in this chapter.
- Section 47C(3)(a) of the *Freedom of Information Act 1982* should be amended to specifically include the social sciences.

4.1 Specify the objective of the analysis

Clarity of objective is self-evidently essential in ensuring that each step in a CBA study is consistent with preceding and successive steps. In particular, it is important that alternative approaches or projects are formulated in a way that is consistent with the desired outcomes of decision-makers. An example might be the implementation of preventative health programs as an alternative to constructing a new hospital in order to address the policy objective of reducing the effect of some debilitating medical condition on the community.

4.1.1 Constraints

An informed approach to identifying realistic alternatives also requires an elicitation of legal, physical, geographic, informational, political and other constraints that could limit achievement of the policy objective. A key feature of the CBA should, therefore, be a specific enumeration and examination of the constraints that may influence achievement of the desired outcome.

4.1.2 Cataloguing alternative projects

All potential alternative projects should be listed at the outset so as to avoid 'first selection' bias. In the words of NSW Treasury (2007, p. 3), 'the economic appraisal should not be a "business case" which simply promotes a preferred approach'.[1] The list should not be limited to a single approach, such as construction of infrastructure or regulation of an activity. Market- or price-based solutions, delayed or staged implementation, and use of a real options approach, should also be considered. For example, a program to encourage people to increase their level of active exercise may be an effective alternative to a proposal to build a dedicated facility to treat obesity or diabetes.

For practical reasons, the full list of alternative projects will need pruning if the CBA is to be conducted within time and resource constraints. In doing so, however, transparency requires that reasons should be given for the rejection of projects that are not shortlisted. In some circumstances, it may also be possible to conduct a 'back of the envelope' or 'rapid CBA' appraisal of the major benefits and costs to assist in the filtering process with the detailed CBA conducted for the key proposals. For complex decisions, each proposal may deserve a standalone CBA to detail the process and results. In those situations, it is necessary to ensure different CBAs use consistent assumptions and unit value in the assessment and an overall CBA report is prepared to summarise all individual analyses.

---

1   If a decision has already been taken by government that a specific project should be undertaken, then a cost-effectiveness analysis may be more appropriate than proceeding with a CBA. A government decision to proceed is presumably based on its perceived benefits. Implementation is then largely a matter of lowest cost, or value for money.

4.1.3 The role of the analyst in choosing alternatives for appraisal

Rather surprisingly, CBA textbooks rarely discuss the issue of selecting alternative projects to include in an appraisal. In practice, an analyst may be asked to evaluate only one project against a base case, but may also be aware of other potentially viable alternatives. If the commissioning agency rules out comparisons of the proposed project with potential alternatives, the analyst may face a moral dilemma. Sugden & Williams (1978, p. 231) examine some of the issues involved, but are unequivocal about the stance to be taken by the analyst:

> The analyst has a dual role to play in relation to the set of alternatives to be compared. He may offer advice at this initial stage, seeking to ensure that important and practicable policy options are not ignored. Here the roles of decision-maker and analyst overlap a good deal. And at the end of the analysis, the analyst should do his best to ensure that his findings are not misinterpreted, or read as implying more than they really do. If important alternatives have not been considered in the study, intellectual honesty requires that the analyst points this out. It is possible that the decision-maker may suppress these, and perhaps other significant qualifications when presenting the analyst's work in support of his decision. This puts the analyst in a difficult position but we believe that the analyst has the professional duty to set the record straight, for otherwise analysis in general is brought into disrepute. If in the special circumstances this is impossible, then it becomes a matter of conscience for the analyst whether he can continue working for that client, and whether he should dissuade other analysts from so doing.

Table 2.4 reveals that more than half the respondents considered that CBAs are not conducted independently and objectively, are used to justify rather than inform, and are not undertaken for important decisions. Requiring CBAs to record explicitly why apparently feasible alternative projects have not been included in an analysis is desirable in maintaining credibility, even if decision-makers do not release this information.

4.1.4 Strategic merit tests

Transport agency guidelines in the various jurisdictions generally specify the conduct of a 'strategic merit test' in an early stage of a project. For example, Transport for NSW (previously the Road Transport Authority) (2013, p. 72) states that:

> Strategic merit testing is a technique used to check if the proposed project aligns with the economic, environmental and social objectives, policies and strategies of the government. This qualitative project appraisal tool used during the strategic planning phase includes a series of questions which try to identify the contribution of the proposed project to the government's objectives, policies and strategies.

On one reading, this advice is not much different to the point made above that constraints, including those of a political nature, should be taken into account in identifying a realistic set of alternative projects. On the other hand, a less sympathetic interpretation might lead one to conclude that there is a considerable risk of bias posed by such 'strategic merit testing', with analysts second-guessing ministers as to what alternative projects might in fact be acceptable to the government. Government policy is not always set in stone, and may change during the course of an electoral cycle, especially if changeable budget constraints dictate a reconsideration of earlier priorities. From this perspective, a full listing of projects that satisfy the government's primary objective is a desirable element of all CBA studies.

A broader, more informative approach to the use of a 'strategic merit test' might be to compare government priorities in all sectors of society — perhaps by applying a rapid CBA assessment — to gauge the relative merit of using scarce resources in the transport sector compared to expenditure on health or education or defence. This may not be practical, however, and may pre-empt government consideration of the merits of broader alternatives. In some cases, governments may have decided formally or informally that they will proceed with a project or program long before a CBA is commissioned.

The national guidelines issued by the Australian Transport Council (2006, Part 3, p. 16) are rather circumspect, acknowledging the subjective nature of decisions made by government. Nevertheless, the risk remains that an unsophisticated approach that considers 'strategic merit' can result in a biased selection of project alternatives. This may especially be the case for inexperienced officials who commission a tendentious CBA study by a commercial consultant.

4.1.5 Peer review

Studies of complex projects can involve difficult issues of a methodological or conceptual nature. In order to ensure a defensible result, it is sometimes the practice to engage a peer body or analyst to review the study to reassure decision-makers or the public of its fidelity. The concept is analogous to the gateway process employed in large government procurement programs.

In general, CBA studies are time-consuming, and may be expensive. There is, therefore, merit in engaging a peer reviewer early in the process, to provide critique and feedback throughout the study, rather than at the end when there may be a reluctance to redress any apparent shortcomings. In doing so, however, it would be prudent to maintain a degree of independence for the reviewer, perhaps with greater use of academics who are not reliant on government agencies for continued work.

4.1.6 Recommendations

A CBA should record explicitly:

- the objective of the proposed project or policy
- a full list of alternative projects and policy initiatives that could be used to achieve the objective, including market-based alternatives to construction of infrastructure or its expansion
- reasons for not including any of the feasible alternative projects in the CBA analysis
- a process of objective and independent peer review be instituted at an early stage of the analysis for all government-funded studies.

4.2 Define 'standing' and scope

Many CBA studies fail to define explicitly the perspective from which costs and benefits are to be included or excluded.

Specification at the outset of the perspective or 'standing' to be taken in an analysis is a key determinant of subsequent steps, especially the inclusion or exclusion of particular benefits or costs. For example, if the analyst or decision-maker decides to conduct the analysis from the standpoint of the city of Auckland, then benefits accruing to residents of Wellington or Dunedin, or costs imposed on them, should not be counted.

The Capital Metro Agency (2014) business case for Canberra's proposed light rail system does not explicitly define standing. It implies in several parts (e.g. p. 69) that a key objective is 'facilitating economic growth for the ACT [Australian Capital Territory]', including job creation. It is therefore unsurprising that the study wrongly includes as a benefit additional tax revenue from an assumed larger workforce (Table 28, p. 102), even though income tax is levied and largely retained by the federal government rather than the ACT. Further, the study does not reveal how much of the additional employed labour is likely to be sourced from residents of the ACT, rather than from neighbouring commuter towns like Queanbeyan, Goulburn or Yass, which are located in New South Wales.

Omission of the critical step of defining standing in a CBA is difficult to condone. However, Whittington and MacRae (1986) argue that:

> The practice of equating standing with citizenship worked reasonably well in most early applications of cost-benefit analysis. For instance, in the appraisal of water resources development projects, it served to broaden the focus of the analysis from the immediate beneficiaries for a project (often limited to a small district or region) to include other citizens who would have to pay the cost of what typically turned out to be porkbarrel projects. Neither the costs nor the benefits commonly spilled over national boundaries. Though the techniques of cost-benefit analysis were often misused, the thrust of the analysis should theoretically have detected narrowly conceived projects that were designed to serve only a few who would gain something at the expense of the majority, who would lose more. The issue of standing may also have been neglected in the literature because economists felt they had little expertise that could be brought to bear on the question. Thus, following Mishan, they attempted to calculate the willingness to pay for 'each person in the defined community', leaving the determination of the 'defined community' to the political process.

The issue of standing was the subject of debate in the early 1990s, primarily by Trumbull (1990), Whittington and MacRae (1990) and Zerbe (1991) in response to an article by Whittington and MacRae (1986). Despite some unresolved contentious issues, Boardman et al. (2011, ch. 2) reflect contemporary thinking in suggesting that standing in CBA should be from a national perspective as a default position, and be based on prevailing social norms and preferences, and legal rights.

Ethical conundrums can bedevil attempts at satisfactory approaches to defining standing. Some examples include the interests of aborted foetuses, the rights of prisoners incarcerated near a noisy airport, treatment of non-human hominids, local pollution that affects neighbouring countries, or non-participation of children in vaccination programs if their parents object.

4.2.1 Standing and the value of statistical life

The human capital approach essentially posits that society values a (statistical) life on the basis of the value of the wages that the deceased could have been expected to earn in their remaining lifetime as measured by their life expectancy at a particular age.

Most Australian road and rail agencies — New South Wales being an exception — have for many years used the human capital approach to value statistical life, or the hybrid approach employed by the Australian Bureau of Infrastructure, Transport and Regional Economics (2009). In New Zealand, the Ministry for Transport specifies the value of statistical life (VOSL), and the same value is used by New Zealand Treasury and other departments and agencies. The New Zealand VOSL has been based on the willingness to pay (WTP) approach since 1990, when it replaced the human capital approach.

One well-known disadvantage of the human capital approach is that the lives of pensioners who no longer earn a wage should theoretically be valued at zero, or worse. If a life is lost, it could be argued that society loses the value of that person's production (as measured by their wage), but that society will also save the resources that would have been consumed by the individual in their remaining lifetime. However, Prest and Turvey (1965, p. 722–23) point out that this issue of consumption forgone poses a conundrum for the analyst:

Ignoring non-materialistic considerations like the grief of family and friends, the loss to society of a decedent is typically taken to be the wealth that the person would have accumulated, plus taxes that would have been paid, minus any transfer payments that he or she would have received. An adjustment sometimes made to this 'value of life' approach is to subtract the value of the resources that would have been consumed by the individual because they can be used by society for other purposes, and are therefore a social 'gain'. But this presupposes that society is defined as it exists *after* the person's death. That is, standing is defined implicitly to exclude the statistically deceased individual.

Prest and Turvey (1965) argue that an alternative perspective might be to consider society as including all current residents or citizens, including those who will die in the future. Imagine these residents considering a proposed safety project and discussing the cost to society of future deaths of residents. Members of this discussion group would still see themselves as part of society into the future. For them individually, the loss due to death would include the consumption that they would forgo. Since they are still part of society, the disbenefit of their loss of consumption into the future would conceptually also represent a loss to society. From this perspective, the private loss of consumption by a prospective decedent should be counted as a social *loss*, rather than an offsetting 'gain'.

4.2.2 Standing and wider economic impacts in transport analysis

The 1980s saw the beginnings of a debate about the broader effects of transport infrastructure improvements on the economy, in addition to the conventional CBA methods employed by transport economists. Analysts and agencies in the United Kingdom began to characterise such effects as 'wider economic benefits', an inappropriate term given that they relate mainly to changes in gross domestic product due to public investment in infrastructure. Appendix 3 examines the issues in more detail.

Recent work, reviewed by Laird and Mackie (2010), has revealed a failing by earlier studies to take into account the standing or 'prism' from which the analysis was conducted. Increased productivity due to infrastructure investment was found to be mainly due to the relocation of the most productive people to larger cities. At a national level, the additional productivity effect due to people relocating would simply be redistributive, with a particular area gaining what another loses, and therefore with no net increase. Local government, on the other hand, could be expected to include any increased productivity in its assessment of an infrastructure project.

The wider economic impacts (WEI) estimated in various sub-national studies were in general comparatively large compared to conventional estimates of net social benefits of transport and other infrastructure projects (Laird & Mackie, 2010). Failure to consider the implications of choice of 'standing' therefore risks significant bias in decision-making about the effect of infrastructure investment on the economy as a whole.

4.2.3 Practice in the jurisdictions

Despite its obvious importance in the aggregation of costs and benefits, the treatment of standing is largely absent from Australian Government manuals for CBA. Even the Australian Government Department of Finance and Administration (2006) handbook on CBA does not deal explicitly with the concept of standing.

Evaluation guidelines issued by the SA Department of Treasury and Finance (2014, p. 31) refer in passing to the need to assess costs and benefits that impact upon the 'state economy and broader community'. A NSW Government Department of Infrastructure & Planning (2012) guideline for the use of CBA in mining and coal seam gas proposals states that costs and benefits should be aggregated 'over the whole community', but without specifying the extent of the community. The Victorian Department of Treasury and Finance (Government of Victoria, 2014) guide to CBA in regulation indicates that impacts on different groups and governments should be identified, but does not deal explicitly with the issue of standing.

In contrast, a European Commission (2008) guide to CBA devotes about half a page to the need to establish standing as part of the socio-economic context and scope of the analysis. A draft CBA guide issued by the Treasury Board of Canada Secretariat (1998), also devoted space to the issue of standing, but the oft-cited HM Treasury (2003) Green Book does not cover the topic. New Zealand Treasury (2005, p. 11) stated its expectation that a CBA would be undertaken from a national perspective, but the revised guide that was issued in July 2015 (New Zealand Treasury, 2015) is more equivocal, citing only some examples of the difficulties involved in defining standing.

Officials interviewed in the various Australian states invariably responded that standing was based on a purely state perspective. Somewhat incongruously, no distinction is made between state residents and visitors from other states or abroad, for example, in estimating the benefits of a faster transport link between a capital city airport and the central business district. The reason generally given was that no data are available to distinguish between different users of infrastructure.

Practice in the various Australian jurisdictions is thus consistent with the Austroads (Rockliffe et al., 2012, Part 2, p. 8) suggestion that standing should include 'all affected persons', including foreigners, because 'few data sources distinguish the residency of affected persons'. One rationale given for not addressing this contradiction is that governments generally wish to promote tourism, so that the practice of including non-residents is not inconsistent with the overall strategic objectives of the government.[2] It is difficult to believe, however, that no adjustment is possible on the basis of available statistics produced by the Australian Government agency Tourism Research Australia.

Counting benefits to non-residents of a particular state when standing is taken as being confined to the residents of that state means that the benefits of the project will be overstated. In the health sector, however, interstate agreements about mutual hospital treatment may make it difficult to justify excluding consideration of project benefits to non-residents, even if 'standing' has been specified as being limited to one state alone.

On the face of it, there appears to be little justification for persisting with a narrow state-based approach to standing when benefits to non-residents are being counted. However, several jurisdictions intimated

---

2   This argument is redolent of the use of apologetics to defend a position that may otherwise be logically flawed. If the government wishes to promote tourism, it should do so directly with a specific project or program, subject to justification through a CBA. Inclusion of benefits to tourists in an infrastructure project is a blunt instrument that may have no significant causal relationships to the number of tourists in the country.

in interviews that their governments would not be keen to take into account any externalities that local projects might impose on another state. For example differences in waste disposal fees between states has seen at least one state accepting a neighbouring state's waste, but any externalities that might be imposed were not taken into account in an evaluation by the sending state. While not presented by interlocutors as a justification for taking a state-only perspective, political reality is that the issue of potential externalities would seem to be a pertinent disincentive to changing the current practice of purely state-based standing.

4.2.4 Recommendations

The need to clearly define standing at the outset of an analysis is important, but it would be inappropriate to offer prescriptive guidelines for areas that involve ethical issues.

Nevertheless, a degree harmonisation of approaches is desirable to promote greater consistency and transparency in economic evaluation. In particular:

- Explicit specification of 'standing' should be provided in all CBA studies. Where more than one perspective is adopted (e.g. to provide additional information requested by decision-makers), results should be shown separately for each specification.
- Adoption of a national perspective for all CBA studies should be the default position. Studies should clearly identify the parties whose benefits and costs are included, as well as those who are specifically excluded from the analysis.
- Consideration should be given to adopting a convention that all residents of Australia, not just citizens, be granted standing in a CBA study.

4.3 Establish the base case: Establishing a reference point

Calculation of additional benefits and additional costs requires an initial or reference case from which to measure the changes induced by implementation of a project or policy. This reference case is often termed the 'base case' in CBA studies, but is also variously depicted as the 'before project situation', 'status quo option', 'do nothing' option, 'business as usual' and 'do the minimum' option. The latter two terms probably best express the underlying concept of a counterfactual situation that would exist if the project or policy were not implemented. In general, all alternative projects specified in Section 4.2 above should be evaluated against the same base case.

A realistic base case does not assume that past behaviour will be replicated infinitely into the future. It recognises that life goes on, even if a particular project or policy is not implemented. Populations may grow or diminish and age profiles will shift, traffic densities may increase, land-use patterns will change, and similar but smaller projects may be implemented.

Nevertheless, political constraints sometimes require use of a base case different to the 'business as usual' or 'do the minimum' scenarios. For example an analysis of the National Broadband Network (NBN) by the Australian Department of Communications (2014, Vol. II, p. 9) eschewed the use of continued rollout of the NBN as being 'clearly not realistic', because the incoming government had explicitly decided not to continue it. The base case adopted was continued rollout, but without any further government subsidy of the operation.

4.3.1 The period of the base case

Establishing the period of the base case — the time of its beginning and the time of its end — determines which, and how many, costs and benefits are counted. Where only one project is analysed, the base case and project periods may coincide naturally, although long-lived projects may require the inclusion of residual or 'horizon' values in order to justify choice of matching periods. If more than one alternative project is analysed and the project life cycles do not coincide, resort to equivalent annual values (s. 5.2), or similar techniques, may be required.

4.3.2 Recommendations

The importance of the base case as a reference point for estimating additional costs and benefits suggests that there would be merit in harmonising the following procedural principles:

- listing and explanation of all assumptions made in choosing or developing the base case scenario
- as a default option, use official sources for key variables employed in projections
- justification for use of estimates that are not based on official sources
- specification and justification of the time period selected for the base case
- where relevant, ensuring consistency of base case assumptions with those used in projections of impacts of the project or policy.

4.4 Predict the effects of the policy or project over its life cycle

The additional benefits and costs of a project are measured in terms of the difference of the effects induced by the implementation of a project, compared to the counterfactual of a base case. In simple terms, the project that generates the highest level of net benefit relative to the common base case is to be preferred.

Even if an analyst is experienced and knowledgeable, there is some likelihood that they may not fully identify all the impacts of a project, particularly if there is novelty in the case being examined. Prudence suggests a wide-ranging consultative process by the analyst, including particularly with operators (the people with the spanners) and those directly affected by the project, in order to avoid bias due to omitted impacts.

Unless the analyst provides readers of the study with information about who has been consulted, however, it is difficult for a decision-maker to form a judgement about the rigour of the results. Overcoming this asymmetry of information is relatively straightforward if the analyst provides a list of those consulted. The same is true of published sources that may have been relied on. A 'belts and braces' approach also requires the analyst to provide reasons for *not* consulting relevant people or sources of information.

Transparency and accountability also require that the identified impacts are presented by the analyst to allow peer reviewers and decision-makers to identify omissions from the analysis. In short-listing the impacts for which economic values are to be estimated, the analyst should provide cogent reasons for all exclusions.

4.4.1 The period of analysis of the project(s)

The period of time chosen for analysis of a project and its alternatives determines the types and number of costs and benefits that are aggregated over time, just as for the base case. Transparency is therefore critical, but is rarely observed in practice. Textbooks are also silent in this area, despite the fact that manipulation of results can be more easily achieved than fiddling with the more obvious aspects of a CBA, such as the discount rate.

The Canberra light rail project is a case in point. Economic analysis conducted by Capital Metro Agency (2014, Table 19) used a 30-year period beginning in 2016, despite positing an 'operating term of 20 years'. Because the analysis begins from construction in 2016, it excludes significant set-up costs.[3] It has been argued informally by Capital Metro that exclusion of preliminary costs accords with accounting standards because the formal Cabinet decision to proceed with the light rail project was not made until after contracts were let for preliminary engineering work and the agency had been established. In effect, the project period has been broken up into separate stages in a way that excludes preliminary project costs.

Where government procurement guidelines set limits to expenditure in the absence of a formal request for tender process, there may be a temptation to break procurement projects up into separate stages that all fall below the limit. To preclude this, guidelines typically require bundling of staged costs to ensure a full accounting of the total costs involved. The *Commonwealth Procurement Guidelines* (2005, s. 8.10), for example, contain the following safeguard clause:

> Where a procurement is to be conducted in multiple parts with contracts awarded either at the same time or over a period of time,

---

3   Specific figures are not readily available, but *Canberra Times* (6 August 2014, p. 2) reported that $30 million had been budgeted over two years from July 2013, including $9.8 million for consultancies and $2.3 million for staff and administration costs.

with one or more suppliers, the estimated value of the property or services being procured must include the estimated total maximum value of all of the contracts.

Employment of a similar approach in harmonising the analytical framework for CBA should be considered to ensure a 'true and fair' view of proposals as a whole. By the same token, all costs relevant to implementation of a government decision to proceed with a project or program should also be included: these may include items such as post-implementation reviews, *in media res* and ex post reviews, auditor investigations, and reports to ministers or parliament.

4.4.2 Transfer payments

Pensions, subsidies to businesses, taxes and unemployment benefits are examples of transfer payments. They redistribute resources or wealth without affecting the overall well-being of society (assuming, for example, that the marginal utility of income is constant). The person providing the payment does not directly receive any goods or services in return for the payment.

Because transfer payments are not considered to affect the overall well-being of society, they are typically treated as being neither a cost nor a benefit. For this reason, it is not uncommon for transfer payments to be ignored in a CBA. Nevertheless, it is useful to identify such transfers at an early stage of the analysis because they are relevant to any discussion of distributional consequences at a later stage of the CBA.

4.4.3 Duality in costs and benefits

There is often an element of duality in CBA. Duck hunters, for example, may welcome the construction of a dam, but campers may regret the loss of trees and land.

An increase in house rents (a change in price) that does not reflect a change in costs involves greater expenditure by the person renting the house. But the tenant's increased expenditure is exactly offset by the additional revenue to the landlord. Such pecuniary effects cancel each other out, so their inclusion in a CBA is effectively superfluous. Nevertheless, there is merit in including them when compiling a list of project impacts, both to demonstrate comprehensiveness, and because they can provide useful information to decision-makers about the distributional outcomes of a project.

Some proponents of transport infrastructure favour the automatic inclusion of WEIs (Appendix 3) in project appraisals. A review of the WEI literature, however, found no reference to the need to also estimate the corresponding deadweight loss (Appendix 7) of a project. This is despite the fact that projects that can be expected to generate significant WEIs are also likely to require significant amounts of government expenditure, suggesting at least some degree of deadweight loss due to government borrowing or increased taxation. Some WEI studies do refer to potential negative effects of agglomeration, such as increased traffic congestion, but with no further investigation of the strength of such offsetting effects.

The Capital Metro Agency (2014) analysis of the Canberra light rail project includes as a benefit the WEI of the light rail, amounting to about 20 per cent of total estimated benefits. These so-called agglomeration benefits are largely calculated on the basis of the effect of government expenditure on the supply of labour. However, there is no countervailing inclusion of the marginal excess tax burden (METB) effects on disposable income, and hence transactions, or on the supply of labour. Costs have therefore been underestimated.

It is important to not only list all the positive and the negative effects that might be expected to arise from a project, but also to justify why some are not rigorously investigated. It need hardly be pointed out that failure to do so invites risk of bias.

4.4.4 Causality

Demonstration of causality is not a common aspect of CBA studies, despite its analytical importance. Methodological harmonisation requires, at the very least, an attempt to demonstrate causation, rather than relying on statistical correlations alone. Transport safety interventions, in particular, require an understanding of the possible range of impacts, rather than relying on experience in other countries.

On the basis of a survey of American regulatory impact statements, a conference paper by Johnston (2015) argued that:

epidemiological evidence alone is highly unreliable as a measure of actual health impacts. This point is made with a detailed analysis of estimates of the impact of fine particulates on excess mortality. The data show that particulates have their biggest impact on cardiovascular mortality among the elderly in the winter months. However, the medical literature reveals a variety of mechanisms that account for the heightened risk of death from cardiovascular causes among the elderly during the winter, and these mechanisms do not involve exposure to elevated levels of fine particulates. If researchers look statistically at only one particular factor — fine particulates — while ignoring others, then estimates are subject to omitted variables bias. A better approach is to look first to identify potential causal mechanisms so that all potential factors are controlled for in statistical studies ...

The cases of WEIs and the METB provide another example. A key qualification in the estimation of WEIs is that the direction of causality needs to be demonstrated for the relationship between effective density and productivity. It is also important to demonstrate that the relationship has not been overestimated because explanatory variables have been omitted. In the case of the estimated deadweight social loss due to increased taxation used to fund a project, a prior condition is the need to demonstrate that the expenditure can be attributed to increased taxes rather than borrowing or a countervailing reduction in expenditure elsewhere in the budget. Automatic inclusion of either effect without appropriate supporting evidence would likely result in a biased estimate of net benefits.

4.4.5 Primary and secondary markets

In listing the expected impacts of projects, it is useful to distinguish as far as possible between primary and secondary markets.

There are no firm rules for such distinctions, but the primary market can usually be divined from the objective of the CBA study. Textbooks such as Boardman et al. (2011) provide guidance on the circumstances in which impacts in secondary markets should be included in the appraisal. WEIs are an example of secondary market benefits, although not all the effects are suitable for inclusion in a CBA. Productivity effects on GDP, for example, are not commensurable with social surplus estimates in a CBA.

4.4.6 Recommendations

The following are worthwhile conventions for analysts compiling a catalogue of expected project impacts:

- provision of a comprehensive list of impacts and an explanation of all assumptions made in predicting impacts
- provision of a list of persons and sources consulted to identify project impacts
- provision of evidence-based justification of causality for all impacts identified
- cogent explanations for excluding impacts that have not been short-listed
- all costs and benefits, including the costs of preliminary analyses or administrative preparation, should be attributed to the project, even where the project is implemented in stages that may appear to be separate projects
- inclusion of all relevant implementation costs, including post-implementation and final ex post review on completion of the project or program
- identification and/or valuation of major transfer payments that are significant enough to include in a distributional analysis
- require the use of official sources for key variables employed in the base case
- explanation of reasons for use of estimates not based on official sources
- ensure consistency of time period used with that of the base case
- where relevant, ensure consistency of project impact assumptions with those used in the base case.

4.5 Estimate the economic value of the costs and benefits

Identification of the costs and benefits of the base case and those of the projects being assessed, needs to be followed by the estimation of their economic values. Costs are valued as opportunity costs, and benefits are valued in terms of social surplus. Boardman et al. (2011)

define the social surplus as consisting of consumer surplus, producer (i.e. factor) surplus, government surplus and externalities, but other categories could also be used.

Various methods are used to estimate WTP in order to estimate various aspects of social surplus. Commonly used approaches include econometric estimation where data are available, travel cost methods, market analogies, contingent valuation surveys, choice modelling, and hedonic pricing (Boardman et al., 2011; Campbell & Brown, 2003). Each of these methods has advantages and disadvantages, so that the analyst needs to choose the one best suited to the project at hand.

4.5.1 Harmonisation of variable values

The transport sector has a predilection for standardised variable values. Austroads, for example, has for many years provided detailed values, most recently in Tan et al. (2012). Similarly, the New Zealand Transport Agency provides evaluation methodologies and benefit parameter values in its *Economic Evaluation Manual*, which is updated annually. The European Commission (2008) guide to CBA also contains detailed instructions and variable values for use in a variety of major projects as part of its cohesion policy, the objective of which is to reduce regional socio-economic disparities.

Whether Australian agencies should adopt harmonised values for key variables is open to question. To ensure consistency and comparability between different projects, there may be some justification for harmonising the value of a variable such as the VOSL, because it is used by two different sectors, transport and health. There may also be a similar rationale for harmonising key variables, such as the value of time, because it is used across different transport modes in road and rail projects, and because larger projects may be federally funded so that their merits should desirably be fully comparable.

One drawback of adopting a set of standardised or harmonised statistics is that they need to be updated regularly. Updating requires not only resources for continued research, but also agreement on methodology. For example, the WTP for a reduction in the risk of premature death due to road crashes in New Zealand in 1991 was estimated at NZD2 million by Miller and Guria (1991) using the contingent valuation method (CVM). This figure has been used since for transport appraisals in New Zealand, but it has been indexed using the ordinary time wage rate. As Guria (2010) points out, this method is flawed because indexation by price inflation should have been used instead.

A further complication may arise in the case of choosing a single default value for a variable, such as the VOSL. A stated preference estimate of a road crash VOSL may differ from one estimated for death due to a plane disaster or terminal cancer, because the risk or contextual factors may be perceived differently.

Sanderson et al. (2007) report on research within Business Economics Research Limited, which was commissioned by the NZ Fire Service Commission to establish 'a technically robust and defensible fire-related ... VOSL for use in Regulatory Impact Statements'. Because of the age of the 1991 car crash estimate, the preferred method of Sanderson et al. (2007) was to estimate the relativity between the fire VOSL and the road VOSL as a reflection of the current preferences of the NZ population. It was argued that a stand-alone estimate may not have been strictly comparable with one carried out some 15 years earlier. Their study found that the value of an additional life saved from fire was perceived to fall in the range of 57 to 66 per cent of the road VOSL.[4]

However, Guria (2010) notes that an Organisation for Economic Cooperation and Development (OECD) study shows that people's willingness to pay for a reduction in the risk of death in a house fire is greater than that for transport accidents. He concludes that:

> To make sure government funds are used to best effect, the VOSLs need to be right. This would best be achieved by developing an appropriate and common methodology for estimating VOSLs for different risks in different areas and establishing the relativities between them.

Clough et al. (2015) also consider that a transport VOSL could be a benchmark for other risk areas, with appropriate adjustment if the value relativity between different risks is appropriately estimated. They further argue, however, that because VOSL is affected by base

---

4   The key question asked in the survey was: 'Suppose the Government could increase funding to safety programmes, which would result in 20 accidental deaths being averted per year. How many of these would you prefer to be saved from reduced car accidents, and from reduced residential fire accidents?' Respondents indicated on average that 12.4 of the 20 lives saved should be from car crashes and 7.6 from residential fire accidents.

risk and income of the affected population, a VOSL is not likely to be the same in transport as in other risk domains, such as workplace safety or health interventions. They therefore recommend that separate VOSLs should ideally be determined for each domain, reflecting its own particular risk characteristics.

4.5.2 Harmonisation of methodology

The VOSL can be estimated in a number of ways, but the two major contenders in Australia and New Zealand are the human capital approach and the stated preference (either choice modelling or the CVM) approach. The human capital method is an ex post present value of identifiable costs, such as earnings forgone, over a standard period (typically 40 years) representing an average working life, hospital care, and property damage. It therefore excludes retirees and non-working-age children. Further, it does not include family grief or pain and suffering, although the Bureau of Infrastructure, Transport and Regional Economics (BITREs) (2009) 'hybrid model' seeks to incorporate such effects. Conceptually preferable to the human capital approach, stated preference methods include all tangible and intangible effects by eliciting people's average, ex ante WTP to reduce the risk of death, based on econometric analysis of survey information.

The methodology used to estimate transport VOSL differs among jurisdictions. Transport NSW employs the WTP approach, as do the New Zealand Ministry of Transport and the New Zealand Transport Agency. Other jurisdictions use the human capital estimate established by BITRE, adjusted for property costs, earlier funerals, and pain and suffering of relatives. Queensland Transport and Main Roads uses the human capital approach, except for safety-related projects (e.g. the Black Spots program) where a WTP figure is used.

Reflecting general agreement among its members that the WTP approach is the most appropriate method for determining VOSL and crash costs, Austroads (Naude et al., 2014) produced a scoping study that explored the process for implementing a WTP study across Australia. It recommended a national WTP survey that 'would provide a set of robust values for the country, based on a sound and consistent methodology' every 8–10 years with regular updating bi-annually. The cost of a national study was estimated at about $1 million at 2012 prices.[5]

Use of CBA in the health sector is comparatively rare. Both clinical and pharmaceutical studies rely on measures such as quality adjusted life years (QALY) and disability adjusted life years (DALY). A QALY combines changes in life expectancy with a composite 'quality of life' index of changes in health states as the result of a treatment. For example, a treatment may extend a person's life expectancy, but, at the same time, reduce their quality of life for the remainder of their life, perhaps because of unpleasant side effects induced by the treatment. Treatment costs are compared to the change in a QALY or DALY in so-called cost-utility analysis, a form of cost-effectiveness analysis that does *not*, however, involve the economic concept of utility (Drummond et al., 1997).

Stated preference methods could be used to estimate people's willingness to pay for changes in risk of death or injury for specific illnesses and treatments. Unless relativities between the different conditions could be established, however, a large number of expensive studies would be required.

Abelson (2012, ch. 32) outlines an alternative approach. An estimated VOSL can be transformed into an annuity over some assumed life span such as 40 years. The equal annual amounts,[6] termed the value of a life year (VLY), can be multiplied by a relevant QALY index number to provide a proxy annual estimate of people's willingness to pay for a specific treatment. Clough et al. (2015), however, argue that VLY should be estimated directly, based on survey results, rather than simply annualising the VOSL. The study also recommends investigating whether VLY varies with different levels of quality of life arising from an injury.

---

5   By way of comparison, the BITRE (2009) estimate, based on the human capital approach, involved four project staff, plus various contributions from another eight departmental officers. Assuming that the study took about two years, the saving in staffing costs had BITRE not undertaken its theoretically questionable approach, could have funded a national WTP study.
6   An annuity 'spreads' a given amount (like the value of life, VOSL) over a given number of years (assumed here as 40 years) so that the value is equal in each of the 40 years.

Given the readily available possibilities, it is only fair to ask why the health sector does not turn to CBA, rather than continuing its use of cost-effectiveness methods. One health sector official interviewed for this publication pointed out that the reason for the inertia is that the current system is based on a balance of incentives among the various vested interests. Large pharma-companies, government officials, and the medical profession are unwilling to change because their current profits, processes and invested knowledge are all geared to the current system. Any change would require authoritative intervention by an entity with an overriding interest in economic efficiency.

4.5.3 Optimism bias

Flyvbjerg (2009), and his earlier work on optimism bias, is well known. Nevertheless, the problem of underestimation of infrastructure costs is enduring. The Capital Metro Agency (2014, Table 1) business case for the proposed Canberra light rail estimated construction costs at less than $600 million in nominal terms, excluding a contingency of $173 million and an 'escalation' provision of $65 million. However, *Canberra Times* (20 July 2015, p. 1) reported that a government letter to an agent engaged to promote the project with international financiers put the cost at $900 million. No explanation for the difference in estimates is publicly available. Moreover, the letter is reported to have been issued two months before publication of the business case,

The issue of cost underestimation is not an easy one to resolve, mainly because of the difficulty of quantifying, ex ante, what the extent of any potential optimism bias might be. The same is true of overestimates of patronage for Sydney's Lane Cove and Cross City tunnels and the Clem Jones tunnel in Brisbane.

But it is at least arguable that, for project cases for large infrastructure projects in particular, author-analysts should be required to explain why they do not consider their work to have significantly underestimated costs or overestimated benefits. For example, a range of similar projects could be cited, with an analysis of any cost blowouts and how the project being proposed will safeguard against similar occurrences. Risk analysis using the Monte Carlo technique should also be used, perhaps with a suitably skewed probability distribution for expected construction costs.

Capital Metro Agency (2014, s. 5.1.2) stated that it used a 'cost estimation firm with deep, recent Australian light rail experience to calculate a non-risk adjusted base cost estimate'. The contingency provision estimate was based on workshopped consideration of risk and likely distributions (s. 5.2.1), with Monte Carlo analysis used to determine confidence levels in a range of cost estimates. This is a useful contribution, but fuller disclosure would have been preferable.

Full disclosure of the identity of experts undertaking estimates of costs and benefits is desirable from both a procurement perspective and from that of a CBA. Over time, it would become readily apparent whether particular experts are prone to optimism bias, especially if ex post CBAs are carried out. Inveterately over-optimistic analysts could be avoided by agencies that commission CBA studies: market pressure would eventually reduce any tendency towards optimism bias among consultants. Further, procurement officers and ministers would be less likely to be placed in the invidious position of having to seek additional funds because of underestimated costs, or criticism of unsuccessful projects.

4.5.4 Replicability

Whatever approach is taken to harmonising values used in CBA, it is important that full information be provided, possibly in detailed appendixes, on the sources of data and the methodology used to derive estimates of variables. The amount of detail provided should be sufficient to allow other researchers to replicate the estimates of economic values used in the study.

4.5.5 Recommendations

Harmonisation could involve the adoption of a set of conventions, including the following:

- provision of explicit justification for the timeframe used for analysis
- explanation of reason(s) for selecting a particular method of estimating benefits, rather than feasible alternative method(s)
- ensure replicability of results by making data publicly available (e.g. online), or providing specific references to sources used
- as a default option, use of official or authoritative sources for variables employed in projections

- comprehensive tabulation of all costs and benefits, including those that are attributable to the project but are incurred outside the period of analysis
- consideration of greater use of stated preference methods on a national basis to permit estimation of benefits on a comparable basis
- recording of all variables that it is not possible or practicable to quantify
- providing a statement explaining measures taken to minimise potential optimism bias in estimating infrastructure construction costs or predicted benefits, possibly by comparison with projects that have been completed in similar circumstances, but also including the identity of the author of the estimates.

4.6 Adjust costs and benefits for risk

Risk is commonly understood to be either a negative event outcome, or its combination with the consequence of the negative outcome. Wikipedia expresses the concept as the potential of losing something of value. Standards Australia and Standards New Zealand (2009) define risk as the 'effect of uncertainty on objectives', with 'effect [defined as] a deviation from the expected — positive and/or negative', although earlier formulations had been framed primarily in negative terms only.

Common usage of the term 'risk' implies a solely negative connotation, involving an adverse outcome for an event. For example, it is normal to speak of the risk of rain spoiling a picnic. In context, this vernacular use of the term 'risk' is valid and has a specific, generally accepted meaning.

Financial analysts and economists, however, envisage risk as meaning that an event can have either a negative or a positive outcome compared to an expectation. In the case of the picnic, the weather forecast may suggest a dry but cloudy day, which, in the absence of other information, is the accepted expectation. The economic concept of risk in this case could involve a negative outcome like rain, or a positive outcome like sunshine rather than cloud. In other words, the outcome could be either better or worse than expected.

In CBA, the concept of risk is generally associated with the statistical measure of variance — the degree of deviation from an expected value like the mean — a unit that can include both positive and negative deviations. For example, a road project may be designed to reduce travel times but a construction flaw may result in the need to impose a low speed limit for safety reasons. The outcome would be higher than expected travel times. Alternatively, a design improvement during construction may reduce the length of the road, or permit smoother traffic flows, so that travel times are reduced below their expected value. Estimation of probabilities of various possibilities could be used to construct a probability function that would allow calculation of its variance. The expected benefit of the road (in this case travel time) can then be calculated in probability-adjusted terms using a technique like Monte Carlo analysis (see Appendix 6).

Economists have generally accepted the distinction between risk and uncertainty put forward by Knight in 1921 (2009, p. 121). In the case of risk, 'the distribution of the outcome in a group of instances is known (either through calculation a priori, or from statistics of past experience)'. Risk is therefore often characterised as the calculable variation — positive or negative — around a point of central tendency of a probability distribution. By contrast, the probability of uncertain events is, by definition, not known or measurable.

A traditional, but increasingly infrequent, means of allowing for risk in CBA has been to adjust the discount factor by some additional amount. A major disadvantage of doing so is the implicit assumption that the level of risk increases exponentially each year over the period of analysis, and that it applies equally to all costs and benefits. Loading discount rates is also potentially open to manipulation of the results of NPV calculations. An alternative is to use a risk-free discount rate after converting all costs and benefits into 'certainty equivalents', but this is generally considered impractical because people's utility functions are not known.

Where probabilities of occurrence of costs and benefits are known or can be estimated, they can be expressed as expected values: the aggregated values of all possible outcomes weighted by their corresponding probabilities. A drawback of the expected value approach is that it is an average that is unlikely to reflect an actual outcome. For example, the likelihood of rain may be a probability-weighted average of rain in different parts of a given area (e.g. 70 per cent), but the actual outcome can only be that it rains (100 per cent probability) or does not (0 per cent) in any particular spot.

Decision trees can be used to model different possible outcomes and their corresponding probabilities. This 'decision theory' approach has the advantage of being able to take into account varying circumstances over different time periods. Because costs and benefits are adjusted for risk through the application of probabilities, discounting takes place using a risk-free discount rate to avoid double counting the effect of risk. However, decision trees are based on expected values, and suffer from the disadvantage of not providing information about the variance associated with their calculated result.

Most modern texts express a preference for the Monte Carlo approach for incorporating risk into estimates of NPVs. Its advantage is that it permits simultaneous variation in multiple variables, yielding a probability distribution of NPV values rather than a single point estimate. A drawback is that the application of Monte Carlo analysis requires knowledge of — or assumptions about — the probability distributions of the variables involved. Nevertheless, the use of the Monte Carlo method is growing in large corporations and among government agencies.

4.6.1 Provision for contingencies

Infrastructure projects often make provision for 'escalation' and for 'contingencies', but details are not always provided. Escalation amounts may refer to price increases for inputs, but disclosure of their exact nature would be desirable to remove any ambiguity in the analysis.

Disclosure is also desirable where 'contingency' amounts are incorporated into costs. The rationale and the method of estimating the contingency is important if it is intended to serve as a proxy for risk analysis. Explicit explanations of the derivation of contingency amounts can help to reduce or avoid estimates based on arbitrary assumptions.

4.6.2 Sensitivity analysis

Some analysts confuse sensitivity analysis with risk analysis. Risk analysis involves the application of probabilities to estimates of costs and benefits. Sensitivity analysis does not involve the use of probabilities, and is limited to testing the effect of a specific change in value of a cost or benefit on the calculated NPV. Sensitivity analysis should be carried out after adjustment of costs and benefits for risk.

4.6.3 Recommendations

Harmonisation could involve the adoption of conventions such as the following:

- risk analysis should, in principle, be undertaken for all CBA studies
- where risk analysis is not used, an explicit explanation should be provided of the reasons for the omission
- Monte Carlo analysis is preferred, provided that relevant probability functions can be specified with sufficient confidence
- the rationale and estimation method for cost 'contingencies' and 'escalation' factors should be disclosed fully
- if the Monte Carlo technique is employed as part of risk analysis, details should be provided regarding the derivation and rationale for the probability functions used.

4.7 Calculate the net present value of the costs and benefits

Calculation of the NPV in a CBA is ultimately a straightforward, mechanical exercise in arithmetic. The basic formula contains four variables: costs and benefits in each time period, the discount rate, and the time period over which discounting takes place. Each of these variables is potentially subject to mis-estimation or to deliberate manipulation. Nevertheless, attention in the last few years has focused almost exclusively on the discount rate.

4.7.1 Discount rates

It is not the intention here to review the numerous approaches advocated for the determination of discount rates. The technical literature is voluminous, but some of the more accessible sources include Zhuang et al. (2007), Portney and Weyant (1999), Boardman et al. (2011), Pearce et al. (2006) and Harrison (2009). Appendix A.4 reviews some of the values used: Australian and New Zealand government agencies appear to have an unexplained preference for a real discount rate of about 7 per cent per annum.

Discount rates are not unimportant in calculating NPVs, especially over long time periods. However, the effect of differences even between rates such as 7 and 4 per cent per annum can be swamped by the uncertainties inherent in estimating future costs and benefits. The question therefore arises whether government agencies should simply adopt a common rate of discount to ensure consistency and comparability between the NPVs for different projects, or whether the search for the holy grail of an ideal rate should continue.

There is an arguable case for harmonising the methodology for setting common discount rates, should that be considered desirable by the various jurisdictions. A lower 'consumption' rate may be considered appropriate for projects in the health or environment sectors if benefits are generally consumed at the time that they accrue (and so cannot be reinvested) and resources used do not have significant opportunity costs. However, if the capital expended on the project represents forgone investment opportunities that would have provided a stream of benefits that could have been reinvested in perpetuity, then the 'producer' (social opportunity cost of capital, or 'investment') discount rate should be preferred (Pearce & Nash, 1981, s. 9.7.1; Abelson, 2012, ch. 8; Department of Finance and Administration, 2006, ch. 5). Central agencies in Australian jurisdictions have generally adopted the 'producer' rate.

Shirking the chore of specifying a discount rate a priori by using the artifice of sensitivity analysis is puzzling.[7] If discount rates reflect social time preferences and opportunity costs, then they are better treated as parameters than variables in CBA (but not necessarily so in financial or investment analysis). It is in any case obvious from the NPV formula that different discount rates will affect the final value of the NPV, so the point of testing NPV for sensitivity to different discount rates is not entirely clear.

Further, plugging in arbitrarily selected higher and lower values of a discount rate cannot edify the decision-maker as to which rate is the more appropriate. The decision-maker is simply left to choose between several differing NPV values without a clear decision rule.

4.7.2 Real and nominal values

Whether NPV is calculated in real or nominal values is immaterial, provided that all the variables in the formula are expressed in the same dimensions. There is, however, a case for presentational consistency in any particular study.

In its business case for the proposed Canberra light rail project, Capital Metro Agency (2014) flips between the use of real and nominal values; for example, tables 1, 18 and 38. The lack of transparency complicates comprehension of the analysis, and leaves the reader wondering if the findings have not been compromised somewhere by a mistake involving the inconsistent use of variable values.

For the sake of both transparency and confidence in the findings of CBA studies, jurisdictions should agree that studies must be expressed entirely in either nominal or in real terms. This requirement would not preclude the presentation of results in both forms in order to suit the

---

7   The Department of Finance and Administration (2006, p. 187) handbook condones the application of sensitivity analysis to discount rates. Boardman et al. (2011, ch. 7) is more circumspect, drawing attention to the conceptual problem of 'mixing uncertainty about predicted effects with uncertainty about how we value those effects' and suggesting that the discount rate be treated as a fixed value. Sugden and Williams (1978, p. 226) indicate that if an analysis is found to be sensitive to the discount rate, then 'the decision-maker will be obliged to commit himself to some statement about the social MTPR [marginal time preference rate], even if only implicitly'.

needs of a particular audience. An implicit condition, however, would be the inclusion in the study of an exposition of the methodology used to derive the expected rate of inflation for future time periods.

4.7.3 Recommendations

To enhance transparency — and hence comprehension — as well as reducing the scope for potential manipulation of results, it would be desirable for jurisdictions to consider harmonisation in the following areas:

- prior to commencement of the analysis, specification of a single social discount rate to be used in the CBA
- adoption of a common discount rate, at least within jurisdictions
- consistency within a CBA study in terms of use of either real or nominal values
- if real values are used, derivation of the expected future rate of inflation for each period should be explained.

4.8 Conduct sensitivity analysis

It is far from unusual for CBA studies to contain a section on sensitivity analysis that consists simply of tables or statements reporting the effect on NPV calculations of some variation in the magnitude or range of all the variables. In such cases, the effort involved in estimating the effect on NPV is entirely nugatory. While tables of sensitivity testing may help pad out a report, and perhaps give the impression of analytical input, the lack of interpretative commentary leaves the analysis incomplete.

Lack of clarity about testing for sensitivity may be a factor in the absence of interpretative analysis of its implications. A confounding fact is that sensitivity analysis is often discussed in textbooks in the context of risk analysis, despite the fact that risk analysis is based on probabilities, while sensitivity analysis is not. The nature and purposes of the two are distinct.

At the simplest level, sensitivity analysis is used to determine whether NPV changes significantly when changes are made in variables used to calculate that NPV. Its ultimate purpose is to identify variables that strongly influence NPV and to check their estimated values for robustness or accuracy. In other words, if NPV is shown to be sensitive to changes in a particular variable, it provides a signal to the analyst to check the robustness of the estimates being used for that variable and possibly also the adequacy of risk analysis.

Some judgement is required as to which variables should be tested. Where a CBA includes, say, 17 variables and the sensitivity analysis considers the most plausible value as well as one level that is higher and one that is lower, the number of combinations will be 3^{17}, yielding over 129 million results. As a first step, then, variables in whose estimation the analyst has confidence, or which are obviously unlikely to influence NPV significantly could be excluded from sensitivity testing to increase tractability.

General practice is to vary the expected or most plausible value by a certain percentage, both up and down. However, this may lead to inconsistent results. A 5 per cent variation in a cost of $50 million per annum, for example, will affect NPV differently to a 5 per cent variation in an annual wage rate of $100,000. The two variables should be tested on the same basis, perhaps by varying the expected value for each by one standard deviation (Perkins, 1994, s. 15.7.2). In many cases, however, relevant probability distributions may not be known for key variables.

Partial sensitivity analysis involves testing the influence on NPV by changing one variable at a time. This is the most common approach, and may involve testing 'best' and 'worst' case values for a variable. It is also possible, however, to change the value of more than one variable at the same time. Where this is done, care is required to ensure that the two variables are independent of each other. Negatively correlated variables, for example, could result in only a small effect on NPV, although their effect when altered separately may be quite large.

Sensitivity analysis can also be used to discover switching points (sometimes also called threshold, crossover or breakeven values) of variables (Sinden & Thampapillai, 1995, ch. 10). If the NPV has been calculated to be positive, for example, then a particular variable may be reduced (or increased) until the NPV falls to zero or switches to a negative amount. If decision-makers consider that it is plausible that the variable in question could in future reach such a switching point, they may not proceed with the project, even if the calculated point NPV is ostensibly positive. Although it is inappropriate to vary social discount rates in sensitivity analysis, the switching point of zero NPV provided by the internal rate of return may be sought by a decision-maker.

4.8.1 Monte Carlo (risk) analysis and sensitivity analysis

Monte Carlo analysis involves random selection of values from the probability distributions of multiple variables at the same time. The result is the generation of a probability distribution of NPV values rather than a single point estimate. However, this simultaneous drawing of sample values from different variables' distributions is confused in some texts as representing multivariate sensitivity analysis. In fact, software programs such as Palisade's @RISK carry out a separate sensitivity analysis *after* completion of the Monte Carlo risk analysis. In the case of @RISK, the sensitivity test results are presented in the form of a tornado chart.

4.8.2 Recommendations

CBA reports should:

- focus sensitivity testing on key variables
- avoid treating social discount rates in CBA as variables to be subject to sensitivity testing
- interpret and analyse the results of sensitivity testing.

4.9 Determine distributional consequences and distributional weighting of costs and benefits

Distributional issues cause confusion and controversy. It is therefore desirable to clarify their role in CBA studies, to facilitate understanding and transparency of results.

A 'positive economics' approach is to examine the implications of a proposed project, including flows of transfer payments, by describing in detail the benefits and costs accruing to the main stakeholders. A normative approach seeks to influence the overall outcome of an analysis by adjusting the estimated benefits and costs in a manner that advantages specific stakeholders in society. Such 'distributional weighting' may involve multiplying benefits that accrue to low-income groups in society with weights greater than one, for example. Where this occurs, the calculated NPV will be increased, so that the project has a greater chance of being accepted.

4.9.1 Distributional consequences

Traditional texts such as Gramlich (1981), Mishan (1988) and Musgrave and Musgrave (1976) tended to address CBA issues from the perspective of society as a whole. If the benefits or gains to all members of society exceeded total opportunity costs, the project or policy was considered to be worthwhile overall. If the gainers in society also compensated the losers and were still left with net benefits, the situation was considered to satisfy the Pareto criterion that there be at least one winner and no losers. Under the so-called Hicks–Kaldor criterion, projects can also be considered to be overall socially beneficial where the *potential* exists for winners to compensate losers, even in the absence of *actual* compensatory transfers.

In order to determine whether it is possible in theory or in practice for the winners from a government project or policy to compensate the losers, it is essential to be able to identify the flow of benefits and costs between different sections of society. In theory, it would be possible to identify the gains and losses accruing to each member of society, but the identification of key groups is usually adequate for most policy considerations.

According to Lichfield et al. (1975, p. 78), a Planning Balance Sheet method was developed by Lichfield in the 1950s to identify the incidence of costs and benefits on various social groups in urban and regional planning proposals. This approach consisted of a conventional CBA, but with detailed accounting of costs and benefits by category of the social groups affected. Alexander (1978) applied the method to a series of development proposals in the Blue Mountains, to the west of Sydney, with 18 categories of producers (mainly government agencies) and a similar number of consumer groups.

Krutilla (2005) adopted a similar disaggregated approach in promoting what he terms a 'Hicks–Kaldor tableau' for presenting the results of a CBA. Tables 4.1 and 4.2 are modified tableau presentations used by Krutilla (2005), illustrating three variants of a public project where labour is hired at a wage W to produce a good or service of benefit value B.

Table 4.1 represents a situation where labour is paid a wage of W by a private or government employer, but also incurs an opportunity cost (OC), perhaps due to loss of leisure time by previously unemployed persons. The wage itself is a transfer from the employer to labour, and nets out in the final column, and hence the overall calculation of net benefits created by the project. Nevertheless, the tableau format records the fact that a financial flow occurred due to the project, and was received by the labour sector. While the financial flow of wage payments does not affect the net social benefit in the simplified Table 4.1 scenario, the information contained is likely to be of interest to decision-makers, especially at the political level.

Table 4.1: Implementation of synthetic project, using labour

	Stakeholders in accounting domain			
	Project beneficiaries (consumers)	Project administrators (producers)	Labour (factor of production)	Net benefit
Benefit	B			B
Financial charge		–W	W	0
Economic cost			–OC	–OC
Net benefit	B	–W	W–OC	B–OC

Source: adapted from Krutilla (2005)

Tableau formats are flexible enough to reflect other features. Table 4.2, for example, indicates that local labour receives a wage as a windfall transfer, but the source of the wage is from an entity that has been excluded from the 'standing' of the project (perhaps a foreign government or investor). The net benefit from a 'local only' perspective is now (B+W–OC).

Table 4.2: Synthetic project, assuming 'standing' is local only

	Stakeholders in accounting domain		
	Project beneficiaries (consumers)	Labour (factor of production)	Net benefit
Benefit	B		B
Financial charge		W	W
Economic cost		–OC	–OC
Net benefit	B	W–OC	B+W–OC

Source: adapted from Krutilla (2005)

Where the distributional consequences of a project are of interest to decision-makers, a tableau format can prove useful. In particular, a tableau can provide an indication of how much compensation may need to be offered to those opposed to a project because they will suffer some detriment. From a broader perspective, the tableau approach also promotes a degree of transparency that may not always be present in a conventional presentation of the efficiency effects of a government policy or project. A particular advantage of using a format that is useful to decision-makers because of the distributional information it contains, is that it would help promote the use of CBA.

Should jurisdictions find the tableau format useful, it could be considered as a standard feature to be used in CBA studies. However, two issues would need to be resolved:

• Greater levels of disaggregation are likely to involve greater analytical effort. It is not immediately obvious where the balance between cost and degree of detail might lie.

• Australian and New Zealand public servants have a duty to remain apolitical. Disaggregating CBA detail to the level of electorate boundaries may be unethical. Whether sufficient detail should be provided to allow ministers' offices to piece together the puzzle themselves is also an issue requiring careful resolution.

4.9.2 Distributional weighting of costs and benefits

Applying weights to the costs and benefits that affect different social groups is contentious at best.

In principle, adjustments to estimated costs and benefits accruing to particular social groups can be made on the basis of various criteria. For example, benefits from a road project that accrue to residents of a regional area may be increased by some factor because decision-makers consider that improved transport links between regional and urban areas are desirable, or that regional residents should be compensated with better transport links to make up for the disadvantage suffered due to isolation. Alternatively, low-income groups may be favoured by increasing the benefits attributable to them. Using choice modelling, Scarborough & Bennett (2008) estimate community distributional preferences favouring younger generations.

Pearce and Nash (1981, ch. 3) argue in favour of the use of distributive weights. Mishan (1988, ch. 30), on the other hand, argues that the use of such weights is ultimately subjective and arbitrary, as well as being a misplaced use of fiscal policy because income redistribution could be better achieved through general taxation policy.

Some safeguards can be adopted to promote transparency and reduce the degree of arbitrariness where decision-makers insist on the use of distributive weighting as part of a CBA.

- Justification for the use of weights, and for their value, should be established and recorded before commencement of the analysis, preferably certified by a high-level decision-maker.
- Because of the scope for potential manipulation of overall results, subsequent changes to the value of weights used should not be permitted.
- Two sets of results for the CBA should be presented: one with, and one without application of distributive weights.

4.9.3 Recommendations

- Jurisdictions should give consideration to the use of extended tableau formats to present the distributional consequences of CBA studies.
- Adoption of comprehensive tableau formats should be subject to safeguards that maintain the apolitical nature of public service advice.

- Justification for the use of weights, and for their value, should be established and recorded before commencement of the analysis.

- Because of the scope for potential manipulation of overall results, subsequent changes to the value of weights used should not be permitted.

- If distributional weights are used, then two sets of results for the CBA should be presented: one with, and one without application of weights.

4.10 Arrive at a conclusion or recommendations for the results of the CBA

It is not uncommon to read a CBA study where the executive summary or the concluding section asserts various findings, but where the claimed results are difficult to find in the body of the text or in the appendices. It is inefficient to search for greater detail, or for the evidence on which any conclusions are based.

In order to reduce search costs, conclusions or summaries of findings should be fully referenced to the section from which they have been sourced. For example, a calculated NPV should be referenced to a specific table or paragraph in Section 4.7 (in this publication), or to a relevant appendix. Some form of such referencing is important not only for transparency, but also to help ensure the internal consistency of the analysis.

An analytically complete study should also record sufficient data and calculations to allow reviewers to check the validity of the conclusions. Replicability is an important means of ensuring the credibility of the results.

More frequent publication of CBA studies would promote their credibility because both consultants and decision-makers would be faced with the 'sniff' or 'pub' test. During interviews a number of jurisdictions pointed out that publication would also assist long-term harmonisation because those commissioning CBA studies would have previous examples as models that could be followed. Commercial confidentiality is often claimed as a reason for not releasing CBA studies, but, given that project expenditure cannot occur without parliamentary appropriation, much of the claimed commercially sensitive information may well be released into the public domain at some stage anyway.

4.10.1 Recommendations

Jurisdictions should consider harmonisation of the following aspects of the concluding or executive summary sections:

- All statements and assertions regarding findings should be referenced to tables or paragraphs in the body of the study, or to relevant appendices.
- Sufficient data should be provided in the body of the study, or in relevant appendices, to permit reviewers to replicate key findings.
- In the absence of genuine commercial or national security sensitivities, studies should be published in full to allow public scrutiny and to facilitate their use as models for evaluating other projects or policies.

5

What not to do: A 'belts and braces' enhancement of harmonisation

Introduction: Common misconceptions in cost-benefit analysis

A range of agencies in the Australian and New Zealand jurisdictions occasionally publish manuals, fact sheets and guidelines to assist their staff in preparing or commissioning studies employing cost-benefit analysis (CBA). Examples include the New Zealand Treasury (2015), Department of Finance and Administration (2006) and Transport for NSW (2013). An obvious advantage of publishing manuals and guidelines is that individual agencies reinforce their advocacy of the use of CBA in evaluating project proposals.

One, possibly unintended, consequence of publishing manuals and guidelines is that they foster a degree of harmonisation between agencies and even between jurisdictions. Most agency manuals cover similar topics and generally cite or copy sections of other agencies' manuals and guidelines. The Department of Finance and Administration (2006) *Handbook of Cost-Benefit Analysis* is an exception in that it refers almost entirely to academic publications, although it is often itself cited by other agencies in their manuals.

Preparation and publication of a manual or handbook requires considerable effort. No matter how skilled an author in a government agency, he or she will inevitably face reviews of multiple drafts by superiors and others in the organisation. Considerable resources are ultimately devoted to the production of a CBA manual. It is therefore pertinent to ask whether publication of manuals by individual agencies is an effective use of resources, and whether the contents could be improved in some way. Several perspectives are relevant.

Given the number and range of textbooks of various levels of sophistication that are readily available, an obvious question to ask is why agencies bother to replicate or rewrite published, peer-reviewed material. One answer might be that manuals are intended to distil concepts and methods that may be expounded at greater length and in a more theoretical context in academic textbooks. Abstraction from a theoretical context in an area like CBA, however, risks misapprehensions and mistakes of the sort dealt with in the examples examined in this chapter.

A second issue relates to the degree of detail and level of sophistication that should be incorporated into a manual. The problem is that a mixed readership requires different levels of information and explanation. Officials in specialised government agencies are likely to become bored with basic material, making little use of a publication. On the other hand, overly succinct explanations or instructions are likely to leave novices puzzled. An example is the frequent reproduction of the present value formula: unnecessary for those who already understand the concept of discounting, but unnecessarily confusing to those not used to interpreting mathematical formulae.

Manuals tend to be written in a prescriptive manner that informs users about what is to be done in an appraisal. Some point to the pitfalls of standard problems such as double counting. In general, however, they fail to clarify or specify what should *not* be done. A 'belts and braces' approach that also advises what should be avoided would aid comprehension and the quality of CBA studies.

It is important to be explicit about undesirable methodologies. An example is the treatment in CBA of employment creation, a topic of interest to most decision-makers at the political level. The need to take into account political considerations has generally been handled adroitly by recommending that job creation should be 'reported separately' to the results of the CBA itself. Despite the neatness of the solution, there is nevertheless a risk of fostering the erroneous perception among readers that 'jobs' are in fact an additional benefit, on top of other quantified benefits.

Recommendations

- Manuals and handbooks on CBA that are produced by agencies should specify methodologies that are not considered to be desirable, with explicit explanations for why this is so.
- Agencies should consider the relative value of supplementing official manuals with training courses that provide a fuller context to the contents of manuals and handbooks.
- Publication of CBAs should be encouraged as a means of fostering wider discussion of methodology and the values used.

5.1 The misconception that the purpose of discounting is 'to allow for inflation'

A not uncommon misconception among public servants is that discounting means 'allowing for inflation'. It is possible that the confusion arises because the arithmetic used in making adjustments for inflation is similar to that used for discounting.

CBA provides a comparison of the sum over time of the additional projected benefits and the sum of the additional attributable costs of a proposed project or policy. Adding up costs and benefits requires that they be expressed in common units or mathematical 'dimensions'. Ensuring commensurability should ideally involve, at a minimum, adjusting values to reflect their receipt or incidence at different periods of time, expressing them consistently in either real or nominal values, and adjusting for risk.

Placing discounting, inflation-adjustment and risk analysis within the broader context of commensurability is a useful means of avoiding confusion among generalists who may not be familiar with the different concepts. There is no single, fixed method of conducting a CBA, so it is important to stress the underlying concept of commensurability, rather than simply prescribing discounting. The following section demonstrates that it is possible to work in either real or nominal values, provided all variables are expressed in consistent units. A similar illustration could be provided for the adjustment of costs and benefits for risk.

5.1.1 Real versus nominal: Does it really matter?

It is typically the case that costs and benefits are first converted to real values and then discounted by a rate that is also expressed in real terms. The same result could be obtained, however, by working exclusively with nominal values for both the benefits, costs and the discount rate, with no adjustments for inflation. Table 5.1 compares the two approaches.

Table 5.1: Discounting with real and nominal values

	Nominal values		Real values (t = 0)	
Period	Annual benefit	Discounted at 5% per annum	Annual benefit inflation 2% p.a.	Discounted at 3% p.a.
1	$10	$9.52	$9.80	$9.51
2	$10	$9.07	$9.61	$9.06
3	$10	$8.64	$9.42	$8.62
4	$10	$8.23	$9.24	$8.21
Present value		$35.46		$35.40

Source: Leo Dobes

Ignoring the difference due to rounding error[1] when working with exponential values, it is clear that the same result can be obtained by working in nominal values only, or in real values alone. The key issue is that the 'dimensions' of the values used (benefits, costs, discount rate) in either approach must be consistent with each other.

In practice, it is difficult to forecast future values in nominal terms. For example, forecasting the cost of petrol for each year for the next 15 years is fraught with difficulty because observed prices at the pump are likely to fluctuate during the year, as well as between years. A workaround is to choose a long-term average value and treat it as a

---

1   The two approaches are in fact mathematically equivalent. Sugden and Williams (1978, s. 3.5) provide a short but elegant proof.

real cost. For example, a cost of about $1.20 per litre might be chosen as a long-run average, without being adjusted any further for inflation on the assumption that it will increase at approximately the same rate as all other prices. The present value of petrol costs over the 15 years would then be obtained by applying a real discount rate.

5.2. Qualification of the decision rule that a BCR > 1 or NPV > 0 indicates that a project should proceed

It is not uncommon for proponents to claim that projects should proceed because their benefit-cost ratio (BCR) is greater than 1. At first glance, such calls seem unobjectionable because a BCR ratio that exceeds unity implies that benefits exceed costs. The use of BCR therefore offers a readily accepted decision rule. In practice, the reality may be different.

5.2.1 The standard benefit-cost ratio and the net present value decision rule

The most common, standard use of a BCR refers to a ratio of the present value of all the benefits, divided by the present value of all the costs (including capital and operating).

$$BCR = \frac{present\ value\ of\ all\ benefits}{present\ value\ of\ all\ costs\ (including\ capital\ and\ operating)}$$

$$BCR = \sum_{t=0}^{n} \frac{B_t}{(1+r)^t} / \sum_{t=0}^{n} \frac{C_t}{(1+r)^t}$$

A better alternative to citing a BCR is to refer to the net present value (NPV) which equals the present value of all social (private plus public) benefits minus the present value of financial operating and capital costs, as well as economic costs like externalities. Table 5.2 illustrates the importance of presenting costs and benefits separately.

Table 5.2: Comparison of standard benefit-cost ratio (BCR) and net present value (NPV)

	Project 1	Project 2	Project 3
Present value of all benefits	11	1100	11
Present value of all costs	10	1000	9
Benefit-cost ratio	1.1	1.1	1.2
Net present value	1	100	2

Source: Leo Dobes

At first glance, Project 3 appears to be the superior alternative in Table 5.2 because it has a BCR of 1.2, while projects 1 and 2 have BCRs of only 1.1. On the basis of BCRs, projects 1 and 2 are also equivalent in merit. On the basis of BCRs alone, a decision-maker would choose Project 3, and remain indifferent between projects 1 and 2 if a second choice were available. The problem is that ratios do not clearly distinguish between the numerator and denominator so it is not clear how relatively attractive they are.

Use of NPV, on the other hand, is comparatively unambiguous, with Project 2 clearly showing the greatest contribution to economic welfare in absolute terms. In comparison, the relatively small NPV values for projects 1 and 3 suggest that they would be eliminated from further consideration. While BCRs may be preferred by some project proponents for presentational reasons, NPVs are a more transparent approach for displaying the result of a CBA and should be preferred to a BCR in presenting the results of a CBA.

It may be argued that an NPV by itself does not inform the decision-maker how large the difference between social costs and social benefits may be relative to the overall social cost. The cost of a project, however, is not itself relevant to decision-making in CBA. What is relevant is the magnitude of the additional benefit that can be gained from an additional social cost, taking into account feasible alternative projects.

Nevertheless, the standard decision-making rule of NPV > 0 that is presented in some texts should not be applied automatically or indiscriminately.

5.2.2 When use of the NPV > 0 criterion alone may be problematic

Even if NPV > 0 or BCR > 1, there may be better projects available with a higher NPV. The point is that a positive NPV or a BCR that exceeds unity are not in themselves sufficient to conclude that a project should be implemented. Overall social well-being can be increased by selecting alternatives with the highest NPVs. For example, a school or hospital may have a higher NPV, even if the focus of a particular study is on the construction of better roads. Special interest advocates typically ignore alternative potential uses of social resources, sometimes in the genuine belief that the social merit of their proposed project is self-evident and should therefore be given precedence.

Further, there are three specific situations when use of NPV > 0 is not necessarily an appropriate decision criterion:

* where there is a budget constraint in a given year that precludes the financing of all the projects that yield a positive NPV
* where two or more projects have different lives: a longer time horizon is likely to involve the accretion of more costs and benefits, so that a project with a shorter life cannot be validly compared with a more protracted one
* if a real (quasi) option is present: the flexibility of not needing to invest fully at the start of the project in a situation of uncertainty generates additional value that should be added to the NPV. The topic is too complex to address succinctly below, but see, for example: Dixit & Pindyck (1994), Trigeorgis (1996), Treager (2014), *The Economist* (1999, August).

5.2.3 Selecting projects under a budget constraint

In a situation of limited budgetary resources, it may not be possible to fund every project that demonstrates a positive NPV. Giving preference to projects with the highest NPV may not maximise overall NPV, especially if projects with high NPV also require a high level of initial funding for their implementation. It is possible that selection of lower NPV-yielding projects can maximise overall NPV. Table 5.3 illustrates this possibility.

Table 5.3: Ranking of projects by NPV and profitability ratio ($ thousands)

Project	PV (K)	PV (B)	NPV (rank)	B/K (rank)
A	100	130	30 (5)	1.30 (2)
B	400	433	33 (4)	1.08 (5)
C	200	303	103 (1)	1.52 (1)
D	400	494	94 (2)	1.24 (3)
E	500	558	58 (3)	1.11 (4)

Note: K = capital cost of investment; B = benefits net of operating costs; B/K = net benefit investment ratio (NBIR): also known as the profitability ratio

Source: reproduced from Table 3.3 in Campbell & Brown (2003)

Table 5.3 compares five fictitious projects ranked by their NPV (4th column) and by their rank on the basis of the net benefit investment ratio (NBIR, 5th column). The NBIR can easily be confused with the standard BCR. However, rather than including only benefits in its numerator and all costs in the denominator, as for the standard BCR, the NBIR includes in its numerator benefits minus operating costs, with the denominator being limited to the capital or investment cost alone. An alternative term for the NBIR could be the profitability ratio because it shows the net return on the initial investment.

$$NBIR = \sum_{t=0}^{n} \frac{(B-C)_t}{(1+r)^t} \Big/ \sum_{t=0}^{n} \frac{K_t}{(1+r)^t}$$

Campbell and Brown (2003) posit an $800,000 limit on financial resources with decision-makers faced with the projects shown in Table 5.3. If the projects with the highest NPV were given preference by decision-makers, projects C and D would be funded first, and then 40 per cent of project E, assuming that it could be part-funded. The overall NPV achieved would be $220,000.[2] If, instead, decision-makers ranked projects according to the NBIR, they would choose projects C, A, D, and 20 per cent of project E, yielding an overall NPV of $239,000.

---

2   NPV = $103 + $94 + 0.4*$58 = $220,000

In cases where projects are indivisible, it may still be possible to choose a set that have generally lower NPVs individually, but together yield a higher overall NPV within the budgetary limit. The NBIR can again be used to rank such 'lumpy' projects.

Brealey et al. (2006, ch. 5.4) point out, however, that the use of NBIR to rank projects subject to a budget constraint is 'inadequate whenever there is any other constraint on the choice of projects'. Examples of constraints include cases where one project depends on another or two projects are mutually exclusive, or there is a budget constraint in more than one year. In such cases, resort to linear programming methods may be required to identify an optimal set of projects.

5.2.4 Comparing projects with different lives

Projects with different timeframes cannot be compared directly on the basis of their NPV values. The longer of the two project periods will accrue a greater number of benefits and costs than the shorter one. It would therefore not be appropriate to compare the two on the basis of NPV alone.

One means of validly comparing projects with different time horizons using only NPV is to replicate them in a way that results in the same period for both. For example, a two-year and a three-year project would be replicated three times and two times respectively, so that both are six years long. However, this approach may not always be practicable — for example, if one project is seven years in length and the other nine years — because the common time period may be too long. A lengthy time period necessarily needs to assume that technology and other conditions remain the same; otherwise a comparison over the extended time period becomes unrealistic.

Table 5.4 illustrates the alternative approach of deriving equivalent annual values (EAV) by converting NPVs into annuities. A government agency needs to choose between two types of motor vehicles its senior management. They are of equivalent quality and performance but differ in price and length of effective life. Vehicle A costs $25,000 to purchase, with annual maintenance costs of $6,000. It is kept for three years and then sold for $5,000 at the end of the third year and then replaced with the same vehicle type. From the annuity table, the annuity factor for 3 years at 5 per cent p.a. is 2.72. Vehicle B costs

$20,000 to purchase, with annual maintenance costs of $7,000. It is kept for only two years and then sold for $5,000 at the end of the second year and then replaced with the same vehicle type. The two-year annuity factor in the annuity table is 1.86 at an interest rate of 5 per cent per annum.

Table 5.4: Using EAVs to compare projects with different time horizons ($ thousand)

	C_0	C_1	C_2	C_3	PV @ 5% p.a.
Vehicle A	25	6	6	(6-5) = 1	37.01
EAV		13.61	13.61	13.61	37.01
Vehicle B	20	7	(7-5) = 2	-	28.48
EAV		15.31	15.31	-	28.48

Note: EAV = equivalent annual value; PV = present value
Source: Leo Dobes

Because the PV of the costs for vehicle A ($37.01) is higher than for vehicle B ($28.48), the decision rule of choosing the least cost vehicle, vehicle B would be chosen. If the vehicles were being bought and replaced over a longer period (e.g. 10 years) then it would be financially more favourable to use vehicle A, because its annualised value of $13.61 is lower than that for vehicle B ($15.31).

Conversion of NPV values to EAVs permits direct comparison of the two machines on the basis of annualised constant costs. The EAVs are derived by dividing the NPV of each by the annuity factor corresponding to the life of each project. For example Machine A has a PV of $28.37. Dividing the PV by the annuity factor for three years at a 6 per cent per annum discount rate (equal to 2.673) provides an EAV of $10.61. Comparing the two machines on the basis of annualised values leads to a decision to choose Machine A, even though the PV of its costs is higher than that of Machine B.

The EAV approach is sometimes also used for projects where there are large costs at the end of the project, as well as large capital costs at the beginning of the project. An example might be a comparison between a nuclear power station and a coal-fuelled one, where decommissioning costs are incurred. In such situations, there is a reversal of the sign of cash flows — from initially negative during construction, to positive during the operational phase, and then to negative again when decommissioning occurs.

In sum, NPV should be used as the decision criterion for CBA. Care is required to ensure that NPVs are used validly, however, especially where projects with different time horizons are being compared. It is also desirable to present as much information as possible to decision-makers, rather than providing only an NPV. Itemising all social costs and social benefits is particularly desirable.

5.3 The furphy that the period of analysis should not exceed 30 years because the effect of discounting is to make any present values negligible after this length of time

There are no hard and fast rules for the time horizon of a project. The relevant timeframe should be determined by the period over which impacts are typically expected, rather than any effects of discounting. Nevertheless, even respected publications like *The Economist* (for example, 26 June 1999, p. 94) may on occasion recommend a time horizon not exceeding about 30 years for discounted cash flow analysis.

Table 5.5: Present values of $1 for selected years and discount rates

Years	3% p.a.	5% p.a.	10% p.a.
10	0.74	0.61	0.39
20	0.55	0.38	0.15
30	0.41	0.23	0.06
40	0.31	0.14	0.02
50	0.23	0.09	0.01

Source: adapted by Leo Dobes from appendix 2, Campbell & Brown (2003)

Table 5.5 presents a selection of years and discount factors for present values. It is clear that, even with a 5 per cent per annum discount rate, the present value of $1 is still almost a quarter (0.23 cents) after 30 years. A similar figure holds after 50 years if the discount rate is only 3 per cent per annum. Even a relatively high discount rate of 10 per cent per annum would see approximately 1 cent in every dollar preserved at the 50-year mark. It is therefore not clear why blanket advice should be given to avoid exceeding periods of 30 years for discounting project costs and benefits.

5.4 Caution required regarding treating increased property prices around a new road or railway as a benefit

It is obviously important to distinguish between the various effects of a project when conducting a CBA.

Primary effects are typically those that reflect most closely the purpose or objective of the project. In the case of a dam that is constructed to reduce flooding, the primary effect will be to reduce flood damage, but there may also be ancillary or associated costs or benefits that need to be attributed to the project. For example, the dam may be constructed in such a way that it also produces hydroelectricity, or it may result in the negative externality of exterminating a fish species that requires a free-running river.

Analysts are sometimes tempted to include in a CBA less direct effects, variously termed 'indirect effects', 'secondary effects' and 'transmitted effects', possibly because of their prominence in the public psyche. A common example is the expected increase in property prices in areas near a new road or railway. The creation of additional jobs due to a project is another impact that is invariably emphasised at the political level.

In the case of a new or improved road or railway, the primary benefit is the reduction in travel cost experienced by existing and new users of the transport route. The benefit may be due to reduced travel time if the route is shorter, or if it is upgraded to permit faster travel. Fuel savings may also be reaped, representing a resource saving. Safety improvements can reduce mortality from crashes.

An increase in property prices is not a separate effect; it simply reflects the value of the primary benefit. People living near the improved road or railway will benefit from faster travel times or reduced fuel costs, so demand for those properties will increase, resulting in increased prices. The increase in property prices is *caused* by the increased benefit of improved transport. It is not additional to it. Another way of looking at this is to consider that the gain from improved transport is distributed, or 'trickles down' to other sectors like real estate or to shops close to a train station. To include both the primary effect of time and fuel savings, as well as increased property prices, would be to double count the benefits of the project.

A second reason why it would not be appropriate to include increased property prices as a benefit of a road or railway improvement project is that the increased demand for properties close to the upgraded transport route may be offset by reduced demand for properties elsewhere. For example, those people wishing to move closer to the upgraded road or railway are likely to sell their existing, more distant residences. The price of those more distant residences is likely to fall, offsetting to some extent the increase in prices closer to the transport route. In a broad sense, there is an element of transfer or pecuniary effect, with price gains in one area being offset in another, and therefore the gains are cancelled out.

A focus on secondary or transmitted effects may be justified, however, when the primary benefits cannot easily be valued. If it were not possible, for example, to estimate travel time and fuel savings due to a road or railway upgrade, then any increase in property prices could serve as a proxy benefit value that reflects the underlying travel benefit. Similarly, if estimating the value of the additional water produced or harvested by the construction of a dam is not feasible, then the value of the resulting additional crop production could serve as a proxy measure.

Care is required in using secondary markets as proxies for primary effects. In the case of property prices, it may be difficult, if not misleading to designate a particular area as benefitting from improved transport, especially if not all the users of the upgraded road or railway live locally. And an improved railway route may reduce road congestion as an ancillary benefit. In the case of the dam, estimates of increased crop production would need to be controlled for the additional cost of fertilisers or altered rainfall patterns due to evaporation from the nearby dam. Further, increased crop production would exclude other benefits of the dam, such as recreational swimming and fishing, as well as negative ones such as the destruction of trees and animal habitats.

5.5 Is it really true that 'you can't monetise things like the environment'?

There is little dispute that it is not possible to monetise environmental services and impacts. It is therefore surprising that critics of CBA should focus on this aspect.

Economists do not attach monetary values to intangibles like environmental services and impacts. But they do seek to establish what values people place on them. The techniques for doing so are covered in most textbooks. Hedonic pricing, for example, is typically presented to explain the valuation of the negative value of noise: prices of houses near an airport can be compared with similar ones further away. The difference in price, other things being equal, is taken to reflect the willingness of people to pay to avoid the 'bad' of noise. The higher house price represents the sacrifice of other goods and services that could have been purchased instead of a house less exposed to noise.

The essence of attaching a value to an intangible environmental quantity lies in determining its opportunity cost. In a world of limited resources and goods, not all wants can be satisfied. It is generally necessary to give up something of value in exchange for another good or service. The maximum amount or value of the forgone good or service thus provides a measure of the value placed on the object that is acquired in its place. Where markets exist, so-called 'revealed preference' methods like hedonic pricing can be used.

In the absence of markets (for example, the value placed by people on the preservation of a wetland), 'stated preference' techniques like contingent valuation methods and choice modelling can be used. Choice modelling considers goods or services in the form of a 'bundle' of constituent characteristics, including price, that can be traded-off in various combinations. It is instructive that commercial firms like supermarkets employ so-called conjoint analysis, a technique similar to choice modelling, to estimate how much customers are likely to pay for a new type of good once it is placed on the shelf.

5.5.1 Choice of numeraire

It may be that critics of CBA are confused because CBA does in fact express costs and benefits in dollar values. However, monetary units are used for cognitive convenience, rather than because of any supposed myopically pecuniary worldview held by economists.

It would be conceptually feasible to measure costs and benefits in terms of alternative units of measurement, such as sea shells or cups of coffee. But dollars are preferred, simply because they are readily understood by most people. Without first translating into monetary units, most people would find it difficult to assess how many cups of coffee they would be willing to trade-off to save a koala or some threatened species. The monetary value of other goods and services that people are prepared to give up in exchange for a koala reflects their willingness to pay to save it.

5.5.2 The non-measurable

Finally, Gramlich (1981, p. 5) addresses several misconceptions about CBA, one being that:

> benefit-cost analysis is a mechanical substitute for common sense. Nothing could be further from the truth. Benefit-cost analysis is really a framework for organizing thoughts, for listing all pros and cons, and for placing a value on each consideration … in the real world there will be some considerations that cannot easily be enumerated or valued … the sensible way to deal with such omitted considerations is not to abandon all efforts … but rather to … quantify what can be quantified, to array and rank nonquantifiable factors, and then to make a decision.

5.6 Can benefits be measured as 'costs (or damage) avoided'?

It is not uncommon to see CBA studies estimating benefits in terms of the damage cost averted, invariably in financial terms. The practice is particularly prevalent in disaster situations and in climate change modelling. The 'costs avoided' approach is also sometimes presented as the 'defensive expenditures method' (e.g. Boardman et al., 2011, ch. 14). It appeals particularly to those who perceive costs and benefits in terms of production function effects. However, the outcome is essentially a cost–cost study, rather than a conceptually ideal CBA.

Flood mitigation benefits are often estimated in terms of the damage avoided. Such estimates tend to focus on the financial cost of replacing or repairing damage to houses, furniture, and infrastructure. They therefore exclude the more subjective value placed by people on items such as family photographs or heirlooms that may have been destroyed and are an underestimate of the likely willingness of residents to pay to avoid a flood event.

Studies of droughts (climate-induced or not), often combined with appraisals of constructing dams, may well overestimate benefits by taking a production-oriented approach. Such studies tend to take as a given the current level of production of a specific crop. A disaster is then assumed to fully destroy the crop, possibly in perpetuity in the case of a climate change effect. Avoiding the total cost of the fully destroyed crop is counted as the potential benefit.

In reality, farmers might not sow a crop in a bad year, saving on seed, fertiliser and other inputs and/or engaging in off-farm employment, or they may substitute a less water-dependent crop. That is, farmers are in reality more likely to adapt to changing conditions rather than continuing to plant their usual crop each year, and waiting passively for it to be destroyed. Benefits estimated as the avoided cost of fully destroyed crops into the future are thus likely to be overestimates.

An example provided by Boardman et al. (2011, ch. 14) is that of a smoggy city where residents periodically hire workers to clean their windows. This 'defensive expenditure' can be used as an estimate of the cost of mitigating or eliminating the negative externality. Avoidance of part or all of this expenditure can be considered to be a measure of the benefit of a policy that reduces the amount of smog. To the extent that 'smog also leads to dirtier shirts and to health problems', the window-cleaning approach will result in an underestimate of the benefit of cleaner air. Hanley and Barbier (2009, ch. 6) point out that modern production function approaches seek to estimate the effect of environmental changes on consumer and producer surplus in response to changes in costs and prices of the final marketed good.

Mishan (1988, ch. 3) refers to an apparently popular practice of estimating the benefit of reducing or eliminating a disease using a 'costs avoided' approach. The approach includes three separate categories:

- expenditures on medical care, including the costs of the services of physicians and other medical personnel, drugs, hospital facilities and equipment
- loss of production, measured in terms of loss of earnings
- pain and discomfort, although this area cannot be measured directly.

Mishan's judgement about the approach is worth quoting in full:

> The ... [averted costs] ... method of calculating the benefits of eliminating a disease cannot strictly be justified by reference to economic principle. A reduction in cost can be directly translated into a benefit for society only when — as in an increment of consumer surplus from a fall in price — we are operating on the demand curve for a specific good. If, for example, the good in question were a standardized health unit which could be purchased on the market, and the unit cost fell by an amount that resulted in a saving of $5 billion a year for the same number of health units bought, then the benefit would indeed be equal to the cost saving of $5 billion a year.

To some extent popular use of the 'damage costs avoided' approach is understandable, because costs are generally easier to estimate than benefits. However, when 'stakeholders' (typically vested interests) are able to marshal political support by producing dramatic anecdotal material or egregious cost estimates, the well-being of the community can suffer. A significant increase in expenditure on a familiar ailment, such as arthritis, may 'crowd out' the introduction of a new, but hitherto unknown cancer drug. It is therefore important to compare alternatives on the basis of additional expenditure and additional benefits rather than just total costs avoided (see Section 5.6).

For some variables, it may be apposite to determine associated dose-response relationships: for example critical concentration levels of specific nutrients in rivers that will cause algal blooms (Read Sturgess, 2000), or vehicle operating costs per kilometre at different speeds (Tan et. al., 2012). A pertinent example is a study by Ludwig et al. (2009), who modelled the effect of a large decline in rainfall on a number of sites in the Western Australian wheat belt. Simulations indicated that not only did crop yields *not* fall, but leaching of fertiliser also decreased, thus reducing costs to farmers, and the spread of dryland salinity was reduced significantly. Further, beneficial profit outcomes were obtained through minor variations in planting periods for two wheat varieties.

5.7 Conjuring up the benefits of jobs — 'it's not what you see, it's what you don't see'

In highlighting job creation as a social benefit of a pet infrastructure project, politicians bear a considerable affinity to magicians. By drawing the attention of the audience to the obvious job-creating effects of a project or policy, they are able to neglect consideration of corresponding, but less visible losses in employment or social well-being.

An oft-cited example of the job-creation fallacy is the 'broken window' allegory by Frederic Bastiat (1850), who distinguished 'between a good and a bad economist [on the basis that] … the one takes account of the visible effect; the other takes account both of the effects which are seen, and also those which it is necessary to foresee'. In effect, Bastiat draws attention to the need to take opportunity costs into account.

Bastiat (1850) posits an angry shopkeeper whose careless son has just broken one of the shop windows. As an inquisitive throng of shoppers mills around the scene commiserating with the shopkeeper, one bystander offers the consolation that 'everybody must live, and what would become of the glaziers if panes of glass were never broken?'. Bastiat points out that this is to focus on the obvious and immediately visible consequence, to the exclusion of other effects. It presupposes that the shopkeeper pays an amount of, say, six francs to the glazier. The shopkeeper gains a good — a new window pane — that he values at six francs, and the glazier gains an equal amount of six francs; so society as a whole is no better or worse off than before.

It is only by taking into account a wider perspective of the whole of society that one appreciates the fallacy, points out Bastiat. Had the window not been broken, the shopkeeper might have fulfilled his original desire to buy a pair of new shoes. One needs to take into account all other third parties, like the shoemaker, or some other tradesman, who suffer by the loss of their potential sale. In other words, the additional employment of the glazier is exactly offset by the forgone opportunity of employment of the shoemaker or some other tradesman. There is no net offsetting gain in employment to society, which simply loses the asset of a previously existing window.

5.7.1 Two less immediately discernible effects that merit consideration

It is not clear why people — even those with some training in economics — are willing to be side-tracked by claims of 'more jobs' as an indicator of social benefit of a project or policy, without considering the wider impacts. Lakoff and Johnson (2003, ch. 13) argue that metaphors such as 'labour is a resource' and 'time is a resource' reflect cultural values about work and the ability to quantify labour. These perspectives even induce a notion of 'leisure time' as a resource not to be wasted, with a whole industry devoted to ensuring that it is used productively. It is also possible that wider public awareness of Keynesian economics has engendered an unwarranted view of government expenditure and employment creation as being 'good things' in themselves and in all situations.

Whatever the reason for the apparent allure of job creation, there are two broad, less visible issues that merit consideration in any claimed job creation benefits. The first of these is analogous to the fallacy identified by Bastiat (1850).

First, while project proponents are keen to emphasise as many job creation impacts of a project as they can, it is rare to see discussion of any countervailing deadweight loss to society due to the funding of the project (Appendix 7). If a major project is unambiguously funded by increased taxation, the aggregate level of both consumption and savings in the economy are likely to fall because people's disposable income is reduced. A reduction in consumption levels, and reduced investment due to reduced savings, will reduce overall economic activity, and consequently employment levels. However, this negative effect on employment levels may be partially offset by an increased desire by some individuals to work more, in order to recoup their loss in disposable income.

An alternative would be for the government to borrow the funds required to finance a project. Whether the funds are borrowed domestically or overseas, they eventually need to be repaid, most likely through increased taxes at some future time. The 19th-century economist David Ricardo argued that public borrowing would be perceived by rational citizens as being a precursor to increased future taxation, and they would therefore curb their consumption from the outset in anticipation. Although not uncontroversial, this concept of 'Ricardian equivalence' is argued to result in reduced consumption due to public borrowing in the same trajectory that would be observed in a scenario of increased taxation at the time of project implementation.

An alternative that involves neither increased taxation nor borrowing is to reduce current government expenditure in other areas of the economy, for example on education or defence. In this case, the social cost of tax financing becomes irrelevant. While this would avoid the problems of deadweight loss and Ricardian equivalence, it would also have a direct, negative effect on employment in those areas where cutbacks occur.

A second issue that requires consideration is the source of the additional labour that is employed on a new project. For example, the government of the Australian Capital Territory (ACT) in October 2014 called for expressions of interest to build and operate a light rail system to connect the north of Canberra with the city centre. A key supporting argument for the project was that it would increase employment opportunities in the ACT. Although the 'standing' or perspective taken by the business case was not specified, the proposition of increased employment opportunities does not necessarily translate into more jobs for Canberra residents. Nor was it explained why the objective of more jobs should be fulfilled by construction of a light rail system — employment could also have been increased by building more hospitals or schools, or even by digging and refilling holes.

In a situation of reasonably full employment in the ACT economy, a Canberra resident employed in the ACT who takes up a newly created position on the light rail system will not increase the total level of employment in the ACT. The net effect will simply be a transfer of employment from one occupation to another within the ACT. Indeed, in a situation of full employment, the vacated position is more likely to be filled by someone from outside the ACT. In this case, the net effect is that the number of Canberrans employed as a result of the project will not change, despite the increase in job vacancies created.

If the vacated position cannot be filled even by workers from outside the ACT because of high employment levels across Australia, there may even be some offsetting loss in production in the ACT. An increase in the wages offered could attract outside workers, but the increased cost of labour may also force some ACT businesses to cease production and hence reduce employment opportunities within the ACT. This reduction will offset some of the additional jobs created by the light rail project.

In a situation of frictional or less than full employment in the ACT economy, it will be possible for at least some Canberrans to accept a position on the light rail system, assuming that they have the requisite skills, or can acquire them on the job. The individual worker will gain the benefit of a wage — including tax that is gained by the Federal government — that exactly offsets the cost to the employer (the so-called 'equilibrium assumption': Mannix, 2013). However, there will be an additional loss to Canberra society because of the individual worker's loss of leisure time on taking up employment.

Leisure time is another of those commonly 'not seen' effects of job creation where previously unemployed workers choose to work. Defined variously as 'non-paid work time' or simply 'non-work time', leisure can include anything from doing absolutely nothing, sleeping, minding children, gardening, or listening to music. All of these are economic benefits, despite the fact that they may not result in the production of marketed goods or services. Depending on an individual's preferences, each item contributes to their personal utility, and hence to the overall well-being of the society to which the individual belongs. Because employment necessarily results in the loss of some leisure, its loss represents an opportunity cost to a previously unemployed individual, and hence to society.

Other issues that might be considered in a detailed CBA would be the transaction costs of a worker changing employment or taking up a job when previously unemployed. Transaction costs could include new clothing, travel costs, possible residential relocation costs, or childminding costs. Employers, too, face additional costs in interviewing job applicants, training new workers, placing vacancy advertisements, and loss of productivity due to errors made by new workers.

5.7.2 How to accommodate politicians' perspectives?

In general, it would be conceptually difficult to argue that job creation in itself generates social benefits. It might, however, be argued that there is some form of 'existence value' gained by people who are happy that unemployed residents have been able to find paid work. If it is accepted that higher employment levels are associated with reduced crime, and causation can be demonstrated, then there may also be a wider social benefit of increased employment levels. Attribution of any of these benefits would, however, require direct evidence of their existence, and some form of measuring their magnitude. Adler (2013), for example, argues that research is required into the nexus between unemployment and physical and psychological health and its monetary equivalent.

Nevertheless decision-makers at the political level invariably require information on the employment impacts of a project or policy. Some Australian jurisdictions accommodate this requirement by providing a separate brief, or a separate section following a CBA, that provides information on likely job creation. This approach satisfies the need to provide employment impacts, without compromising the integrity of the CBA by including job creation as a benefit in calculations, or in presentation.

5.8 True or false?: Taxes are just transfer payments, so they can be disregarded

It is true that a tax collected (or subsidy provided) by government is a transfer payment.[3] Taxes in themselves do not constitute a social benefit or a social cost. Analogous to a voluntary charity donation, a tax is simply a transfer from taxpayers to government. Subsidies involve transfers from government to a particular segment of society.

---

3   A transfer payment differs from a normal market transaction in that resources are transferred from one party to a second party, but nothing is provided in return by the second party to the first.

Nevertheless, taxes, and their obverse, subsidies, represent economic distortions that create differences between prices paid by producers and consumers for a particular good or service. It is therefore important in estimating the social cost or social benefit of goods or services to take into account the taxes and subsidies that apply to them.

The subject of adjusting market prices for taxes and subsidies is not always entirely straightforward. Sinden and Thampapillai (1995, p. 50) whimsically provide a guideline to the effect that 'Taxes and subsidies should sometimes be included, and sometimes be excluded'.

Prices adjusted for taxes and subsidies are typically referred to as 'shadow prices'.[4]

The concept of willingness to pay (WTP) can be used to determine how benefits (outputs) should be adjusted for taxes and subsidies. Opportunity cost can be used to adjust the costs of inputs. In each case it is important to also identify whether a project results in an increase in outputs or inputs, or whether it displaces the quantity of existing inputs or outputs in the market. Table 5.6 provides a broad categorisation.

Table 5.6: Adjusting for taxes levied (and subsidies provided) on inputs and outputs

Supply/demand	Increase in availability	Displacement or diversion of existing units
Outputs	**A** Market price, including taxes less subsidies, to reflect willingness to pay to acquire the output.	**B** Market price plus subsidies less taxes. The benefit is the value of the units saved by not producing the existing units of output.
Inputs	**C** Market price less taxes plus subsidies. The benefit is the resource (opportunity) cost of the additional inputs.	**D** Market price, including taxes less subsidies, to reflect productivity in previous use.

Source: adapted from Department of Finance (1991), Department of Finance and Administration (2006), and Sinden and Thampapillai (1995)

---

4   Boardman et al. (2011, ch. 4) describe shadow pricing as a means of assigning benefit or cost measures 'when observed prices fail to reflect the true social value of a good accurately or observed prices do not exist … thereby finding "in the shadows" needed values that are not readily observable'. It is also useful to note that shadow prices used in CBA are not the same concept as the one used in linear programming.

Quadrant A represents an increase in availability of an output, which would be valued at the market price. For example an increase in the supply of water from a newly constructed dam should be valued on the basis of farmers' willingness to pay for it; that is, the market price inclusive of taxes but excluding any subsidies. At least some of the dam water would have previously formed part of the flow of a river and has now been diverted to agricultural use (quadrant B). It is therefore likely to have displaced the benefits of recreational use by people swimming or fishing in the river that has now been dammed. In other words, part of the benefit to farmers is gained at the expense of the output of water (a benefit) that is no longer available to recreational users. The benefit that is diverted from (lost to) recreational users to farmers is the resource value that is 'saved' by reducing recreational use and would therefore exclude taxes. Determining the resource cost of the river water, however, may be problematic.

Shadow pricing the cost of inputs depends on whether there is an increase in availability of the input (quadrant C), or whether existing uses of the input are diverted (quadrant D) to the new project. The value of additional inputs is determined by the opportunity cost of the resources. An example is the employment of additional workers who were previously unemployed: the cost of these additional workers is the opportunity cost of the loss of their leisure time. The use on a project of workers already employed elsewhere is the opportunity cost of the marginal revenue product that they would have generated in their previous employment had they not been displaced: reflected in the wage — including income and payroll tax minus any subsidies — their previous employer was willing to pay them.

Perkins (1994, ch. 7) provides a range of further examples for both distorted and undistorted markets of the Harberger approach to estimating shadow prices, including relevant formulae. The Harberger approach involves calculation of weighted averages of increased outputs or inputs and the corresponding amounts that are displaced or diverted. As might be expected, economic benefits and costs depend on the relative elasticities of demand and supply, changes in quantities and prices, and the presence of taxes and subsidies. However, the Department of Finance and Administration (2006, s. 3.5) points out that it is not uncommon for project demand for inputs to be relatively small compared to total production, and the price elasticity of demand is usually large ('flat' demand curve), so that shadow prices 'will be close to the market price and this sort of analysis is unnecessary'.

5.8.1 Correctional (Pigovian) taxes

One purpose of taxation is to raise revenue. An alternative rationale for levying taxes is to encourage or discourage consumption or production of goods and services.

However, the distinction may not always be clear cut. Campbell & Brown (2003, p. 111) pose the question whether a tax on tobacco is intended to raise revenue because of its inelastic demand, or whether it is a correctional tax intended to reduce consumption to avoid imposing costs on the health system. In assessing this distinction, a degree of judgement is required on the part of the analyst conducting the CBA.

Corrective taxes[5] or charges imposed unambiguously to reduce negative externalities, such as traffic congestion, should be set to reflect the additional cost imposed by each driver on other car drivers. By not taking into account (internalising) the cost imposed on others, drivers demand an increased amount of output in the form of additional trips. The corrective tax is intended to reduce the demand for road trips to a socially optimal level, by equating the marginal benefit to the marginal social cost. Imposition of the corrective tax therefore diverts resources that would otherwise have been used for car travel to other uses. However, the correct shadow price of road usage should include the corrective tax, in contrast to the approach of excluding a purely revenue tax in Table 2.8 for a diversion or displacement of existing outputs.

A subsidy on diesel used by farmers will see farmers paying a lower price than the market price paid by other users at the bowser. If the government reduces distance travelled by building new wheat silos closer to farms, farmers will save on fuel. Campbell & Brown (2003, ch. 5) point out that value of the fuel saving should be calculated on

---

5   Sometimes called Pigovian taxes after AC Pigou (1920, Vol. 1, ch. 9), who proposed the imposition of compensatory payments on private individuals who produce negative externalities to reflect social costs of production.

the basis of the market price because it reflects the cost of production. In other words, the subsidy needs to be removed from the price paid by farmers in order to obtain the resource cost.

5.8.2 Marginal excess tax burden (deadweight loss due to taxation)

When a project is funded through increased taxation, the level of economic activity will be reduced because of the negative effect on consumption and/or investment. The resulting loss of social surplus is a deadweight loss. Appendix 7 deals with this issue.

5.8.3 Discount rates

Harberger (1976, ch. 2) argues in favour of the investment-oriented social opportunity cost of capital over the consumption-oriented social rate of time preference for discounting, but emphasises the need to adjust private returns for taxes. The argument is analogous to including taxes when considering the value of additional production or diverted use of inputs in Table 5.6 above. Part of any additional product is skimmed off by government in the form of taxes:

> There are a number of possible sources of divergence between the social and private benefits of private investment; but of these, by far the most important consists of taxes ... Of two investments with the same private yield, one of which generates corporation income tax payments equal to its private yield, and the other of which generates no tax payments at all, the former is clearly socially preferable, as it either enables the public sector to have more command over real goods and services or, alternatively, it permits the public sector to reduce some other tax and thus permits the private sector to buy more real goods and services. The indicated procedure is therefore to include corporation tax payments generated in any industry as part of the social return to capital in that industry. And if the social rate of return to capital is estimated for the private sector as a whole, the entire yield of the corporation income tax should be added to the income perceived by private enterprises in order to convert the latter to a social concept of 'income generated by capital'.

> Where indirect taxes exist on a final product, they lead to a situation in which the value of the marginal product of each factor of production involved in that good's production exceeds the income earned by

that factor by the percentage rate of indirect tax. In this case, the income from capital (gross of corporation tax) should be augmented by a fraction of the receipts from the indirect tax, the fraction being capital's share in the value added in the industry in question.

Harrison (2010) explores in more detail tax adjustments from the perspective of discount rates.

5.9 Another misconception: Sensitivity analysis should be used to adjust for risk in a CBA

Sensitivity analysis is distinct from the adjustment of costs and benefits for risk. It is specifically directed at ascertaining how the NPV of a project would change if the magnitude of one of the variables included in the calculation was altered.

5.9.1 Adjustment for risk

To aggregate costs or benefits requires that they be expressed in commensurate units or 'dimensions'. Values are routinely adjusted for inflation by conversion to real values, and for time by discounting. Adjustment for risk is also worthwhile because receipt of a risky dollar is unlikely to be valued in the same way as the certain receipt of an identical amount: a bird in the hand is invariably worth two in the bush.

Following Knight (2009 [1921]), risk is generally conceptualised as variation from a measure of central tendency, such as the mean. It therefore requires knowledge of the associated probabilities of events — such as the size of a benefit, or timing of a cost — occurring. Adjustment for risk can be carried out by calculating expected values in the form of probability weighted averages. An extension of this approach is to employ decision trees and to attach probabilities to different scenarios. Boardman et al. (2011, ch. 7) provide an exposition of both expected values and analysis using decision trees.

Monte Carlo analysis offers a more sophisticated form of risk analysis, but requires specification of associated probability distributions, rather than single-point estimates of probabilities of occurrence.

Repeated random sampling from the probability density functions attached to the variables included in estimating the CBA generates a probability distribution of possible NPV, rather than producing a single-point estimate of the NPV. Software such as @RISK (www. palisade.com/risk/) allows straightforward application of the Monte Carlo method.

5.9.2 Sensitivity analysis

Despite a common misconception, sensitivity analysis is *not* a form of risk analysis; nor is it a substitute for risk analysis. Risk analysis requires the application of probabilities to input variables. Sensitivity analysis can be carried out whether or not risk analysis has been undertaken. Its primary objective is to discover the extent to which each of the constituent variables of the CBA influences the final result, the calculation of NPV. Some analysts also vary input variables to determine 'break-even', 'switch-over', or output 'switching points', such as the point when NPV becomes zero or changes sign.

Sensitivity analysis can be carried out simply by changing the value of one variable at a time, or even several or all the variables together. Some sensitivity analyses choose 'worst case' and/or 'best case' values. Alternatively, it is possible to use an absolute or percentage variation either side of the input variable values used in the calculation of the NPV, although Perkins (1994, s. 15.7.2) points out that comparability of the sensitivity of NPV to different input variables should be based on equivalent variations, such as one standard deviation from the mean. Software like @RISK produces a sensitivity analysis of the Monte Carlo result in the form of a tornado chart. That is, sensitivity analysis can, and should be applied after any adjustment of input variables for risk.

In the case where a change in the value of a particular input variable exhibits a substantial influence on the calculation of NPV, sensitivity analysis provides a valuable signal. If the analyst is not fully confident that the value of that particular input variable has been robustly estimated, then it would be prudent to revisit the estimation method to ensure that the variable value is as accurate as possible. If the estimation cannot be improved, then the CBA report should draw the decision-maker's attention to the fact that a particular variable is influential in determining the NPV, but its value may benefit from improved estimation.

Where an NPV has been estimated as a probability distribution on the basis of risk analysis, sensitivity testing can be applied in a more sophisticated form than mere absolute or percentage deviations from estimated values of input variables. Software such as @RISK can also be used to vary the parameters of the probability density functions that have been used to define the risk attached to each input variable. In other words, advanced sensitivity analysis can involve not only the most plausible or expected value of each input variable (the first moment of the distribution), but also its variance (the second moment of the distribution) and the degree and direction of skewness (the third moment).

5.10 Confusing marginal and average: Does a positive mid-term economic appraisal indicate that a program should continue, or be expanded?

A CBA is typically carried out before a project is implemented (and ideally before a decision is made to implement it). This ex ante approach is (less frequently) supplemented by an ex post appraisal, after finalisation of the project. It is much rarer still for a mid-term (*in media res*) evaluation to be carried out.

A particular advantage of a mid-term CBA evaluation, perhaps as part of an implementation review of a project, is that it offers the option of terminating or expanding the project, as well as simply continuing it as originally envisaged. An example of a mid-term review is the evaluation of the Australian Government's Rural Transaction Centres program (Dobes, 2007). The CBA found that the provision of a range of government and commercial services to about 50 smaller regional towns was socially beneficial.

It can be tempting, but wrong, to consider a positive NPV result obtained from a mid-term review to be an indication that an expansion of the project or program would consequentially also be socially beneficial. The fallacy here of course is that the mid-term review will estimate an NPV based on the average results of the project. However, an expansion of the project or program requires consideration of all *additional* costs and *additional* benefits attributable to the expansion.

The base case is no longer the original 'do minimum' counterfactual, but rather the project that has already been (partially) implemented. Any attempt to carry out the CBA simply for an expanded project against the original counterfactual would be misguided, even if the overall result still produced a positive NPV.

The distinction between average and marginal results is also important in the case of inputs accounted for in a CBA, whether ex ante, ex post, or *in media res*. It is often the case that average values are used because market prices can be readily observed. A large project that draws heavily on a particular input (e.g. concrete, or highly specialised workers), however, may see an increase in cost. It is the increased cost that should be used in the CBA, not the average price that exists before the project is implemented.

The distinction between marginal and average values of benefits is equally important. The Washington State Institute for Public Policy (2014, p. 172) puts it well:

> One important concept for long term portfolio analysis is that of diminishing returns. This is the precept that, as a program serves more and more of its eligible population (that is, as it reaches market saturation), the effectiveness of the program for each new participant may be reduced.

The Rural Transaction Centres program analysed in Dobes (2007) provides a concrete example. At the outset of the program, smaller towns that are distant from regional centres were provided with government assistance. As the number of assisted towns grew, it was inevitable that the additional towns receiving assistance would be larger and closer to regional centres. Because a key determinant of benefits was the generalised cost of transport between the assisted town and a proximate regional centre, the additional benefit to the overall program contributed by each extra town would be lower. At some point, further expansion of the program would be ineffective, once additional costs outweighed the additional benefits.

Finally, choice modelling (see s. 5.5 above) has the useful attribute of yielding estimates of the additional WTP if one or more characteristics of a good or service are increased. CVMs, on the other hand, are generally restricted to estimating a single WTP value for a good or service. In terms of estimating the benefit of program expansion, therefore, choice modelling has an advantage over the CVM approach.

6

Conclusions and recommendations

It is possible at present to obtain virtually any desired result that one might wish from a cost-benefit analysis (CBA) study. Although the methodology and concepts in CBA are well established, their practical application leaves much to be desired, at least in some Australian jurisdictions.

To accept the current situation as merely a practical matter of little import in the real world would involve a misplaced sense of complacency. Anecdotal evidence indicates that public servants and their political masters are not averse to hiring consultants with a flexible disposition.

For example, Craig Emerson (2015), a former Australian minister for trade and competitiveness, writing about bilateral and regional trade agreements, recalled recently:

> in what might seem a perverse decision, the Labor government rejected a recommendation that a cost-benefit analysis be done on all trade deals before they were locked into place. The reason was not based on opposition to transparency. It was a repudiation of the farcical approach that had been adopted by previous governments of hiring a favoured private consulting firm to produce pre-determined results in support of negotiated agreements.
>
> Absurdity reached dizzying heights when a quantitative analysis of the trade-liberalising effects of the US–Australia free trade agreements was unable to produce any tangible positive results. With little else

to show its client, the consultant threw in a massive positive effect on the Australian economy of a decision by the Howard government to increase the amount of American investment that would be free of screening by the Foreign Investment Review Board from about $240 million to $1 billion. Professor Ross Garnaut described this analysis as failing to pass the laugh test.

Worse still, there is a tendency for some politicians to refuse to obtain information on which to base a decision about the net social benefits of a pet project. Senator Stephen Conroy, the then Minister for Broadband, Communications and the Digital Economy, famously refused to commission a cost-benefit study of the major National Broadband Network project (e.g. Jones, 2010). Similarly, in discussing the mooted Mt Isa to Tennant Creek railway project, the Chief Minister for the Northern Territory stated that '[we] don't need a feasibility study to tell us that we should open up opportunities to develop the significant resources we know exist in this region' (Giles, 2015).

A survey of economists and other professionals (Chapter 2) confirms the view that all is not entirely well in the area of CBA studies.

Two aspects in particular afford considerable leeway in determining the results of a CBA:

- the use of a diversity of values in the various jurisdictions allows analysts and consultants to pick and choose those that may suit a specific purpose or desired outcome. Values of variables, such as the value of statistical life and the social cost of carbon emissions are common examples. In the absence of harmonised values — or at least ranges of values — it is possible to justify any particular value, either by reference to usage in another study, or by more nebulous reference to claimed plausibility

- the absence of a 'belts and braces' analytical framework. For example, it is currently acceptable to nominate only the basic project — such as funding a new road — and to compare it to a hypothetical base case situation. This binary approach automatically excludes other possible projects, such as a rail link, or a market-based solution like congestion charging. A 'belts and braces' framework would require analysts and consultants to provide a list of all feasible strategies that address a specified objective, and then to both list those chosen for analysis *and* to justify the exclusion from further consideration of the remainder.

It would be unrealistic to expect an overnight development of scrupulously honest and rigorous analyses in the case of every government project of policy. Organisational culture and governance play a key role, irrespective of formal guidelines. However, a greater degree of confidence could be engendered through the adoption of a harmonised CBA framework that provides more detailed and specific guidance than that currently presented in government manuals and guidelines.

As a first step, the adoption of a common framework for presenting the results of all CBA studies would improve transparency. Finding relevant assumptions, data and results in idiosyncratic CBA studies is difficult because there is no pattern or location to assist readers to find information. Adoption of a common framework, like that proposed in the 10 sequential categories below (see Chapter 4), would be a useful first step.

1. specify the objective of the analysis
2. define 'standing' and scope
3. establish the base case: establishing a reference point
4. predict the impacts of the policy or project over its life cycle
5. estimate the economic value of the costs and benefits
6. adjust costs and benefits for risk
7. calculate the net present value of the costs and benefits
8. conduct sensitivity analysis
9. determine distributional consequences and distributional weighting of costs and benefits
10. arrive at a conclusion or recommendations for the CBA.

Based on discussion in the body of this monograph and in the appendices, it is recommended that jurisdictions should consider adopting a framework CBA harmonised around the following points:

1. Specify the objective of the analysis

- record explicitly the objective of the proposed project or policy
- provide a full list of alternative projects and policy initiatives that could be used to achieve the objective, including market-based alternatives to construction of infrastructure or its expansion

- provide reasons for not including alternative projects in the CBA analysis
- ensure that a process of objective and independent peer review is instituted at an early stage of the analysis as a matter of course for all government-funded studies.

2. Define 'standing' and scope

- explicit specification of 'standing' should be provided in all CBA studies. Where more than one perspective is adopted (e.g. to provide additional information requested by decision-makers), results should be shown separately for each specification
- adoption of a national perspective for all CBA studies, should be the default position. Studies should clearly identify the parties whose benefits and costs are included, as well as those who are specifically excluded from the analysis
- consideration should be given to adopting a convention that all residents of Australia, not just citizens, be granted standing in a CBA study.

3. Establish the base case

- a list and full explanation of all assumptions should be made in choosing or developing the base case scenario
- as a default option, use official sources for key variables employed in projections
- require specific justification for use of estimates that are not based on official sources
- require specification and justification of the time period selected for the base case
- where relevant, ensure consistency of base case assumptions with those used in projections of impacts of the project or policy.

4. Predict the effects of the policy or project over its life cycle

- provision of a comprehensive list of impacts and an explanation of all assumptions made in predicting impacts
- provision of a list of persons and sources consulted to identify project impacts

- provision of evidence-based justification of causality for all impacts identified
- cogent explanations for excluding impacts that have not been short-listed
- all costs and benefits, including the costs of preliminary analyses or administrative preparation, should be attributed to the project, even where the project is implemented in stages that may appear to be separate projects
- inclusion of all relevant implementation costs, including post-implementation and final ex post review on completion of the project or program
- identification and/or valuation of major transfer payments that are significant enough to include in a distributional analysis
- require the use of official sources for key variables employed in the base case
- explanation of reasons for use of estimates that are not based on official sources
- ensure consistency of the time period used with that of the base case
- where relevant, ensure consistency of project impact assumptions with those used in the base case.

5. Estimate the economic value of the costs and benefits

- provision of justification for the timeframe used for analysis
- explanation of reason(s) for selecting a particular method of estimating benefits, rather than feasible alternative method(s)
- ensure replicability of results by making data publicly available (e.g. online), or providing references for sources used
- require use of official or authoritative sources for variables employed in projections
- comprehensive tabulation of all costs and benefits, including those that are attributable to the project but are incurred outside the period of analysis
- consideration of greater use of stated preference methods on a national basis to permit estimation of benefits on a comparable basis

- recording of all variables that it is not possible or practicable to quantify
- provide a statement explaining measures taken to minimise potential optimism bias in estimating infrastructure construction costs or predicted benefits, possibly by comparison with projects that have been completed in similar circumstances, but also including the identity of the author of the estimates.

6. Adjust costs and benefits for risk

- risk analysis should, in principle, be undertaken for all CBA studies
- where risk analysis is not used, an explicit explanation should be provided of the reasons for the omission
- Monte Carlo analysis is preferred, provided that relevant probability functions can be specified with sufficient confidence
- the rationale and estimation method for cost 'contingencies' and 'escalation' factors should be disclosed fully
- if the Monte Carlo technique is employed as part of risk analysis, details should be provided regarding the derivation and rationale for the probability functions used.

7. Calculate the net present value of the costs and benefits

- prior to commencement of the analysis, specification of a single social discount rate to be used in the CBA
- adoption of a common discount rate, at least within jurisdictions
- consistency within a CBA study in terms of use of either real or nominal values
- if real values are used, derivation of the expected future rate of inflation for each period should be explained.

8. Conduct sensitivity analysis

- focus sensitivity testing on key variables
- avoid treating social discount rates in CBA as variables to be subject to sensitivity testing
- interpret and analyse the results of sensitivity testing.

9. Determine distributional consequences and weighting of costs and benefits

- consideration should be given to the use of extended tableau formats to present the distributional consequences of CBA studies
- adoption of comprehensive tableau formats should be subject to safeguards that maintain the apolitical nature of public service advice
- justification for the use of weights, and for their value, should be established and recorded before commencement of the analysis
- because of the scope for potential manipulation of overall results, subsequent changes to the values of weights used should not be permitted
- if distributional weights are used, then two sets of results for the CBA should be presented: one with, and one without application of weights.

10. Arrive at a conclusion or recommendations for the CBA

- all statements and assertions regarding findings should be referenced to tables or paragraphs in the body of the study, or to relevant appendices
- sufficient data should be provided in the body of the study, or in relevant appendices, to permit reviewers to replicate key findings
- in the absence of genuine commercial or national security sensitivities, studies should be published in full to allow public scrutiny and to facilitate their use as models for evaluating other projects or policies.

Implementation

- CBA manuals and handbooks produced by agencies should specify undesirable methodologies
- agencies should consider supplementing manuals with training courses that provide a fuller context to the contents of manuals and handbooks.

- publication of CBAs should be encouraged as a means of fostering wider discussion of methodology and the values used
- jurisdictions should adopt a common approach in presenting the results of CBA studies, using a harmonised framework, such as the 10 steps outlined above
- in the absence of a formal inter-jurisdictional agreement, a central agency should take an informal leadership role by adopting a framework along the lines outlined in this chapter
- section 47C(3)(a) of the *Freedom of Information Act 1982* should be amended to specifically include the social sciences within the meaning of 'technical matters', in order to permit the release of CBA studies.

Appendices

Appendix 1:
Sources of information

Information and professional perspectives for this publication were obtained from a range of sources:

- a desktop literature survey. This avenue yielded only a limited amount of directly relevant material on the topic of harmonisation of CBA values and methodologies
- manuals and guidelines published by government agencies and industry bodies, such as Austroads
- semi-structured, face-to-face interviews with government agencies responsible for the health, environment and transport sectors, as well as central agencies such as Treasury, Finance, premiers' departments or equivalent. Interviews were conducted in Wellington, Canberra, Melbourne, Brisbane, Hobart, Sydney, Adelaide, Perth, London and Paris. It was not possible to conduct interviews in the Northern Territory
- a survey of members of the Economic Society of Australia and the New Zealand Government Economics Network
- feedback was obtained on an exposure paper on harmonisation presented to the annual conference of the American Society for Benefit Cost Analysis in Washington in March 2015.

Manuals and guidelines published by portfolio agencies provided an important source of information regarding CBA practice. They did not, however, always provide a complete picture of the information sought. In some cases — for example the Queensland Treasury — the guidelines at the time of interviews were non-prescriptive and did not contain any CBA input variable values, whereas those of some other jurisdictions do. In some cases, agencies stated that the guidelines were being updated, so that they could not validly be used as an accurate record of current practice. Some guidelines — for example, those of the NSW Treasury — contained instructions to consult the Treasury on particular issues, such as application of real options.

Information collected during semi-structured interviews was not always as complete or productive as might have been hoped. Larger groups of interlocutors often made it difficult to keep the focus of the group on the questions of immediate interest to this publication because participants were often keen to tell their own stories and to ensure that they were part of the conversation. Combined with time limits, acquisition of relevant data and information was therefore occasionally rather limited. Discussion notes were compiled as soon as possible after interviews, and were sent to interlocutors to afford them the opportunity to confirm or amend the record of discussion.

On the other hand, the broad nature of a portfolio like health meant that it was possible sometimes to only obtain information about one area. For example, the interlocutor available at an agency may have been from the clinical evaluation side, or from the pharmaceutical evaluation side. While they occasionally commented on studies conducted in other areas, they were often able only to provide detailed explanations of practice in their own field.

The problem of arranging interviews with the most informed officials within agencies was compounded on occasion by the absence on leave of relevant interlocutors, a fact that sometimes only became known at the last minute, and despite prior arrangements. In some cases, agencies responded to requests for interviews by stating that CBA expertise was not available. In one or two cases, agencies failed to respond to requests for interviews, despite multiple approaches by phone and email.

Ideally, all government portfolios would have been included in the interview process, but this was not possible with the resources available. Time and logistics limited interviews to three target sectors: transport, health and environment. By interviewing Treasury and Finance officials as well, more general information was obtained, but time constraints on both sides again precluded more than an hour's discussion at most. Further attempts to fill in gaps were made by initiating discussions with research agencies such as the National

Health and Medical Research Council, the Bureau of Infrastructure, Transport and Regional Economics, and some interested public servants from portfolios outside the three target sectors.

The results of interviews with agency personnel have not been tabulated because of requests by a number of interlocutors to maintain confidentiality. The results of the surveys of members of the New Zealand Government Economics Network and the Economic Society of Australia are reported in Chapter 2.

Appendix 2:
Multi-criteria analysis

The rapid growth of composite indexes in recent decades attests to their seductive qualities. Popular indexes include a species that ranks the 'world's most liveable cities', including one version published by the Economist Intelligence Unit. World university rankings attract considerable attention among tertiary education aspirants, while the Worldwide Governance Indicator, the Global Slavery Index, the Climate Change Vulnerability Index, the Global Democracy Ranking, and many others, regularly attract the attention of the media.

Composite indexes seek to summarise disparate data about a specific topic or issue, typically conflating them into a single numerical value. Numerical rankings are based on various measures for different characteristics or criteria, generally weighted by their relative importance in the index, and then aggregated. Multi-criteria analysis (MCA) is ultimately based on the same approach.

Detailed critiques of composite indexes and MCA can be found in Luskin and Dobes (1999), Vincent (2007), Cox (2009), Dobes and Bennett (2009), and Pollitt (2010), amongst others. It is not the intention to replicate these arguments here, but rather to illustrate the arbitrariness of analyses based on composite index methods by presenting a simplified example of an MCA process. We are not aware of any textbooks that present comparable material.

Dobes (1999) bemoaned the fact that it was not possible to obtain a 'live specimen' of an MCA, despite the fact that at least one state road agency was then using the method. This circumspection on the part of governments was noted again by Dobes and Bennett (2009) after a futile request for a copy of the unpublished MCA that was used by the Victorian Government to justify diversion of Goulburn River water to Melbourne in the Sugarloaf Pipeline Project.

Due to the paucity of published government MCAs, a simplified example of an MCA is used below to illustrate the essential approach. Proponents of the MCA method would rightly point out that there is a considerable body of mathematically and statistically sophisticated superstructure related to the selection of criteria, weights and scores (Chankong & Haimes, 1983), but the intention here is to examine the underlying fundamentals.

Table A2.1 portrays a hypothetical approach to a road-widening project in the form of a goals-achievement matrix (GAM) that is typically used in MCA. The first column is the key to the process, because it specifies the factors — termed attributes or criteria — that are to be taken into account in the analysis. There is no theory or specific guideline governing their choice, so their selection is essentially arbitrary and may reflect the priorities of politicians, decision-makers or special interests (i.e. 'stakeholders'). Cost-benefit analysis, on the other hand, requires that the costs and benefits that affect all members of society must be taken into account.

Apart from the temptation for an analyst to second-guess the preferences of decision-makers, there is considerable risk of double counting in MCA due to its emphasis on a set of desired outcomes specified by the analyst. In Table A2.1 this is deliberately illustrated by including both the creation of jobs and the growth in local business revenue, a not unusual set of policy-desirable attributes. Sophisticated MCA practitioners, however, would undoubtedly seek to reduce the scope of double counting by, for example, checking on correlation levels between attributes.

No specific numeraire is used in MCA, with attributes assessed by allocating a score to the estimated impact of the project on each attribute. In Table A2.1, a Likert scale that ranges from −4 to +4 has been used. The weight allocated to each attribute reflects its relative importance in the expected outcomes from the project. Scores and weights may be determined by the analyst, a focus group, or a decision-maker, but there is no theory to guide their determination so that they are essentially subjective and arbitrary. The final step is shown in the right-hand column, where the products of the scores and weights in Table A2.1 are shown and aggregated, giving a unitless total weighted score of 190.

Table A2.1: Simplified goals-achievement matrix for a road-widening project

Attribute	Units	Impact	Score (–4 to +4)	Weight %	Weighted score
Travel time saving per trip	Minutes	13	2	10	20
Growth in local business p.a.	Revenue ($)	56,000	4	40	160
Reduction in crashes p.a.	Number	4	3	10	30
Employment	Jobs	23	3	20	60
Cost of project	$	89,000	–4	20	–80
Total				100	190

Source: Leo Dobes

Table A2.2 demonstrates the effect of a change in the nominated attributes of the project. In this case, a different hypothetical analyst may have decided to take into account the environmental aspects of the road-widening project by including wombat mortality rates and greenhouse gas emissions. Because there is no underlying theory to guide the selection of attributes, or their number, there is no reason to either exclude or include these environmental effects. The scoring scale remains the same, but the weights have necessarily been adjusted to ensure that they continue to add up to 100: a different analyst might also have chosen different weights for each of the attributes. The total weighted score has now changed to 30. Because the weighted aggregate score is unitless, it is not possible to conclude whether it is slightly worse, much worse or not at all worse than the previous result of 190. Nor is it possible to compare either result to an alternative use of resources like building a hospital or a school.

Table A2.2: Selection of different attributes for the project

Attribute	Units	Impact	Score −4 to +4)	Weight %	Weighted score
Travel time saving per trip	Minutes	13	2	10	20
Growth in local business p.a.	Revenue ($)	56,000	4	10	160
Reduction in crashes p.a.	Number	4	3	10	30
Employment	Jobs	23	3	10	60
Cost of project	$	89,000	−4	20	−80
Dead wombats	Number	27	−4	20	−80
More CO_2	Tonnes	55	−4	20	−80
Total				100	30

Source: Leo Dobes

A different scoring scale has been used in Table A2.3, but with no other change from Table A2.1. The extension of the scoring range from −4 to +4 to the new range of −5 to +5 yields a total weighted score of 250. Again, there is no theory to guide a decision to use one or the other scoring scale, or to assess the significance of the difference in results.

Table A2.3: Different scoring scale used to assess the project

Attribute	Units	Impact	Score −5 to +5)	Weight %	Weighted score
Travel time saving per trip	Minutes	13	3	10	30
Growth in local business p.a.	Revenue ($)	56,000	5	40	200
Reduction in crashes p.a.	Number	4	4	10	40
Employment	Jobs	23	4	20	80
Cost of project	$	89,000	−5	20	−100
Total				100	250

Source: Leo Dobes

As would be expected, a change in the weights used in Table A2.1 will produce a different total weighted score, as shown in Table A2.4. As before, there is no method grounded in theory that allows the determination of the relative significance of the results.

Table A2.4: Different weights attached to each attribute

Attribute	Units	Impact	Score (–4 to +4)	Weight %	Weighted score
Travel time saving per trip	Minutes	13	2	20	40
Growth in local business p.a.	Revenue ($)	56,000	4	20	80
Reduction in crashes p.a.	Number	4	3	10	30
Employment	Jobs	23	3	40	120
Cost of project	$	89,000	–4	10	–40
Total				100	230

Source: Leo Dobes

Proponents of MCA sometimes argue that it is preferable because it does not require the monetisation of factors that are considered in assessing a project. Unless all cost considerations are fully excluded, however, MCA does in fact produce implicit monetary values. In Table A2.4, for example, the project cost of $89,000 is estimated to create 23 jobs, a cost per job of about $3,870. A similar calculation can be made for the number of crashes avoided, or for travel time savings, raising the question of whether these outcomes could not have been achieved at lower cost by some other means.

The MCA approach is also attractive, if not seductive, because it is relatively easy to carry out. It essentially requires only an ability to specify criteria, scores and weights. The production of numerical scores also provides a semblance of systematic analysis. The mathematical appropriateness of aggregating disparate attributes measured in incommensurable units by linking them to scores and weights must, even so, be subject to serious reservation.

Absent the aggregation of weighted scores, the least desirable aspect of MCA would be avoided because incommensurable units would not be combined mathematically. Nevertheless, the selection of criteria to be addressed, and the allocation of weights and scores still involve a degree of arbitrariness. The MCA approach therefore begs the question of why one should expend effort on employing numerical values when a simple qualitative comparison of the positive and negative criteria of a project could achieve the same outcome.

If, despite the above reservations, MCA is used as an analytical tool, its use will present decision-makers with a dilemma because there is no consistent way of choosing between, say, a road-widening project and the construction of an art gallery or the preservation of a wetland. Each project has different attributes, so that comparisons of their aggregated weighted scores would be meaningless.

Appendix 3:
Wider economic impacts
in the transport sector

A conventional cost-benefit analysis (CBA) of transport projects invariably focuses on items such as savings in travel time and fuel costs, as well as on changes in externalities, like negative environmental outcomes. The 1990s, however, saw a growth in calls by Australian transport infrastructure proponents for the inclusion of 'additional' benefits of road and rail projects. Interest centred on logistic improvements, such as reduced trip times and just-in-time delivery, which were claimed to reduce warehousing and inventory costs (e.g. Rockliffe, 1996).

More recently, proponents of transport infrastructure projects have sought to broaden the conventional analytical perspective to encompass the effects of large projects on the economy as a whole, rather than limiting the estimation of benefits to particular routes alone. Initially referred to as wider economic benefits (WEBs) (e.g. Department for Transport, 2005), the literature has more recently adopted the term wider economic impacts (WEIs), which reflects the fact that many of the posited impacts relate to changes in GDP and employment, rather than to the social welfare measures used in CBA.

Various authors recognise that a number of the effects initially categorised as WEBs may be better treated separately as complementary outcomes of transport projects (e.g. Department for Transport, 2014; Laird & Mackie, 2010; Worsley, 2011; Abelson, 2011). This recognition is based on the lack of definitive evidence in posited WEBs of the direction of causality (e.g. higher wages in large cities), onerous data requirements for modelling, confounding effects (e.g. the effect on productivity or competition of the internet), limitations of many transport models (e.g. fixed-trip matrices and lack of responsiveness to changes in land use), double counting, and potential ambiguity (transport projects may result in dispersion of economic activity as well as agglomeration).

A3.1 Categories of wider economic impacts for transport

A generally accepted taxonomy of WEIs includes the three major categories, which are examined below. A fourth category — increased competition as a result of improved transport links between different markets — was identified in the Department for Transport's (DfT) 2005 *Transport, Wider Economic Benefits and Impacts on GDP*, but was abandoned in the updated, 2014 version (p. 1, fn. 3) because it was not considered to be relevant in the United Kingdom, where transport links were already well developed and existing transport networks were 'unlikely to be a significant constraint on competition'.

A3.1.1 Agglomeration economies

As the generalised cost of transport (travel time, fuel, externalities) falls, firms and workers in their existing locations will effectively be brought closer to each other. In other words, the 'effective density' of the area where production occurs will increase because workers can more easily reach it, even if they live elsewhere.

Although simple distance (e.g. kilometres) or travel time (e.g. minutes) are sometimes used as proxies, DfT (2005, annex 1, para 153) defines the effective density of a location more realistically as 'the employment in and surrounding the area, weighted by their proximity (in generalised cost of transport) to the location'. It is recognised, however, that reduced generalised costs of transport may also result in some countervailing reduction of effective density if workers or firms relocate further away from the central business district.

Increased 'effective' proximity of firms and workers to each other as a result of better transport links is seen as raising productivity due to positive spillovers. Firms are considered to learn more from other firms and about innovations generally if they are 'clustered' physically close to each other, especially because of face-to-face interaction between employees.

O'Flaherty (2005, ch. 2) argues that workers in cities can more easily change jobs, bringing new knowledge to their destination firms when they move. Jaffe et al. (1993) show that new patent applications are five to 10 times more likely to cite patents from the same metropolitan area compared to patents from outside it. Proximate firms are more likely to have available a greater variety of inputs from local suppliers, and can therefore choose those that best suit their production processes. They can also benefit from lower transport costs, search costs and sharing of costly infrastructure. Firms that can draw on a larger pool of workers benefit from greater opportunities for matching available specialised skills with their particular needs. Workers on the other hand, can more easily move to the jobs they prefer.

A3.1.2 Increased output in imperfectly competitive product markets

Conventional transport CBAs implicitly assume a situation of perfect competition throughout the economy, including in sectors that use transport services to obtain inputs and deliver outputs. In a perfectly competitive situation, users of transport services for commuting and for freight pay a price that matches the value to them of the services. Conventionally estimated consumer surplus provides a satisfactory measure of social surplus.

The situation is different in the case of business users operating in imperfectly competitive markets. Where business users of transport services have monopoly power in their various markets, a reduction in transport costs is likely to have two separate effects. One effect, already captured in conventional CBA, is an increase in consumer surplus accruing to users of transport services from additional (generated or induced) trips. The other, additional, effect is an increase in social welfare because lower costs may induce transport-using monopoly industries to increase their output and, hence, the quantity of goods and services available to society.[1] The literature (e.g. Vickerman, 2007a, p. 603; Kernohan & Rognlien, 2011, pp. 116–21) generally illustrates

---

1   To induce customers to buy the extra output, the monopolist must reduce its price. Consumers benefit from the lower price. But society also benefits from the larger number of units of output made available compared to a monopoly output. The monopolist also benefits from the additional output. Although the price reduction cuts into monopoly revenues, the additional units sold increase overall receipts.

this situation by presenting a standard monopoly-type diagram and then deriving an 'uprate factor' based on the Ramsey (1927) pricing model (Brown & Sibley, 1986). The 'uprate factor' is intended for scaling up benefits that have been calculated for business-related trips in a conventional CBA.

A monopoly-style diagram is also relevant to the Cournot solution for a duopoly, which is an approach adopted by Kernohan and Rognlien (2011), among others. Two perfectly cooperating duopolists can jointly achieve a monopoly price and output by sharing market output equally. Each effectively maintains a monopoly over their own share of the market. In the case of a homogenous product, an attempt by either duopolist to reduce price or increase output will need to be followed by their competitor, taking both away from the monopoly position towards the perfect competition equilibrium. There is no single, determinate position, however, especially once the assumptions of a homogenous product and identical cost of production are discarded.

By adding more firms, the Cournot solution can be extended to represent an oligopoly. But a larger number of firms will reduce the likelihood of a durable collusive agreement on price or output, while increasing the likelihood of product differentiation (e.g. through branding). As Leftwich (1970, p. 239) points out:

> As a practical matter, sellers in most oligopolistic industries sell differentiated products … Industries approaching pure oligopoly include cement, basic steel and most other basic metal-producing industries. Even here there are elements of differentiation among the products sold in a particular industry. Locational factors, service, and even personal friendships may differentiate the products of the various sellers in an industry.

And reactions of oligopolists in claiming market share are less likely to be based on the assumption that the other firms will not react in turn and will keep their output and prices fixed. However elegant, it is at least arguable that a Cournot solution is an unrealistic portrayal of the real world.

An oligopolistic market may, therefore, be better portrayed in terms of the classic 'kinked demand curve' case, where products are differentiated, and individual firms find it unrewarding to alter prices because of the potential reactions of their competitor oligopolists. The discontinuous, vertical marginal revenue curve below the kink suggests a degree of price and output rigidity for the industry whether marginal costs increase or decrease. If the kinked demand curve interpretation of an oligopolistic industry's structure and conduct is preferred to the Cournot approach, then it would be less convincing to argue that reductions in the generalised cost of transport will result in welfare improvements in imperfect markets. In such situations, any automatic application of 'uprate factors' based on a Cournot model would be decidedly misguided.

In practice, price wars do occur between oligopolists. On the other hand, non-price competition in various forms is also feasible, obviating the need for price and output adjustments, and hence retaliatory price wars. Advertising, changes in quality and design, use of technology to reduce barriers to entry, and issue of loyalty cards to customers, are some forms of this competition. Price wars, product differentiation, and other potential real-world oligopolistic practices mean that there is no single approach to modelling oligopoly. Serious doubt must again be cast on the wisdom of the automatic application of 'uprate factors' to increase estimated benefits of transport services used by oligopolistic industries.

A simple analysis of monopolistically competitive markets is also tricky. Products may be highly differentiated, with a large number of independent sellers who tend to equate marginal costs with marginal revenues. According to Leftwich (1970, p. 275), 'some slight restriction of output and increase in prices may occur under monopolistic competition, as compared with pure competition', so that there may be some welfare gain from increased output following a reduction in costs. The degree of ease of entry into the industry and the extent of advertising and other forms of non-price competition that are used will, however, influence actual outcomes. No unique modelling approach is available.

In discussing imperfect competition generally, Vickerman (2007a, p. 602) cautions that:

> In order to be able to apply CBA in these circumstances, we need first to assess the way in which any transport improvement will affect different activities, then assess the competitive structure of those activities in order to be aware both of the markup and the likely competitive response of firms or other agents, and only then can we hope to evaluate the benefits accurately.

DfT (2005, para 101) is equally explicit about the need for evidence and the facts of a situation before estimating benefits associated with imperfect competition:

> Two steps are required to estimate the impact of these additional effects on welfare. First we need to know how firms respond to transport cost savings, specifically what the impacts are on output. Then we need to know the size of the additional benefits delivered by the additional output.

A3.1.3 Changes in the labour market

Lower transport costs may induce more workers to travel in order to enter employment, or seek more remunerative employment. This is a benefit to travellers that is captured in conventional CBA in the 'generated demand' triangle. Worker-travellers take their decision to increase travel (or not) on the basis of after-tax earnings. The wage paid to the worker by the employer, however, includes payroll and income taxes, because it is the total before-tax wage that reflects the worker's contribution to the value of their output for the employer.

Although the tax component is not captured in conventional CBA analysis of transport projects, it reflects part of the additional value of production attributable to new commuting trips of workers, or to those now earning higher wages in different jobs. Additional tax revenues can be used to fund other socially desirable projects that would otherwise not have been funded, or they can be used to reduce taxes imposed elsewhere in the economy. They therefore constitute an additional social benefit, an impact that is not captured in the conventional analysis.

Rather puzzlingly, the other side of the taxation coin is ignored in the literature on WEIs and by proponents of increased spending on transport infrastructure. Infrastructure projects that raise significant amounts of additional taxation receipts because of the postulated increase in labour supply, would arguably also be significant enough to require substantial financial resources.

Whether the funding for infrastructure construction and operation is raised by general taxation, printing money, or by loans, there will be some consequential opportunity cost to the economy. Government borrowing will reduce consumption and divert resources away from the private sector. Inflation generated by excessive printing of money will distort resource use. Taxes distort markets and may reduce the supply of labour. Whether the deadweight loss of these effects outweighs the additional tax raised from an increased labour supply — or indeed all WEI effects — depends on the particular circumstances of each project. Failure to include both the positive and negative effects of an infrastructure project can only result in a less than impartial analytical approach.

A3.2 Some empirical issues

Estimation of posited WEIs is largely an empirical issue. A preference for harmonisation of the parameters or variables employed, therefore, needs to take into account issues that are relevant to empirical analysis.

A3.2.1 Agglomeration economies

Conceptually, agglomeration benefits are measured as the increase in output (GDP) due to the implementation of the transport project. A key variable that requires estimation is, therefore, the elasticity of total productivity with respect to the effective density of employment for industry i in area j. Evidence of causality is thus required to establish that changes in productivity or output are due to an increase in effective density generated by a specific transport project, but this is rarely, if ever, provided in the transport literature or CBAs. Paucity of data and the effort that is required to estimate agglomeration benefits, however, encourages use of 'uplift'; factors derived from large cities, whether they are appropriate or not. Mare and Graham (2009, p. 4) add that confounding effects in correlations may also bias estimated productivity impacts upwards.

Effective density is estimated as a gravity model, with agglomeration factors falling away exponentially with generalised travel cost. Definition of zones used by transport models is therefore critical: many models include only origin–destination data for trips between zones, so that larger zones will exclude more within-zone trips. Some models also rely on physical distances between zone centroids rather than on generalised costs of travel.

A further concern is that changes in productivity may be attributed solely to transport projects, potentially risking a form of confirmation bias. Supporting infrastructure, such as the availability of high speed internet, may not be as conspicuous as a major highway or rail upgrade, but may play a key role in increasing urban productivity. Some, (e.g. Florida, 2003) might similarly argue that entertainment, high level educational facilities and life-style ambience are also essential to attracting the 'creative class' of high-productivity individuals to jobs in cities.

Nor does the WEI agglomeration literature typically feature in its modelling the constraint of travel time budgets (TTB). Based on detailed analysis of historical data, Zahavi (1979), Marchetti (1994) and others have argued that people will only travel a daily total of about an hour from home to work and return. Unless a transport project improvement captures a significant additional number of workers who can now reduce their daily travel time to an hour or so, the number of additional workers may not increase enough to change productivity levels. Improved transport modes may also result in increased fares, thus dissuading some workers from travelling.

Mean travel times of between 60 to 90 minutes per day are considered to be historically stable, but Milthorpe (2007, Table 1) found that they had increased in Sydney from about 73 minutes in 1981 to 81 minutes in 2005. As Milthorpe (2007, s. 2.2) notes, increased TTBs may involve use of mobile phones and laptops, either for recreation or work. The ready availability of technology in urban areas, as well as transport improvements, may therefore also play a role in determining effective densities and agglomeration economies.

On a broader level, use of GDP or its sub-national equivalents is not compatible with the welfare approach adopted in CBA. But even the fundamental issue of standing appears to have been neglected in the literature. Reporting on studies of transport projects in Germany and China (Laird & Mackie, 2010, para 2.2.4) that do not address the issue explicitly, Laird and Mackie (2010, para 2.1.5) comment more generally that:

> An improvement in transport supply in one region will make that region more accessible to other regions and potentially result in the displacement of economic activity to the 'other' regions. This is known

as the two-way road effect. Thus an improvement in transport supply in one region may increase the size of the economy at the national level but reduce it at a sub-national level.

In sum, empirical analysis of WEIs can be problematic due to deficiencies in available transport models and the paucity of data relevant to specific projects. Detailed critiques are provided by DfT (2014); Worsley (2011); Laird and Mackie (2010); Graham et al. (2009) and Byett et al. (2015), among others.

A3.2.2 Output change in imperfectly competitive product markets

It is not clear why the WEI literature has focused so strongly on the aspect of imperfectly competitive markets. The implication is that it is ignored in conventional CBA. However, standard texts, such as Boardman et al. (2011, ch. 5), inform readers in some detail of the need to examine secondary markets that are distorted by taxes or other government interventions, externalities, or imperfect competition. The outcome differs for factor markets, primary markets and secondary markets, and depends on the efficiency of each. Further, Rouwendal (2012) examines different forms for demand functions (not just the straight line) for a number of different models of imperfect competition, finding that the indirect effects 'may have the same order of magnitudes as the conventionally measured direct effects, may be much smaller, or may exceed them substantially'.

DfT (2005, para 204) derives an expression that it recommends should be used as an 'imperfect competition uprate factor' that is the product of the elasticity of demand of the imperfectly competitive firm and the percentage mark-up of the price in excess of the marginal cost. The uprate factor is used to scale up travel time savings and any transport reliability gains to businesses (but not commuters).

Drawing on a number of price-cost studies for UK manufacturing industries and economy-wide elasticities, DfT (2005) recommended an uprate factor of 0.1, based on a price-cost margin of about 0.2 and a price elasticity of demand of 0.5. That is, for imperfectly competitive firms, any welfare gain due to business travel time savings, as well as transport reliability gains, should be increased by 10 per cent above values estimated using the conventional analysis in CBA. Although it refers to an 'uplift factor', rather than an 'uprate factor', DfT (2014) confirms this recommendation.

Abelson (2011) notes that improved transport infrastructure may also result in economies of scale that reduce costs and hence increase welfare gains. He points out, however, that 'because the gains from economies of scale are particular to each situation, these economies cannot be incorporated simply into a standard appraisal. They must be justified and estimated on a case-by-case basis'.

Tyers (2014) examined the economy-wide effects of oligopolistic service industries in Australia. In particular, his analysis explored the effect of government price-cap regulation and price surveillance of the sectors that had been privatised or made more competitive since the 1980s: telecommunications services, transport, health, education, utilities and finance. According to Tyers (2014, p. 6), the privatised services (electricity, gas, water, finance, transport and telecommunications) account for at least 20 per cent of Australia's GDP, but 'the precise extent of imperfect competition in Australia's service industries is difficult to quantify'.

Oligopolistic vehicle manufacturing in Australia is being wound down under the Australian Government's Automotive Transformation Scheme. Increasingly sophisticated use of the internet by producers and distributors (*The Economist*, 2 May 2015) is likely to increase the degree of competition in a range of other industries. Companies like Uber and Lyft, for example, are pressuring governments to allow individuals to offer passenger transport services in competition with taxis. Napster and Spotify (music sharing), PayPal (electronic payments), Prosper and Lending Club (peer-to-peer lending), and multiple online sites for rating restaurants, toilets, and performances, are just some of the growing number of suppliers and information providers. Even where entry of competitors has not yet occurred, the mere threat of the possibility is likely to constrain less than competitive behaviour.

Another relevant issue that has not been addressed directly in modelling WEIs is the effect of government regulation, rather than market structure, in limiting competition. Australian examples of legislated rigidities and imperfect competition include chemists, newsagents, taxis, centralised wage determination mechanisms, some postal services, trade union and professional association restrictions, after-hours penalty rates, occupational health standards (such as truck driver hours and maximum weights of bags that may be lifted manually). Institutional rigidities preclude significant increase in production or fall in prices, even if a producer's transport costs are reduced.

While not denying that reduced transport costs in imperfectly competitive industries can generate benefits additional to those estimated in conventional CBAs, there is an arguable case for considerable caution in automatically applying multipliers like the DfT (2005) 'uprate factor' in an analysis. Given the diversity of firms within an industry, and differences between industries and countries, mechanistic application of standardised WEI factors is unlikely to produce a robust, defensible analysis.

A3.2.3 Changes in the labour market

DfT (2005, paras 109, 118) summarises the effect of improved labour supply as follows:

> If a transport improvement facilitates increased GDP, there will be tax consequences, whether the additional work involves more people in employment, additional hours, or moving to more productive jobs. The welfare effects of small changes in time savings will be marginal for individuals, but the GDP effects can be more substantial for the minority of people affected … in some cases, relatively small welfare benefits from time or cost savings can lead to significant GDP effects. There is no theoretical reason to be certain whether the welfare effect of such savings will be smaller or larger than the GDP effect … [It is] likely to be significant only where a transport scheme relieves a significant transport constraint, and then only for a minority of individuals (insofar as transport cost changes lead to a change in employment or in employment patterns).

A transport intervention that reduces the generalised cost of transport to a commuter can be thought of as an increase in the effective wage. It is therefore possible to estimate an elasticity of labour supply with respect to effective wages, and to use it to estimate a change in the level of employment. The product of the change in employment and GDP per worker (average labour productivity) yields the overall change in GDP. Studies relevant to the United Kingdom find that the labour supply elasticity with respect to wages ranges from 0.5 to 0.15, so DfT (2005, para 241) proposes 0.1 as 'best estimate'. In a UK study, Venables (2007, p. 186) concluded that increased incomes due to workers moving to higher productivity jobs 'typically yield[s] total gains several times larger than those that would be derived from a standard cost-benefit analysis'.

DfT (2005, paras 245–47) refers to evidence that time savings on commuting journeys tend to result in longer commuting distances, and that 'workers are not very responsive to changes in wages when choosing how much to work'. It therefore recommends that the GDP effect should be assumed to be zero. DfT (2014, para 4.1.25) states, however, that 40 per cent of the change in GDP is due to the labour supply impact, and 30 per cent of the change in GDP is due to moves to jobs of different productivity levels.

A3.3 Wider economic impacts in the Australian and New Zealand jurisdictions

A report to the Council of Australian Governments Reform Council by SGS (2012a) reviewed the literature on agglomeration economies and provided estimates of projected changes to metropolitan GDP. The report was based on case studies of proposed transport projects in Melbourne and Adelaide, and greenfield housing development in urban fringe areas of Sydney.

The SGS (2012a) report adopts an approach similar to overseas studies by estimating changes in state gross value added (GVA) based on correlation between effective job density (EJD) and labour productivity by statistical local area (SLA). EJD is derived using travel time rather than generalised cost of travel.

However, SGS (2012a) also proposes a different approach to estimating 'uplift' in GVA, based on elasticities of changes in human capital due to changes in EJD. This approach is based on the hypothesis (SGS, 2012a, p. 2) that households are 'knowledge intensive enterprises' in their own right, and that transport projects will open more opportunities to learn and acquire skills. It is not entirely clear from the report whether the acquisition of additional human capital is hypothesised as being due to better access to educational centres or to on-the-job training, but the calculated elasticities are based on the incidence of formal tertiary qualifications in each SLA.

With regard to productivity effects of agglomeration, the points made by SGS (2012a) are similar to those by DfT (2014), Worsley (2011), Laird and Mackie (2010), and Graham et al. (2009), among others. For example, 'rather than firms being more productive because they are in a central location, firms that are more productive can command central locations', so that the direction of causality runs in the opposite direction to the one usually hypothesised. A further problem is that researchers are not able to obtain access to detailed firm-level productivity data in Australia, whereas overseas studies have been able to do so. Indexes of EJD also do not distinguish between 'jobs' and their relevance to a particular sector in terms of their contribution to GVA: for example, a bank teller and an investment banker will be treated as equivalent occupations. SGS (2012a) also acknowledge that the use of cross-sectional data at a particular point in time to estimate elasticities may not be appropriate for projecting changes in future productivity due to a transport intervention or land-use strategy.

Given these uncertainties, it is incongruous that SGS (2007, Table 14) should attribute over $17 million out of a total of $85 million in present value benefits to urban consolidation benefits as a result of replacing a railway level crossing with an underpass in suburban Springvale in Melbourne. Capital Metro Agency (2014, Table 18) attributes a similarly high proportion of about 20 per cent in WEIs to its estimate of the total benefits for a 13-kilometre light rail connection between a suburb that is already served by a rapid bus service and one out of the four existing Canberra town centres.

Some other reports on WEIs commissioned by Australian jurisdictions, but not reviewed here include SGS (2012b), KPMG (2012), and Hensher et al. (2012). At the time of writing, a detailed study of elasticities of productivity with respect to employment density was being undertaken by SGS under the aegis of the Australian Government's Bureau of Infrastructure and Transport Economics on behalf of Austroads.

Studies have also been undertaken in New Zealand. Mare and Graham (2009) used more detailed data than those available to researchers in Australia to estimate agglomeration elasticities. Kernohan and Rognlien (2011, Table 8.2) analysed imperfect competition through the prism of a Cournot model using the price-cost differences of New Zealand firms. They recommend an uplift factor of 10.7 per cent be applied to business-user benefits. Agglomeration impacts or externalities are included in the NZ Transport Agency's (2013, p. 5: 406–411) *Economic Evaluation Manual*. It includes weighted average agglomeration elasticities for New Zealand by industry, as well as the procedure to apply the agglomeration elasticities to estimate productivity changes by location.

Discussions with transport agencies in Australia and New Zealand indicate a general acceptance of the need to include WEIs in evaluations of transport projects. Manuals issued by government agencies in a number of jurisdictions contain sections on WEIs or WEBs. Central agencies are typically more guarded, emphasising the need to avoid the application of elasticity and other values obtained from overseas studies or from other projects, although current methodologies are broadly supported. Most of those interviewed recognised the potential pitfalls of double counting, the need to demonstrate causality, and the limitations imposed by data availability.

Infrastructure projects that are sufficiently large to generate WEIs are, however, also likely to require considerable funding resources. Raising substantial funds is also likely to have a negative effect on economic activity (see Appendix 7 on marginal excess tax burden). Somewhat worryingly, the apparent enthusiasm of government agencies to apply the WEI approach is not matched by a corresponding willingness to adjust costs and benefits for the opportunity costs of increased borrowing or taxation.

Infrastructure Australia (2013, p. 11) notes that WEIs may not always be positive and that 'the availability of Australian specific data needed to calculate WEBs is currently sub-optimal'. It states that it will treat estimates of WEBs 'separately to the traditional CBA', but is nevertheless broadly supportive of their inclusion in proposals for infrastructure spending.

A3.4 Issues for consideration in harmonising approaches to wider economic impacts

Vickerman (2007b) provides a comprehensive review of the debate regarding the existence of WEBs, distinguishing between macro-level and micro-level approaches, and noting the difficulty of 'knowing whether an elasticity obtained from the macro-study is in any way applicable to a single investment decision'. After reviewing differences in approach in the estimation of elasticities in macro-studies (output, productivity, or employment), the issue of direction of causality, and use of land use transport interaction (LUTI) models versus computable general equilibrium (CGE) models, he points out that most of the empirical evidence relates to ex ante studies. He cites 'one of the relatively few ex post studies' by Hay et al. (2004) to the effect that 'a very significant project, the Channel Tunnel, has not produced significant wider benefits over its first ten years of operation, at least on the regional economies close to the tunnel'.

Reviewing the effects of a number of Train à Grand Vitesse (TGV) projects between pairs of major French cities, Vickerman (2007b) finds that traffic levels generally increased in both directions, but that there was no overall net impact on these major cities, although there was a tendency for increased concentration of economic activity towards them from their regional hinterlands. Vickerman (2007b, p. 16) concludes that 'what is clear is that there is little evidence of there being standard transferable [wider economic benefits] multipliers region to region or project to project' that can be applied to estimated benefits in individual ex ante analyses.

DfT (2014, s. 5.2) reviews a number of data and modelling issues in the United Kingdom that can affect the robustness of estimates of WEIs. Lack of modelling of intra-zonal travel in transport models is likely to produce inaccurate estimates of agglomeration effects. Where transport models do not employ generalised cost matrices, there is likely to be bias in WEI assessments because changes in agglomeration effects depend on costs. Insufficient segmentation of modes in transport models may affect estimates of effective density; for example, if the model does not include a public transport mode. Finally, models may not cover the geographic area under consideration, leading to unreliable results.

Laird and Mackie (2010, pp. 1–2, para 5.1.3) report on British studies where estimates of the growth in GVA attributed to transport investments:

> are significantly in excess of the Present Value of Benefits used in conventional cost benefit appraisal ... Clearly these GVA estimates are large and, on the basis that they also exceed welfare benefit estimates, give rise to questions of consistency with the methods used to appraise transport projects ... the methods available to estimate the potential GVA impact of a region post a transport investment are still in their infancy and need work to ensure they pass internal consistency and robustness tests.

In a detailed review of using the UK GVA approach, rather than GDP, Byett et al. (2015, p. 94) noted that:

> One issue that was not fully resolved was whether the benefits measured are additional or inclusive of the rule-of-half benefits measured within the standard transport appraisal ... Hence at this stage it is recommended that the GVA approach be used alongside the EEM [Economic Evaluation Manual, NZ Transport Agency], rather than as an additive effect.

More particularly from the perspective of this publication, in a summary table of pros and cons of the GVA methodology, Byett et al. (2015, Table 10.1, p. 95) also conclude that:

> The GVA approach is not consistently defined across different studies. Likewise density measures also differ across studies. These inconsistencies reduce the ability to compare model outcomes and calibrate model parameters.

Abelson (2011) concludes that 'searching for wider economic benefits is something of a holy grail in transport economics' and that transport infrastructure:

> often disperses employment rather than concentrates it; correlations of wage and employment density overstate the density effect on wages; attribution of significant agglomeration economies to a small number of generated trips is not very plausible; and the empirical basis for agglomeration economies driven by effective densities is thin and subject to unresolved technical issues. This paper concludes that agglomeration benefits should generally not be included in an appraisal.

Just as there is sometimes unjustified aversion to new ideas, it can sometimes be the case that a new idea or approach is adopted without sufficient critical review. In the case of WEIs, enough caveats have already been expressed by various specialist observers to signal that a thorough review of the approach is desirable before its acceptance and automatic application to transport projects in Australia and New Zealand. Nevertheless, transport agencies appear to be willing to forgo more detailed review.

To ensure consistency and robustness in CBA studies of transport projects, a harmonised approach should be adopted to the following:

- review of the basic methodological principles used in the WEI approach, particularly from the perspective of its application to cost-benefit analysis
- review of the desirability of complementing the WEI approach with a corresponding application of METB estimates to costs and benefits
- peer review by non-transport econometrics experts of estimates of WEI variables and parameters.

Appendix 4:
Social discount rates

Discounting is essential in cost-benefit analysis (CBA) because it provides a way to express all costs and benefits in terms of their present value. It does so by assigning smaller weights to values that occur further into the future than the present. Unless the values of costs and benefits are made commensurable by being expressed as present values, they cannot be aggregated.

Social discount rates reflect society's preference or valuation on current well-being versus future well-being. Despite a voluminous literature, however, there is no consensus on the methodology for determining social discount rates, or their value.

It is not the intention here to review the literature, or to recommend specific values for discount rates. An outline of the main conceptual approaches is provided below, but the focus is rather to record the range of rates that are used in Australia, New Zealand and other countries. This diversity of rates is problematic because the discount rate is a key factor, albeit not necessarily the most important factor, in determining the net present value of a project.

A4.1 Conceptual approaches to establishing social discount rates

The so-called consumption and investment rates are the two major approaches to conceptualising social discount rates. Other perspectives tend to be some form of combination or extension of these approaches. Zhuang et al. (2007), Pearce et al. (2006) and Boardman et al. (2011) provide readable introductions to the topic.

The social rate of time preference (SRTP) reflects the rate at which society is willing to forgo current consumption in return for more consumption in the future. It therefore assumes that all costs and benefits are consumption goods and services. Benefits are consumed rather than being reinvested.

One method of estimating the SRTP empirically is by estimating the after-tax return on government or other low-risk bonds or securities. Individuals may, however, have preferences that go beyond those expressed in their participation in financial markets. Moreover, individuals' preferences are unlikely to be the same as those of society's collective attitude to trading off current consumption for more consumption in the future. An alternative method of estimating the SRTP is to use the Ramsey (1928) formula, but this approach is contentious because it requires the specification of a 'pure' rate of social time preference, as well as other variables.

The other major alternative method for estimating the social discount rate takes an investment or producer perspective. Society's resources are scarce. Their use by government will thus deny or reduce their availability to private investors. If private investors can obtain a higher rate of return than that achieved by the public sector project, society's welfare could be improved by allowing the private sector to use the resources (or funds) instead of the government. Put another way, government projects should only proceed if they are feasible when discounted at the marginal social opportunity cost (SOC) of capital, which is the rate of return on private sector investment.

Most countries, including the Australian and New Zealand jurisdictions, tend to use either the SRTP or the SOC approach (tables A4.1 and A4.2). It is also possible to calculate an average of the SRTP and SOC, weighted by the respective shares of tax funding (assumed to reduce consumption) and domestic borrowing (assumed to crowd out private investment). Some formulations of the weighted average approach include borrowing from other countries. The SRTP and SOC can also be combined into a shadow price of capital, defined by Boardman et al. (2011, p. 256) as the ratio of SOC to SRTP, and multiplying relevant costs and benefits to convert them to 'consumption equivalents' that can then be discounted using the SRTP.

Other approaches, such as the use of intergenerational discount rates, are based primarily on subjective equity justifications. An approach that seeks to incorporate uncertainty about the future (interest rates or the state of the economy) by extending the Ramsay equation is 'time-declining discount rates' (Pearce et al., 2006, ch. 13; Freeman et al., 2013). Time-declining rates, however suffer from the problem of time-inconsistency, which is the incongruence in behaviour between successive time periods.

A4.2 Diversity in discount rates

Table A4.1 demonstrates clearly the diversity of discount rates that have been adopted for use in transport projects by selected Organisation for Economic Cooperation and Development (OECD) countries. Table A4.2 reveals that considerable diversity exists within and between Australian and New Zealand jurisdictions, but discount rates are generally higher than those used in other countries.

Table A4.1: Discount rate used by transport agencies
in selected OECD countries

Jurisdiction	Method	Discount rate (real)
France	Risk-adjusted social rate of time preference	4.5% (or project specific rate)
Germany	Social rate of time preference	3% (for short-term effects) and 1% (for long-term effects)
Japan	Social cost of capital	4%
The Netherlands	Risk-adjusted social rate of time preference	4% to 5.5%
Norway	Risk-adjusted social rate of time preference	4% reducing to 2% over 75 years
Sweden	Social rate of time preference	3.5%
United States	Certainty equivalent	2.5%, 3% and 5% (for estimation of social cost of carbon)
United Kingdom	Social rate of time preference	3.5% reducing to 1% over 300 years

Source: OECD (2015)

Table A4.2: Discount rates advocated by selected Australian and NZ government agencies

Jurisdiction[1]	Rate (% p.a, real terms)	Basis	Source
Commonwealth of Australia	3% (SRTP) and SOC (not specified)	3% used for consumption-only stream (SRTP), with no opportunity cost of resources. SOC is not specified, but investment examples used for illustration utilise 8 % p.a. real.	Department of Finance and Administration (2006, ch. 5)
	4%, 7%, 10%	For infrastructure project proposals by the states. 7% (central value, SOC) with 4% and 10% for sensitivity testing. The 7% central estimate 'is in accordance with the majority of national, state and territory guidelines on cost benefit analysis ...'	Infrastructure Australia (2013, p. 9)
	Government bond rate	The Australian Transport Council (ATC) states that the Bureau of Transport Economics (Luskin & Dobes, 1999, p. 78) 'concludes that the most appropriate discount rate to use for BCA is the government bond rate'. But this is not the case: the citation refers to the allocation of program funding and the need to avoid adding a risk premium.	ATC (2006, vol. 5, p. 84)
	7% p.a. real for public transport infrastructure projects	Recommendation of 7% is followed by the statement that 'Discount rates are determined by state Treasuries'.	Austroads (Rockliffe et al., 2012, p. 7)
	3%, 7%, 10%	7% is 'central', with 3% and 10% for sensitivity testing. Office of Best Practice Regulation (OBPR) notes that 7% is consistent with the US Office of Management and Budget, as well as the NSW Treasury.	OBPR (2014, pp. 7–8)
	3%, 8%, 10%	3%, 8%, 10% represent 'the weighted average riskless rate of return, the weighted average rate of return and a rate of return for a riskier asset or that reflects the marginal productivity of capital during the 2000s' (Harrison, 2010, p. 61).	(Harrison, 2010, pp. 59–61). No other separate official Productivity Commission guidance on discount rates appears to have been published.

Jurisdiction[1]	Rate (% p.a, real terms)	Basis	Source
New South Wales	Central rate 7% (SOC), with 4% (SRTP) and 10% for sensitivity testing	'While there may be no universally accepted "correct" discount rate, interpretation of appraisal results will be impossible if different agencies use different discount rates. The solution is the application of a standard set of real discount rates of 4%, 7% and 10% to see if the outcome is sensitive to such variations and, if it is, to make the critical "break-even" rate clear in the analysis results.'	New South Wales Treasury (2007, p. 52)
	7%	Capital asset pricing model (CAPM) and other calculations suggest SRTP rate is about 5% and SOC 9.3%, but use 7% p.a. real for consistency across the NSW transport portfolio.	Transport for NSW (2013, p. 210)
Victoria	Category 1 (4%) Category 2 (7%) Category 3 (Department of Treasury and Finance (DTF) provides)	Category 1: core areas like public health, justice, education where benefits are not easily quantified; rate based on long-term government bond rate. Category 2: services like public transport, roads, public housing; rate based on long-term government bond rate plus 'modest risk premium'. Category 3: commercial investments with risk similar to private sector. DTF to be consulted on appropriate rate.	DTF (2013, Table 7, p. 25)
	4%	Regulatory proposals should use 4%, like Category 1 in DTF guidelines. Other rates can be used if warranted.	Government of Victoria (2014, p. 11)

Jurisdiction[1]	Rate (% p.a, real terms)	Basis	Source
New Zealand	8% default rate for projects that are difficult to categorise, including regulatory proposals; 5% general purpose office and accommodation buildings; 7% infrastructure and special purpose (single-use) buildings (e.g. prison, hospital); 9% R&D, media, IT, telecoms, technology.	SOC: 'Treasury's policy is to use a pre-tax discount rate equal to the long-run return on investments made by share-market companies … [the Government could, and does, invest in the share market] this guide recommends the use of a discount rate that is based on the rate of return of the next best alternative investment. The most convenient "alternative investment" is the share market.' Assumptions: statutory tax rate: 28%; effective marginal tax rate: 24%; equity risk premium: 7%; risk-free rate: 3.82% at 5 December 2014; inflation 2% p.a.; equity beta: 1.0; gearing: 33% default, 30% buildings, 23% infrastructure, 24% technology.	New Zealand Treasury (2015, pp. 34–36) www.treasury.govt.nz/ publications/guidance/ planning/costbenefitanalysis/ currentdiscountrates [published 17 March 2015.;
Queensland	6% with sensitivity analysis at 4%, 7%, 10%	'Traditionally, infrastructure projects in Queensland have used 6% as the standard discount rate including sensitivity analysis at the 4%, 7% and 10% discount rates. Before any discount rate is applied in a CBA, it is advisable to seek confirmation of the appropriate discount rate from the relevant authority.'	Department of Transport and Main Roads (2011, p. 2.9)
	Not specified — subject to discussion with Queensland Treasury	'The discount rate(s) to be used in a cost-benefit analysis should be agreed between the agency and Queensland Treasury.'	Queensland Treasury (2015, p. 14)
Western Australia	4%, 7%, 10% but other rates sometimes used.	Aligns with Infrastructure Australia, but may use a weighted average cost of capital for commercially oriented projects. The Western Australian Program Evaluation Unit (2015) does not specify a discount rate.	Personal communication, 2014

Jurisdiction[1]	Rate (% p.a., real terms)	Basis	Source
South Australia	Examples of CAPM-based real discount rates range from 2.7% (very low) to 6.7% (high). Section 3.3.3 of DTF (2014) suggests ± 2% sensitivity.	Department of Treasury and Finance (DTF) recommends CAPM-based rates range with sectoral or project risk premium included. One line agency claimed that DTF specifies 6% as default rate.	DTF (2014) part B, Table 3 of *Guidelines*.
Tasmania	Agencies generally use 7%	No guidelines issued by Treasury	Personal communication, December 2014
Australian Capital Territory	4%, 7%, 10%	CBA to be applied to projects greater than $10 million (i.e. Tier 2 and Tier 3). 'The stream of costs and benefits should … be discounted by a real discount rate of 7% with sensitivity testing using discount rates of 4% and 10%. ACT Guide for preparing RIS (2003 version) proposes discounting, but does not specify discount rate.	ACT Government (undated, p. 27)

Notes: 1. Jurisdictions listed in order of size of population; 2. Selection of rates was limited approximately to the period 2000 to 2015, with most recent information available used for each agency.

Source: compiled by Leo Dobes from the sources cited

A4.3 The issue of harmonisation

The choice of approach to determine the public sector discount rate as well as the discount rate value has been, and is subject to continuing debate. It is unlikely that the matter will be resolved in the near future.

Given the unsettled theory and practice about appropriate social discount rates, agreement on harmonised values is unlikely, particularly between different jurisdictions. A degree of de facto harmonisation is occurring, however, in a number of Australian states, which have adopted the NSW 4 per cent, 7 per cent (central rate) and 10 per cent per annum approach. Infrastructure Australia also uses these rates, so that jurisdictions applying for federal funding are of necessity required to use them.

Over time, the 4 per cent, 7 per cent and 10 per cent rates may become standard practice, but a considered review would nevertheless be worthwhile to ensure that the central rate at least is an appropriate and justifiable one.

Appendix 5:
Greenhouse gas emissions and the carbon price

Climate change is an important policy issue for many countries. Despite considerable uncertainty regarding the extent, timing, intensity or frequency of expected changes in climate and extreme weather events, it has become commonplace in economic appraisals to include a monetary value for the greenhouse gas emissions generated by a project. The value is treated as a negative externality in cost-benefit analyses (CBA).

There has not, however, been work done to resolve some of the problems inherent in using any particular value. The purpose of this appendix is to raise issues that should be addressed in establishing consistent valuation of the so-called 'carbon price'.

A5.1 Consistency in measurement

The range of greenhouse gases includes, among others, water vapour, carbon dioxide, methane and nitrous oxide and ozone. The radiative forcing effect of each of these is measured with respect to the reference gas, carbon dioxide. The total effect of any emission scenario is therefore expressed in the common unit of carbon dioxide equivalents, $CO_2(e)$. Nevertheless CBA reports are rarely clear on which greenhouse emissions have been included. It is generally not the practice, for example, to include water vapour, which is a potent greenhouse gas. An obvious area for harmonisation is to establish a common set of gases to be considered, thus allowing projects to be considered on a comparable basis.

The change in radiative forcing caused by greenhouse gas emissions is a function of their addition to the atmospheric concentration of all greenhouse gases. This fact is often overlooked, which leads to the inappropriate measurement of the volume of emissions of greenhouse gases and the attribution of some negative 'carbon price' annual value to a project's 'bubble' of emissions. The additional externality cost will in theory differ each year as the atmospheric concentration of greenhouse gases changes. Given the difficulty of forecasting future global concentration levels, it may be necessary to develop an adjustment factor for future project emissions, perhaps based on the representative concentration pathways (Moss et al., 2008) adopted in the *Fifth Assessment Report* of the Intergovernmental Panel on Climate Change.

Even less tractable is the joint nature of climate change cost due to an increase in emissions in a particular project. In cases where the standing of the project is defined as being national, it is not clear how much of any global change in climatic conditions should be attributed to a local project. Nor is it clear whether there may be a risk of exaggeration in current estimates of carbon prices if they are determined on the basis of damage cost avoided on a global basis.

As well as these conceptual issues, there are four main methods that are currently used to estimate the 'cost of carbon'. Each has advantages and disadvantages.

A5.1.1 Damage cost avoided approach

The 'damage cost estimate' aims to measure the present value of the stream of future damages associated with a marginal increase (e.g. a tonne) in CO_2 emissions. In other words, this approach aims to measure the social cost of CO_2 emissions. The damages considered typically include both market and non-market aspects, covering health, environment, crops and other property damage potentials (e.g. due to increased flood risk or adverse weather patterns) and wider social aspects (e.g. United States Government, 2013).

A frequent problem with the damage cost avoided approach is its reliance on the so-called 'dumb farmer' assumption: that farmers or other actors will not adapt in some way that will reduce or limit the assumed damage incurred. Some of the adaptation framing issues are canvassed in Dobes et al. (2014), including the more realistic modelling approach by Kurukulasuriya and Mendelsohn (2008) to estimating damage to agricultural production.

Estimating the total or marginal damage cost of greenhouse gas emissions involves estimating how they contribute to atmospheric concentrations and hence on associated climatic effects. Integrated assessment models (IAM) have been developed to assess the damage impacts of an increase in global greenhouse gas concentrations, based on different assumptions. Their complex 'black box' nature, however, can mean that the level of transparency around how these models work is generally not particularly high. Pindyck (2013) provides a summary of their key characteristics:

> Most economic analyses of climate change policy have six elements, each of which can be global in nature or disaggregated on a regional basis. In an IAM-based analysis, each of these elements is either part of the model (determined endogenously), or else is an exogenous input to the model. These six elements can be summarized as follows:
>
> 1. Projections of future emissions of a CO_2 equivalent (CO_2e) composite (or individual GHGs) under 'business as usual' (BAU) and one or more abatement scenarios. Projections of emissions in turn require projections of both GDP growth and 'carbon intensity', i.e. the amount of CO_2e released per dollar of GDP, again under BAU and alternative abatement scenarios, and on an aggregate or regionally disaggregated basis.
>
> 2. Projections of future atmospheric CO_2e concentrations resulting from past, current, and future CO_2e emissions. (This is part of the climate science side of an IAM.)
>
> 3. Projections of average global (or regional) temperature changes — and possibly other measures of climate change such as temperature and rainfall variability, hurricane frequency, and sea level increases — likely to result over time from higher CO_2e concentrations. (This is also part of the climate science side of an IAM.)
>
> 4. Projections of the economic impact, usually expressed in terms of lost GDP and consumption, resulting from higher temperatures. (This is the most speculative element of the analysis, in part because of uncertainty over adaptation to climate change.) 'Economic impact' includes both direct economic impacts as well as any other adverse effects of climate change, such as social, political, and medical impacts, which under various assumptions are monetized and included as part of lost GDP.

5. Estimates of the cost of abating GHG emissions by various amounts, both now and throughout the future. This in turn requires projections of technological change that might reduce future abatement costs.

6. Assumptions about social utility and the rate of time preference, so that lost consumption from expenditures on abatement can be valued and weighed against future gains in consumption from the reductions in warming that abatement would bring about.

IAMs are typically developed for assessing the outcomes of mitigation options to inform related policy decisions, rather than to determine the damage cost of CO_2 emissions. For models that provide such cost estimates, the range is typically high. For example, in the United States the estimates of the social cost of CO_2 ranged from US$11 to US$109 per tonne of CO_2 in 2015, increasing to between US$26 and US4$220 per tonne of CO_2 by 2050 (US Government, 2013).

Key limitations of the damage cost approach include the uncertainty in predicting climatic impacts, as well as assumptions about adaptation, mitigation measures and feedback processes, the discount rate and the robustness of the damage functions used in the assessment process (Pindyck, 2013; OECD, 2015). For global models that look at the effects of climate change on different countries or regions, the weighting used to aggregate the cost estimates and the assumptions around whether decision-makers are altruistic towards other countries can also affect the final results (Anhoff & Tol, 2010).

A5.1.2 Abatement cost estimate

Another approach to costing greenhouse gas emissions is 'abatement cost'. This approach aims to measure the marginal cost of achieving a given level of CO_2 emission reduction (either target based or individual mitigation policy based), rather than estimating the social cost of CO_2.

The abatement cost approach essentially involves estimating how much emissions and costs will change over time, with and without a specific mitigation policy. Its major limitation is its inability to measure the social cost due to climate change. It is, therefore, used primarily to compare the cost-effectiveness of different policy options for achieving target levels of emission reductions. Its use in CBA is correspondingly limited.

According to a review conducted by the Organisation for Economic Cooperation and Development (OECD), countries that use the abatement cost approach include France, United Kingdom, Norway and the Netherlands. In the United Kingdom, the abatement cost estimate of CO_2 ranged from £30 to £91 per tonne of CO_2 in 2015, increasing to £110 to £329 by 2050 (OECD, 2015).

A5.1.3 Market price of carbon

The market price of carbon is sometimes used to inform policy decisions. If the market price of carbon truly reflected the social cost of carbon emissions, it could potentially offer an effective means of incorporating it into CBA. However, carbon market prices are affected by a range of political and other considerations that control the emission allowances and exemptions for certain sectors or industries.

For example, in the past year, the traded carbon price in New Zealand was below NZ$10 per tonne of $CO_2(e)$. This low value may not represent the social cost of climate change due to emissions.

A5.1.4 Willingness-to-pay estimates

Predicting the future climate at local levels is constrained by the lack of knowledge of the extent, timing, intensity or frequency of expected changes in climate and extreme weather events. Equally problematic is prediction of the effect of current mitigative actions on future climatic change. These problems make valuing the social cost of carbon emissions extremely difficult.

Stated preference techniques typically involve asking respondents directly about their willingness to pay (WTP) (or accept) a good or services (or for the removal of a good or services) under a hypothetical situation. For example, Veldhuizen et al. (2011) conducted a pilot choice experiment in Australia to understand how people trade off the type and amount of a tax or levy they would be willing to pay for specific 2050 emission outcomes expressed in terms of $CO_2(e)$ concentration levels.

Another approach is to impute WTP from market data (e.g. using vehicle-purchasing decisions to impute WTP for lower fuel consumption). Market-based estimates of damage due to climate change, such as lower agricultural production due to changes in temperatures and rainfall, could be gained using hedonic pricing (Howard, 2014 p. 16). However, hedonic pricing requires market data, and these are only available for contemporary or past situations; application to future conditions would require subjective judgement or extrapolation.

Since climate change due to carbon dioxide and related emissions can affect different sectors and have different impacts, integrated assessment models are sometimes used to combine WTP estimates for different impacts to establish the overall impact.

A5.1.5 Current practice

Table A5.1 presents estimates of the social cost of carbon dioxide equivalent emissions that are used in different countries.

Table A5.1: Current international valuation practice for carbon dioxide equivalent emissions

Jurisdiction	Department	Method	Mid-range value per tonne of $CO_2(e)$	PPP USD 2013	Remarks
Australia	Transport	Abatement cost	€25 (or A$34.75)	22.8	Source: Austroads (2014)
New Zealand	Transport	Damage costs	NZ$40	27.2	
	Health and Environment	Carbon prices	NZ$6.5 (March 2015)	4.4	For cost effectiveness analysis
France	Transport	Abatement costs	€42.40 (2010 € for 2015)	51.1	Source: OECD (2015)
Germany		Damage and abatement cost approach	€80 (2010 € for years to 2030)	105.6	
Japan		Damage cost approach	US$25.70 (2013 $)	25.7	
The Netherlands		Abatement costs	€78 (2010 € for 2015)	96.5	

Jurisdiction	Department	Method	Mid-range value per tonne of $CO_2(e)$	PPP USD 2013	Remarks
Norway	Transport	Abatement costs	NOK210 (2013 NOK for 2014)	22.8	Source: OECD (2015)
Sweden		Fuel tax on CO_2	SEK1.08 per kg (2010 SEK for 2015)	126.6	
UK	All departments	Abatement costs	£61 (non-traded) (2013 £ for 2015)	92.2	
US	All departments	Damage cost approach	US$11 (2007 $ in 2015)	12.1	

Note: $CO_2(e)$ values for Australia and New Zealand were first inflated to 2013 prices in domestic currency using GDP deflators and then converted to USD using PPP conversion factors. GDP deflators and PPP data are sourced from The World Bank. Other $CO_2(e)$ estimates were sourced from OECD (2015). The Austroads (2014, table 5.3) figure is based on estimates of European Union data by CE Delft et al. (2011).

Source: compiled by Joanne Leung from the sources cited

A5.2 Harmonisation

Due to the uncertainty surrounding the nature of future climate change and its effects, it is difficult to establish a robust social cost for greenhouse gas emissions. Any attempt at strict harmonisation of a value for a 'carbon price' would be contentious, given the wide range of values that are shown in Table A5.1.

If jurisdictions consider it acceptable to include in CBA studies values that reflect the social cost of greenhouse gas emissions, despite the deep level of inherent uncertainty, then it would be desirable to initiate early discussion about the best method of estimating an acceptable value, or range of values.

Appendix 6:
Uncertainty, risk and sensitivity

Although his focus is on sensitivity testing of economic models, Pannell (1997) notes the paucity in the literature of 'discussion and procedures and methodological issues for simple approaches to sensitivity analysis'. Even classical cost-benefit analysis (CBA) textbooks such as Harberger (1976), Mishan (1988), Sugden and Williams (1978), and Gramlich (1981) have limited discussion of sensitivity analysis per se, with generally minimal attention paid to uncertainty and risk.

Some government-sponsored manuals conflate the concepts of risk analysis and sensitivity analysis. For example, the Austroads-sponsored project evaluation guide by Rockliffe et al. (2012, p. 24) states that sensitivity analysis 'is the simplest kind of risk analysis', although the following pages do in fact separately discuss quantitative risk analysis in probability terms. More disconcerting is the confounding by Rockliffe et al. (2012, pp. 29, 46–54) of the technical economic concept of risk that is used in CBA risk analysis with the more prosaic concept of a qualitative or quantitative combination of likelihood and negative impact. In everyday language, too, risk is generally perceived to constitute a negative outcome.

While the term 'uncertainty' is generally used in different ways to denote lack of precise knowledge or certainty, 'risk analysis' and 'sensitivity analysis' have specific and distinct meanings in CBA. The distinction is ostensibly based on definitions of risk and uncertainty originally put forward by Knight in 1921 (2009), and which have since become conventional usage among economists. Following Knight, risk is generally conceptualised as positive or negative variation in outcomes from a measure of central tendency, where the probabilities of deviations are known.[1] Uncertainty is associated with unpredictable variation because the probability of events is not known. Recent usage, including in military circles and the climate change literature, may also refer to 'deep uncertainty' (an 'unknown unknown'), which implies lack of knowledge even of the nature of a future event.

A6.1 Sensitivity analysis

Sensitivity analysis is a traditional aspect of project evaluation. Sinden and Thampapillai (1995, ch. 10), devote a chapter to the topic, and define it as follows:

> A sensitivity test is a recalculation of net social benefits with different data, together with the reinterpretation of the relative desirability of the alternatives.

An analyst has varying degrees of confidence in the values used to estimate the net present value of a project. For example, if the purchase of a standard item of equipment that is supplied in a competitive market is to occur soon after commencement of a project, then its price is likely to remain close to the initial estimate. Costs and benefits incurred or reaped further out into the future, on the other hand, are more likely to deviate from current estimates.

In principle, the analyst could assume a number of different values for each variable. In the case of the cost of a standard item of equipment early in the project, it could be assumed that the upper and lower bounds might be 1 per cent either side of the current

---

1   Knight (2009, p. 121) distinguishes risk and uncertainty in a number of places. However, the most cogent distinction is at the beginning of Chapter 8:

> To preserve the distinction which has been drawn in the last chapter between the measurable uncertainty and an unmeasurable one we may use the term 'risk' to designate the former and the term 'uncertainty' for the latter. The word 'risk' is ordinarily used in a loose way to refer to any sort of uncertainty viewed from the standpoint of the unfavourable contingency, and the term 'uncertainty' similarly with reference to the favourable outcome; we speak of the 'risk' of a loss, the 'uncertainty' of a gain … The practical difference between the two categories, risk and uncertainty, is that in the former the distribution of the outcome in a group of instances is known (either through calculation a priori from statistics of past experience), while in the case of uncertainty this is not true, the reason being in general that it is impossible to form a group of instances, because the situation dealt with is in a high degree unique.

estimate. An estimate for a cost 20 years into the future may merit a range that is 15 per cent either side of current expectations. Rockliffe et al. (2012, Table 5.3) suggest ranges for sensitivity analysis such as a plus or minus 50 per cent variation either side of the estimated traffic diverted or generated by a transport project, but only $\pm$ 0.3 for estimated average car occupancy.

Having set the likely range or bounds for each variable, the analyst would then estimate the net present value (NPV) for the lowest (perhaps 'worst case'), highest (perhaps 'best case') and expected ('most likely' or plausible) levels of each variable. However, the number of results increases exponentially with the number of variables tested. If three levels (e.g. high, medium, and low) are used for each variable, then two variables will require $3^2 = 9$ separate calculations. Four variables would require $3^4 = 81$ calculations of NPV. Whether a decision-maker would find it useful to be presented with 81 separate possible values of NPV is open to doubt. Because it does not involve probabilities, sensitivity analysis provides no guidance as to which one of the 81 results is to be preferred.

Because comprehensive application of sensitivity analysis is subject to diminishing returns in a large, complex project, Sinden and Thampapillai (1995, ch. 10) recommend the exercise of judgement by limiting testing to so-called 'critical' variables that are likely to affect the calculated NPV so much that the project may be abandoned, or an alternative project chosen. Nevertheless, they acknowledge that the only reliable method of identifying critical variables is by systematic recalculation of NPVs, a task that is made easier by the use of spreadsheets and computers.

Little and Mirrlees (1974, p. 309) are explicitly sceptical about the usefulness of sensitivity analysis to decision-makers faced with more than one estimate of NPV. Squire and van der Tak (1975, p. 45) point out that different variables may be positively or negatively correlated, but sensitivity analysis assumes that variables are independent of each other (Campbell & Brown, 2003, p. 197). Perkins (1994, s. 15.7.2) considers that a key weakness of sensitivity analysis is its use of 'randomly selected percentage values, such as 10 per cent or 20 per cent', rather than by standardised amounts such as one standard deviation. Finally, selection of 'best' and 'worst' case limits for a variable implies the selection of low-probability events that may be highly unlikely to occur, but are likely to alter the calculated NPV noticeably, bringing into question the purpose of any sensitivity analysis conducted on the basis of extreme values.

Despite these complications, sensitivity analysis can play a useful role in CBA. If a small change in a particular variable produces a large change in NPV, then a prudent analyst will check the method and data used to estimate that particular variable. If appropriate, some re-estimation may be justified. Even if there is sufficient confidence in the robustness of the estimated value, there may be a case for applying risk analysis to the evaluation of the project.

An alternative application of sensitivity analysis is to identify the value of a variable, or group of variables, where NPV falls to zero; the so-called 'switching', 'cross over', or 'break-even' value. Knowledge of switching points can assist a decision-maker to assess the plausibility of the evaluation results.

Of particular relevance to possible harmonisation of the approach to conducting sensitivity analysis is the identification by Sinden and Thampapillai (1995, ch. 10) of potential misuses of the technique. They recommend that analysts should:

- summarise in the main report break-even values of variables, leaving the presentation of large numbers of NPVs from recalculations based on 'several levels of several variables' to an appendix
- provide an interpretation of the results of sensitivity analysis, avoiding just the presentation of arithmetic results of such things as recalculations of NPVs or break-even values
- integrate sensitivity tests into the overall analysis by demonstrating which variables are critical to making choices between the project at hand and any alternatives
- not use sensitivity tests as a substitute for the valuation of unpriced outcomes.

It is important to note that sensitivity analysis is carried out without involving the use or application of probabilities. Risk analysis, on the other hand, is based explicitly on the application of probabilities. The specification of probabilities, or probability distributions, however, is also subject to uncertainty (in the everyday usage of the term). It is therefore appropriate that sensitivity analysis be applied even to the results of risk analysis — a topic that is addressed below.

A6.2 Risk analysis

Risk analysis can be carried out using expected values (probability weighted values of different variables) or with decision trees: Boardman et al. (2011, ch. 7) provide a detailed exposition. The availability of modern software facilitates the application of Monte Carlo analysis. Campbell and Brown (2003, ch. 9) provide an accessible explanation of Monte Carlo analysis using snapshots of spreadsheets based on the @RISK software (www.palisade.com).

In essence, risk analysis requires the specification of probability distributions for some or all of the variables utilised in a project evaluation. Section A6.1 on sensitivity analysis cited Rockliffe et al. (2012, table 5.3) suggesting a 50 per cent variation either side of the estimated traffic diverted or generated by a transport project. The traffic volume variable could be represented by a symmetrical triangular distribution with its peak at the most likely or expected value of, say, 100,000 vehicles per period, and the range ±50 per cent either side of this value, as illustrated in Figure A6.1. Note that sensitivity analysis would only have utilised the three values shown on the horizontal axis, but risk analysis further specifies the probability of observing those three values, as well as the intermediate ones.

@RISK provides a menu of different probability distributions (e.g. normal, log-normal, binomial, Poisson) that can be specified as appropriate for each variable in an evaluation. The program then draws values randomly from each of the specified distributions and calculates NPV by combining the randomly selected values. The first draw may produce an NPV = x_1. The second draw may result in NPV = x_2, the third a different NPV = x_3, and so on. A large number of draws (e.g. 10,000) will produce a histogram of NPV values. The histogram, or its smoothed probability distribution can be used to determine the probability of achieving any particular NPV value.

In other words, the representation of variable values by probability distributions rather than point estimates permits the analyst to incorporate risk directly into the calculation of NPV. The advantage of the Monte Carlo method is its combining of the risks attached to all variables into a single distributional outcome. It also has the advantage of avoiding more dubious approaches to allowing for risk, like adding a risk premium to the discount rate. But a particular disadvantage of the Monte Carlo method that cannot be easily or totally overcome is the treatment of correlated variables.

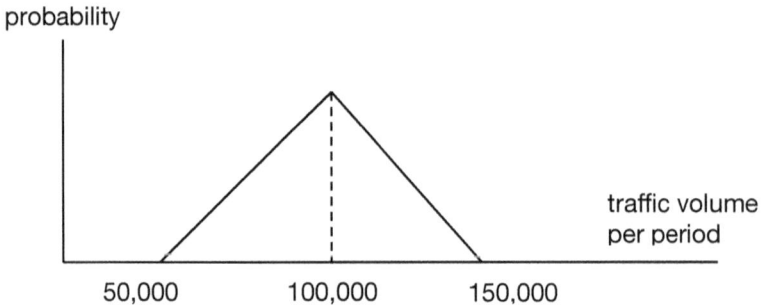

Figure A6.1: Illustration of use of triangular distribution to represent estimated traffic volumes in a transport project evaluation
Source: Leo Dobes

A6.2.1 Sensitivity testing of a risk analysis result

Sensitivity testing need not be limited to non-probabilistic point estimates of variable values. It can, and should, also be applied to the results of risk analysis.

The triangular distribution shown in Figure A6.1, for example, can be subjected to sensitivity analysis. The triangular distribution is defined by two parameters: the extremes of its range (50,000 and 150,000) and the most likely value (100,000). Standard sensitivity testing of point estimates might have investigated the effect of changing the value of the traffic volume variable from the point estimate by also calculating NPV for the two values at either end of the range. The decision-maker would have been presented with three results, rather than one NPV value.

There is no reason, however, why risk should be represented by a single, static probability distribution. An analyst might just as well have set the range of traffic volumes at, say, from 40,000 to 160,000, forming a different symmetrical triangular distribution with a greater variance. Selection of a value range like 30,000 to 110,000 would generate a skewed triangular distribution.

By specifying a set of values starting, for example, at 30,000 and increasing by increments of 10,000 up to 170,000, it is possible to allow @RISK to select randomly from a range of different triangular probability distributions for the variable 'traffic volume per period'. Sensitivity analysis can now be carried out on changes in the most likely value of 100,000, as well as on its associated probability distributions. In principle, the sensitivity analysis of Monte Carlo results will incorporate the first three moments of the distribution — mean, variance and skewness — when testing the sensitivity of calculated NPVs.

A6.2.2 Discount rates and sensitivity analysis

Australian practice is typically to vary the discount rate as part of sensitivity tests. Infrastructure Australia (2013, p. 9) requires the use of 4 per cent, 7 per cent, and 10 per cent per annum in real terms for submission of project proposals, and justifies these values on the basis of common usage in the majority of Australian jurisdictions. The 4 per cent and 10 per cent real per annum rates are based on the assumed social rate of time preference and the social opportunity cost of capital approaches respectively. Nevertheless, specification of multiple discount rates for use in sensitivity analysis would merit extensive deliberation in harmonisation of approaches to CBA.

Market rates of interest can encompass a range of values, depending on the nature of various specialised financial markets. They can also vary with short-term market conditions. On this basis, one could surmise that sensitivity analysis applied to financial or investment analysis would include more than one value for the discount rate. The section on sensitivity analysis in a key text on corporate finance by Brealey et al. (2006, pp. 245–56), however, focuses on a range of project variables, but does not refer at all to varying the discount rate.

Most textbooks on CBA, on the other hand, include some reference to varying discount rates as part of sensitivity analysis. Yet the same CBA textbooks also devote space to discussing an appropriate social discount rate, or some average or shadow value, implying that society has a specific or particular time preference rate, absent complications like tax wedges, expression of costs and benefits in consumption or investment equivalents, and intergenerational issues. Conceptually, a social discount rate is presented implicitly as a point estimate parameter rather than a variable.

Accounting for risk by adding a risk premium to a risk-free discount rate in CBA would require project-specific rates that justify sensitivity testing different rates, but adding risk premiums is rarely recommended in CBA textbooks for reasons summarised by Harrison (2009, ch. 4). Alterations to discount rates may also raise concerns about potential resort to 'fudge factors' in calculating the net social benefit of a project.

Variation of the discount rate in a sensitivity analysis is unlikely to add value or knowledge in the evaluation of a project. The present value formula guarantees that changing the discount rate will result in some change in the calculated value of net social benefit, commensurate with the extent of the variation in discount rate. There is no objective or unambiguous method for choosing the extent of the variation, however, any more than there is for choosing a 'correct' discount rate. And if the discount rate is subjected to sensitivity analysis and found to be influential in determining the NPV, it is not clear how a decision-maker can or should choose between the different results, particularly if the calculated NPVs differ in sign.

Government CBA manuals and textbooks rarely, if ever, provide an explicit justification for sensitivity testing of discount rates. Harrison (2010, p. 61), who supports the application of sensitivity analysis to the discount rate, argues that:

> If the sensitivity analysis reveals that the choice of discount rate is important (changes the sign of the project's net present value), then more consideration should be given to the choice of an appropriate rate — such as the risk characteristics of the proposal (for example, the extent of fixed costs and how costs and benefits vary with the

state of the economy). Project flows that are more sensitive to market returns and other factors should have a higher discount rate, while projects that are less sensitive should have a lower one.

There are two significant problems with this justification. First, it is not clear how risk premiums are to be determined for public sector projects on the basis of their sensitivity to market returns. The problem is obvious for non-marketed goods like health and education, at least in terms of the fact that government provision of such services differs substantially from limited market counterparts. Private hospitals and schools, for example, may be run on non-profit lines or be held by private owners with no exposure to equity markets.

The second problem with Harrison's (2010) justification is that it is circular. Having presumably chosen an appropriate discount rate, the decision-maker may find that sensitivity testing with different rates yields NPVs of different signs. The recommended solution is to give further consideration to the 'appropriate' rate, an approach that might be interpreted by a sceptic as fiddling with the discount rate to get the desired answer. It further begs the question of the basis for the initial choice of sensitivity values of 4 per cent and 10 per cent per annum. As Harrison (2010, p. 61, fn. 16) correctly points out, the increasingly conventional use of discount rates of 4, 7, 10 per cent per annum appears to represent equal, symmetrical deviations from the 'central' rate of 7 per cent per annum, but in fact produces non-symmetrical effects in present value terms.

Appendix 7:
Deadweight economic loss caused by raising revenue for projects and programs

Government projects and programs can be financed by drawing on a variety of sources: taxes on incomes, payrolls, land, sales, domestic and overseas borrowing, petrol excise, mining royalties, stamp duties, parking fines, driving licences, reduced expenditure, and, ultimately, just by printing money. Table A7.2 provides a list of taxes, and Albon (1997) reviews a wide range of taxes imposed specifically by the states and territories.

Raising revenue from any of these sources will affect the economy in some way. Raising revenue is itself not costless, because of collection and compliance costs that add to the amount required to fund a project or program. Moreover, revenue-raising measures will impose opportunity costs on the community to the extent that they preclude activity or transactions that would otherwise have occurred, with consumer and producer surplus being forgone.

A simple illustration of the concept of deadweight loss is provided by Bates (2001, pp. 50–51), reproduced in Box A7.1.

Box A7.1: A simple example of the excess burden of taxation

The following example illustrates how a tax can impose an excess burden (or deadweight loss) by eliminating market transactions and the economic surplus associated with those transactions.

Let us suppose that Jack mows Jenny's lawn each week for $30, which is the going rate in the city where they live. Jenny would actually be prepared to pay Jack up to $33 to mow her lawn, taking into account the income she would forgo and the costs (including displeasure) she would incur if she mowed the lawn herself. Jack would be prepared to mow Jennys lawn for $28, because Jenny lives close to many of his other clients and the cost of mowing her lawn is, therefore, lower than for clients in another area, whom Jack regards as marginal to his business. This means that there is an economic surplus of $5 ($33 minus $28) associated with this transaction.

Now, consider what happens when the government introduces a tax of 30 per cent, which applies to the income that Jack earns from lawn mowing. To keep the example simple, we will assume initially that Jenny does not have to pay the tax on her own income.

After the tax is imposed, Jack tells Jenny that, in order to pay the tax, he will have to raise the price that he charges her to a minimum of $36.40 ($28 plus 30 per cent of $28). Jenny responds that the most she is prepared to pay is $33. Jack calculates that this would leave him with only $25.38 after paying the tax, which is not sufficient to compensate for the time involved in mowing Jenny's lawn. So, the result is that Jenny mows her own lawn and both Jack and Jenny have lower levels of well-being. No tax is collected, but the economic surplus of $5 is lost. This is the excess burden that is incurred by Jack and Jenny because the tax has discouraged a mutually advantageous transaction.

The rate of tax is an important factor determining whether or not the transaction continues to occur following introduction of the tax. It could be expected to continue with tax rates of up to almost 18 per cent — that is, at rates that would not entirely remove the economic surplus that makes the transaction mutually beneficial. Substitution possibilities are also important. If Jenny were unable to substitute her own services for Jack's by mowing the lawn herself, the initial economic surplus on the transaction would have been larger and she might have been willing to accept a pre-tax price of $36.40, or even higher. Similarly, if Jack's potential earnings in alternative occupations were a lot lower than in lawn mowing he might be prepared to continue to mow Jenny's lawn for a post-tax return of $25.38, or even less.

When Jack's clients also have to pay tax on their incomes, transactions with larger economic surplus are also eliminated. Let us suppose that, prior to introduction of the tax, Jenny's neighbour, Bill, has to work an additional 30 minutes at his job in the market economy in order to pay Jack $30 for mowing his lawn. Rather than mow his own lawn, Bill would be willing to work for up to an additional 50 minutes in the market economy. This means that there is an economic surplus of $22 ($50 minus $28) on Bill's transaction with Jack. If the tax applied only to income from lawn mowing, Bill would have to work for 36.4 minutes in order to pay Jack $36.40. When Bill also has to pay the tax, he would have to work for 52 minutes in order to earn the $52 he would require before tax in order to pay Jack $36.40 (and the tax authorities $15.60). This is not acceptable to Bill, however, so, like Jenny, he mows his own lawn. The tax results in loss of the $22 economic surplus on Bill's transaction with Jack.

Source: Bates (2001, p. 50–51)

Different financing arrangements have differential effects on social surplus, but all of them involve some element of deadweight loss. Even reducing government expenditure in other areas to finance a new project is likely to reduce benefits (e.g. social security payments) in some way. More efficient revenue measures entail lower loss of benefits in the form of social surplus for any given amount of revenue raised. A land tax, for example, is often regarded as being relatively efficient because the low price elasticity of demand results in a relatively lower loss of consumer surplus. If the land is owned primarily by foreigners, who are excluded from a 'national' standing in a cost-benefit analysis (CBA), the loss of social surplus would be even lower.

The relative efficiency of a revenue-raising measure — or, more specifically, a tax — is termed the marginal excess tax burden (METB). It is the ratio of the loss of social surplus (the deadweight loss) due to imposition of the tax, divided by the total amount of revenue collected. Such ratios can be calculated for various revenue-raising measures including, for example, a government bond issue (Campbell & Brown, 2003, ch. 10), royalties (Ergas & Pincus, 2012), land and other taxes (Cao et al., 2015). In the case of a tax with an METB of 1.30, for example, raising $1 in revenue would impose a cost of $1.30 on the economy.

A key question in CBA is whether costs should be adjusted by the METB — a form of shadow pricing — in order to take into account the wider economic effects of a project. Most textbooks indicate that an adjustment for the METB should be used (e.g. Brown & Campbell, 2003; Boardman et al., 2011), but this rarely occurs in practice. Moore et al. (2010) is one of the few exceptions. Boardman et al., (2011, p. 65) also draw attention to the fact that projects can generate revenue for the government. Society benefits because the additional revenue allows the government to avoid raising public funds for other projects through taxation, so the revenue should also be multiplied by the factor (1 + METB).

One valid reason for not including the METB in a CBA — apart from avoiding an undesired increase in the cost side of the estimate of net present value (NPV) — is likely to be that governments tend to fund projects from general revenue. It is not possible to attribute the expenditure on a project directly to any specific revenue-raising measure. However, Campbell and Brown (2003, p. 224) argue that:

> If the government is rational and informed it will use each of these three sources of funds [taxes, borrowing, printing money] up to the point at which its marginal cost is equal to the marginal cost of each of the other two. In this way the total cost of collecting any given quantity of public funds is minimised. This implies that if we work out the marginal cost of funds obtained through, say, taxation, we can assume that this is the marginal cost of public funds from any source. There is some evidence that governments are rational and informed in the way that we are assuming: there has recently been much less reliance on inflation to fund public expenditures than previously. The reason is not so much that the cost of this resource has risen but rather that governments are better informed of its costs in terms of economic instability and resource misallocation. Since bond finance eventually leads to higher taxes to pay for interest and principal repayments we may be on reasonably solid ground if we use the marginal cost of tax revenues to approximate the marginal cost of public funds.

Boardman et al. (2011, pp. 65–66) provide a simple numerical example of how METB is calculated from changes in labour supply. Campbell and Brown (2003, ch. 10) illustrate the calculation of deadweight loss for both government borrowing through a bond issue, and the deadweight loss of producer surplus due to an income tax.

A7.1 Estimates of deadweight loss due to taxes and other imposts

Conceptually two sources of deadweight loss may flow from higher taxation: through changes in consumption patterns and through changes in the supply of labour. Calculations of METB tend to focus on the labour supply effect, as it is not clear exactly how net consumption will be affected by the provision of a government project or program and the associated form of taxation.

Empirical studies have produced a wide range of values for the METB that may result from changes in labour supply (Table A7.1).

Table A7.1: Estimates of the marginal excess burden of taxation

Study (year)	Country	Estimated METB	Data	Tax used
Findlay and Jones (1982)	Australia	23% to 65%	1978–79	Labour income
Diewert and Lawrence (1995)	New Zealand	14% to 18%	1971/72–1990/91	Labour income; general consumption, motor vehicle consumption, import duties
Freebairn (1995)	Australia	2.6% to 72.7%	1993	Labour income
Campbell and Bond (1997)	Australia	19% to 24%	1988–89	Labour income
Bates (2001)	New Zealand	50%	Unstated	Labour income
KPMG Econtech (2010)	Australia	–8% to 92%	2008	See Table A7.2 below
Cao et al. (2015)	Australia	–10% to 75%	2007–08 and 2013–14	Company income, personal income, goods and services, land, stamp duty and conveyances

Source: compiled by George Argyrous from the sources cited

As might be expected, attempts to estimate the METB in Australia and New Zealand require specific assumptions, so that the results are 'very sensitive to the estimation model and the parameter assumptions' (Freebairn, 1995, p. 127). Key assumptions that affect these estimates are the particular tax that is assumed to be used to finance a public program, the rate and uniformity of the tax, and the elasticity of labour supply to changes in the after tax real wage rate.

Despite the range of estimates for the METB, the New Zealand Treasury's *Cost Benefit Analysis Primer* stipulates 'a rate of 20% as a default deadweight loss value in the absence of an alternative evidence based value' (2005, p. 18). The NZ Treasury adopts this default rate even though it acknowledges the wide range of estimates provided by Diewert and Lawrence (1994) and Bates (2001).

Similarly, the Australian Government's *Handbook of Cost-Benefit Analysis* cites Campbell (1997) to suggest an METB of 25 per cent (Department of Finance and Administration, 2006, p. 37).

Campbell's (1997) work provides a summary of the analysis in Campbell and Bond (1997), which found METB to range from 19–24 per cent. Their methodology was to construct a representative agent model for each of the 10 gross income deciles and then to simulate for each group the labour supply effects of a 1 per cent increase in marginal income tax rates. Their main conclusion is that 'a project proposed to be undertaken by the Australian federal government needs to have a benefit/cost ratio in the range 1.19–1.24 if it is to receive serious consideration' (Campbell & Bond, 1997, p. 32). Subsequent analysis by Campbell and Brown (2003, p. 229) adjusts these values to a range of 1.20–1.25.

It is worth noting that this analysis by Campbell and Bond (1997) drew upon data from 1988–89, and also from the findings of an earlier study by Apps and Savage (1989). This earlier study provided the parameters for labour supply elasticities from which the welfare loss from higher tax rates were calculated by Campbell and Bond. Apps and Savage used income data from 1981–82, and marginal income tax rates for the same period. Their analysis is based on a restrictive set of assumptions about the structure of households and the way that they allocate resources, including income, among their respective members. Specifically, they model the effects of tax rates by using data from 'couple income units with a male head aged 25–54 years earning labour income solely from wages and salary and working over 624 hours per year' (1989, p. 341).

Given these detailed assumptions for the estimates in Campbell and Bond (1997) it seems inappropriate that the Commonwealth Treasury should uncritically adopt an METB of 25 per cent, well over a decade from the data upon which Campbell and Bond base their analysis. Moreover, studies for Australia have shown a general decline in the METB over time, as income tax rates fall. Campbell and Bond's (1997) decades-old estimate would benefit from updating and re-estimation prior to further use.

A7.2 The use of METB estimates in CBAs

Many CBAs simply ignore the issue of METB altogether (e.g. Department of Infrastructure and Regional Development, 2011). Others (White et al., 2012; Abelson & Joyeux 2007) tend to cite Campbell and Bond (1997), although White et al. (2012) use a value of

10 per cent with no explanation for the difference between that and Campbell and Bond's estimates. Moore et al. (2010, p. 9) simply defer to the 'default deadweight loss recommended by the [New Zealand] Treasury' of 20 per cent.

Other CBAs may have applied the METB without a proper consideration of whether it is relevant or fit for purpose. For example, the *Independent Cost-benefit Analysis of Broadband and Review of Regulation Volume II – The Costs and Benefits of High-Speed Broadband* (Department of Communications, 2014, p. 42) applied a METB of 0.24 cents per dollar, which assumes that the full cost of each option is financed by labour income tax. The financing arrangements for the NBN, however, are through government-issued equity that would be repaid through user-charges; not through increases in tax. Bonds may generate a deadweight loss if they displace investors' consumption and because of the tax wedge on equity earnings (Campbell & Brown 2003, ch. 10) but there is no reason to believe that the METB value will be the same as that for tax increases.

A7.3 Issues for consideration

There are three key issues that are worth noting in arriving at a harmonised value for the METB:

- changes in the labour market and how these might affect labour supply elasticities
- changes in income tax rates and the distribution of tax collection
- greater awareness of the economic impact of various government programs.

One of the arguments for the use of METB in CBA is that higher tax rates create a labour supply disincentive, since they act in a way similar to a fall in the real wage rate. The labour supply response creates a net loss in welfare, and it is the value of this loss that empirical estimates of labour supply elasticities attempt to capture.

The nature of the labour market in Australia and New Zealand has changed dramatically since the 1980s. The classic single-earner/male-breadwinner household is not as common and there has been a noticeable shift from full-time to part-time and casual employment, corresponding with a growth in employment for females (see Harding et al., 2009 for a detailed breakdown of these changes and implications for tax rates). Moreover, the labour supply effects of taxation changes vary across groups in the labour market (Creedy, 2003). Indeed for some groups, such as working wives, the labour supply curve might be backward bending. As Miller (1985) found in an early study for Australia, labour supply may increase for this group as the effective wage rates goes down. Many of the estimates for the METB listed in Table A7.1 avoid this issue by using a single representative household computable general equilibrium (CGE) model facing a single labour supply elasticity and marginal tax rate (see, for example, Cao et al., 2015, p. 3).

Calculating the METB to be applied to government programs also depends on the choice of tax assumed to be used to raise finance. For example, KPMG Econtech (2010, p. 5), using a CGE framework, provides the estimates in Table A7.2 for the marginal excess burden of taxation (see also Ballard et al., 1985, p. 136). Cao et al. (2015, p. 54) point out that different results for METB estimates for GST (8 versus 12 cents per dollar of revenue) may be due to differences in model calibration and data updates.

Table A7.2: Marginal excess burdens of Australian taxes (cents of consumer welfare per dollar of revenue)

Tax	Marginal excess tax burden
Tobacco excise	−8
Import duties	−3
Petroleum resource rent tax	0
Municipal rates	2
GST	8
Land taxes	8
Alcohol excise/wine equalisation tax	9
Fuel taxes	15
Stamp duties other than real property	18
Luxury car tax	20
Labour income tax	24
Conveyancing stamp duties	34
Motor vehicle registration	37

Tax	Marginal excess tax burden
Motor vehicle stamp duties	38
Corporate income tax	40
Payroll tax	41
Insurance taxes	67
Royalties and crude oil excise	70
Gambling taxes	92

Source: KPMG Econtech (2010, p. 5)

The sensitivity of the METB to the choice of tax is reinforced by Hayes and Porter-Hudak (1987), who show that, even for large excise taxes, deadweight loss can be small. Similarly, Diewert and Lawrence (1995) have shown, for New Zealand, that the METB only differed by up to 5 per cent between labour tax and consumption tax rates. Shifts in the tax base over time suggest a need to revise assumptions that feed into the calculation of METB.

Gabbitas and Eldridge (1998, p. 37) provide a similar range of estimates for some Australian state taxes.

Table A7.3: Marginal excess burden of state taxation in the presence of Commonwealth taxation and externalities, Australia

State tax	METB
Leaded petrol	6
Unleaded petrol	4
Diesel	4
Tobacco	28
Normal strength beer	14
Low alcohol beer	15
Wine	12
Spirits	58

Source: Gabbitas, O. and Eldridge, D. 1998, *Directions for State Tax Reform*, Productivity Commission Staff Research Paper, AusInfo, Canberra, May

These wide variations in METB have led the Victorian Department of Treasury and Finance (2013, p. 51) to adopt a default METB of 1.08, on the basis that the government could finance its projects from the most efficient state tax source (i.e. land tax).

Noticeably, the rates in Table A7.3 are lower than those they calculate without factoring in externalities that flow from the activities being taxed. This reinforces the point made by Boardman et al. (2011) that the welfare consequences of higher tax rates depend on the nature of the activities upon which these tax rates fall. For example, they argue that if taxes are increased on activities that have a large negative externality, they actually may be welfare improving.

The calculation of METB, especially when conducted through CGE models such as KPMG Econtech (2010), rest on the assumption that the economy operates, or at least tends to operate over the long run, at the full employment level. If this is not the case, then increases in public spending may lead to higher than otherwise output levels, which may at least partially generate the tax revenue to fund the program. For example, programs being analysed through a CBA may roll out during a period of the business cycle when they generate a net increase in output and tax revenue. As Freebairn (1995) illustrated, the existence of involuntary unemployment affects estimates of the METB.

A7.4 Conclusion

Estimates of deadweight loss are fraught with assumptions and data issues. They are also influenced by the specific type of revenue-raising instrument being used and various flow-on effects that may not be immediately obvious in a partial equilibrium analysis.

Conceptually at least, estimates of deadweight losses should be conducted on a project-specific basis. The cost of doing so, however, would be prohibitive. This factor is probably the reason why studies that incorporate the opportunity costs of raising revenue tend to use estimates conducted by others as 'plug-in' values.

Given the essentially 'rubbery' nature of estimates of deadweight loss, jurisdictions should consider a more harmonised approach that includes the following issues:

- the extent to which deadweight losses should be included in CBA
- the desirability of agreement on deadweight loss factors for a number of the more common revenue-raising instruments
- an agreed approach for easy updating of METB estimates between periodic major reviews.

References

Abelson, P. 2003a. *Cost-Benefit Analysis of Proposed New Health Warnings on Tobacco Products*. Report prepared for the Commonwealth Department of Health and Ageing. Applied Economics, Sydney.

———. 2003b. 'The value of life and health for public policy', *Economic Record* 79 (special issue): S2–S13.

———. 2005. 'Surveying university student standards in economics', *Economic Papers* 24(2): 116–32.

———. 2011. *The Wider Economic Impacts of Transport Infrastructure*. Applied Economics, Sydney.

———. 2012. *Public Economics: Principles and Practice*. 3rd edn. McGraw Hill, Sydney.

Abelson, P. & Joyeux, R. 2007. 'Price and efficiency effects of taxes and subsidies for Australian housing', *Economic Papers*, 26(2): 147–69.

ACT Government. n.d. *The Capital Framework (TCF). Single Assessment Framework. SAF Business Case Guidance Notes*. version 1.0. Australian Capital Territory Government, Canberra.

Adler, M.D. 2013. 'Happiness, health and leisure: valuing the nonconsumption impacts of unemployment', in *Does Regulation Kill Jobs?*, C. Coglianese, A.M. Finkel & C. Carrigan (eds). University of Pennsylvania, Philadelphia.

Albon, R. 1997. 'The efficiency of state taxes', *The Australian Economic Review* 30(3): 273–87.

Alexander, I., 1978. 'The planning balance sheet: an appraisal', in *Australian Project Evaluation: Selected Readings*. ch. 3. Australia and New Zealand Book Company, Sydney.

Allen Consulting Group. 2006. *Phasing out Lightweight Plastic Bags: Costs and Benefits of Alternative Approaches*. Report to the Environment Protection and Heritage Council, Canberra.

Anhoff, D. & Tol, R.S.J. 2010. 'On international equity weights and national decision making on climate change', *Journal of Environmental Economics and Management* 60: 14–20.

Apps, P. & Savage, E. 1989. 'Labour supply, welfare rankings and the measurement of inequality', *Journal of Public Economics* 39(3): 335–64.

Argyrous, G. 2013. *A Review of Government Cost-Benefit Analysis Guidelines*. Australian School of Business, UNSW.

Arnell, N.W., Tompkins, E.L. & Adger, W.N. 2005. 'Eliciting information from experts on the likelihood of rapid climate change', *Risk Analysis* 25(6): 1419–31.

Ashe, B., de Oliveira, F.D. & McAneney, J. 2012. 'Investments in fire management: does saving lives cost lives?', *Agenda* 19(2): 89–103.

Australian Transport Council (ATC). 2006. *National Guidelines for Transport System Management in Australia*. Commonwealth of Australia, Canberra.

Austroads. 1996. *Benefit Cost Analysis Manual*. AP-42/96. Austroads, Sydney.

——. 2014. *Updating Environmental Externalites Unit Values*. Technical Report AP-T285-14. Austroads, Sydney.

Ballard, C.L., Shoven, J.B. & Whalley, J. 1985. 'General equilibrium computations of the marginal welfare costs of taxes in the United States', *American Economic Review* 75(1): 128–38.

Banks, G. 2014. *The Governance of Public Policy: Lectures in Honour of Eminent Australians*. Australia and New Zealand School of Government, Melbourne.

Bastiat, F. 1850, *That Which Is Seen, and That Which Is Not Seen.* bastiat.org/en/twisatwins.html.

Bates, W. 2001. *How Much Government?: The Effects of High Government Spending on Economic Performance.* New Zealand Business Roundtable, Wellington.

Bennett, J. 2008. 'Defining and managing environmental flows: inputs from society', *Economic Papers* 27(2): 167–83.

Bickel, P.J., Hammel, E.A. & O'Connell, J.W. 1975. 'Sex bias in graduate admissions: data from Berkeley', *Science* 187(4175): 398–404.

Boardman, A.E., Greenberg, D.H., Vining, A.R. & Weimer, D.L. 2011. *Cost-Benefit Analysis. Concepts and Practice.* 4th edn. Pearson Prentice Hall, USA.

Brealey, R.A., Myers, S.C. & Allen, F. 2006. *Principles of Corporate Finance.* 8th edn. McGraw-Hill Irwin, New York.

Brown, S.J. & Sibley, D.S. 1986. *The Theory of Public Utility Pricing.* Cambridge University Press.

Bureau of Infrastructure, Transport and Regional Economics. 2009. *Cost of Road Crashes in Australia 2006.* Research Report 118. Commonwealth of Australia, Canberra.

Bureau of Transport Economics. 1976. *Mainline Upgrading: Evaluation of a Range of Options for the Melbourne–Serviceton Rail Link.* Australian Government Publishing Service, Canberra.

——. 2000. *Road Crash Costs in Australia.* Research Report 102. Commonwealth of Australia, Canberra.

Burgman, M., Fidler, F., McBride, M., Walshe, T. & Wintle, B. 2006. *Eliciting Expert Judgments: Literature Review.* First Project Report ACERA 0611. Australian Centre for Excellence for Risk Analysis, Melbourne. www.acera.unimelb.edu.au/materials/endorsed/0611.pdf.

Byett, A., Laird, J., Stroombergen, A. & Trodd, S. 2015. *Assessing New Approaches to Estimating the Economic Impact of Transport Interventions Using the Gross Value Added Approach.* Research Report 566. New Zealand Transport Agency, Wellington.

Campbell, H. 1997. 'Deadweight loss and the cost of public funds in Australia', *Agenda: A Journal of Policy Analysis and Reform* 4(2): 231–36.

Campbell, H.F. & Bond, K.A. 1997. 'The cost of public funds in Australia', *Economic Record* 73(220): 22–34.

Campbell, H.F. & Brown, R.P.C. 2003. *Benefit-Cost Analysis. Financial and Economic Appraisal Using Spreadsheets*. Cambridge University Press, Melbourne.

Canberra Times. 2014. 'Inquiry calls for more clarity on light-rail spending', 6 August, p. 2, author: Kirsten Lawson.

——. 2015. 'Leaked government letter puts cost of light rail line at $900 million', 20 July, pp. 1, 2, author: Tom McIlroy.

Cao, L., Hosking, A., Kouparitsas, M., Mullaly, D., Rimmer, X., Shi, Q., Stark, W. & Wendel, S. 2015. *Understanding the Economy-Wide Efficiency and Incidence of Major Australian Taxes*. Treasury Working Paper 2015-01. Australian Government, Canberra. www. treasury.gov.au/~/media/Treasury/Publications%20and%20 Media/Publications/2015/Working%20Paper%202015%2001/ Documents/PDF/TWP2015-01.ashx.

Capital Metro Agency. 2014. *Full Business Case*. Australian Capital Territory Government, Canberra.

CE Delft, Infras & Fraunhofer ISI. 2011. *External Costs of Transport in Europe. Update Study for 2008*. CE Delft, Delft, Netherlands.

Chankong, V. & Haimes, Y.Y. 1983. *Multiobjective Decision Making: Theory and Methodology Series*. 8. North-Holland, New York.

Clarke, R. 1995. 'Computer matching by government agencies: the failure of cost/benefit analysis as a control mechanism', *Information Infrastructure and Policy* 4: 29–65.

Clinton, W. 1993. 'Regulatory planning and review. Executive order 12866 of September 30, 1993', Federal Register, vol. 58, no. 190.

Clough, P., Guria, J. & Bealing, M. 2015. *Approaches to Valuing Injury and Mortality Risk in Transport Assessments*. Research Report 571. New Zealand Transport Agency, Wellington.

Coglianese, C., Finkel, A.M. & Carrigan, C. (eds). 2013. *Does Regulation Kill Jobs?* University of Pennsylvania Press, Philadelphia.

Coleman, W.O. 2002. *Economics and Its Enemies. Two Centuries of Anti-Economics.* Palgrave Macmillan, New York.

Coleman, W. & Hagger, A. 2001. *Exasperating Calculators. The Rage over Economic Rationalism and the Campaign against Australian Economists.* Macleay Press, Sydney.

Commonwealth of Australia. 2014. *The Australian Government Guide to Regulation.* Department of the Prime Minister and Cabinet, Canberra. cuttingredtape.gov.au/handbook/australian-government-guide-regulation.

Commonwealth Procurement Guidelines — January 2005. Financial Management Guidance No. 1. Department of Finance and Administration, Australian Government, Canberra.

Commonwealth Treasury. 1966. *Investment Analysis. Supplement to the Treasury Information Bulletin.* Commonwealth Government Printer, Canberra.

Cox, L.A. Jr. 2009. 'What's wrong with hazard-ranking systems? An expository note', *Risk Analysis* 29(7): 940–48.

Creedy, J. 2003. *The Excess Burden of Taxation and Why It (Approximately) Quadruples When the Tax Rate Doubles.* NZ Treasury.

Department for Transport. 2005. *Transport, Wider Economic Benefits and Impacts on GDP.* United Kingdom.

———. 2014. *Wider Impacts.* Transport Analysis Guidance (TAG) Unit A2.1, United Kingdom.

Department of Communications. 2014. *Independent Cost-Benefit Analysis of Broadband and Review of Regulation. Volume II — The Costs and Benefits of High-Speed Broadband.* Commonwealth of Australia, Canberra.

Department of the Environment and Heritage. 2003. *Triple Bottom Line Reporting in Australia. A Guide to Reporting against Environmental Indicators.* Commonwealth of Australia, Canberra.

Department of Finance. 1991. *Handbook of Cost-Benefit Analysis*. Australian Government Publishing Service, Canberra.

Department of Finance and Administration. 2006. *Handbook of Cost-Benefit Analysis. January 2006*. Financial Management Reference Material 6. Commonwealth of Australia, Canberra.

Department of Infrastructure and Regional Development. 2011. *High Speed Rail Study. Phase 2 Report*. Australian Government, Canberra.

Department of Infrastructure and Transport. 2011. *Community Aviation Consultation Groups Guidelines*. National Aviation Policy White Paper, Australian Government, Canberra.

Department of Transport and Main Roads. 2011. *Cost-Benefit Analysis Manual. Road Projects*. Queensland Government, Brisbane.

Department of Treasury and Finance (Victoria). 2013. *Economic Evaluation for Business Cases. Technical Guidelines*. Government of Victoria.

Department of Treasury and Finance (South Australia). 2014. *Guidelines for the Evaluation of Public Sector Initiatives. Part B: Investment Evaluation Process*. Government of South Australia, Adelaide.

Diewert, W.E. & Lawrence, D.A. 1995. 'The excess burden of taxation in New Zealand', *Agenda* 2(1): 27–34.

Dixit, A. & Pindyck, R.S. 1994. *Investment under uncertainty*, Princeton University Press, NJ.

Dobes, L. 1999. 'Multi-criteria analysis', in *Facts and Furphies in Benefit-Cost Analysis: Transport*, D. Luskin & L. Dobes. Bureau of Transport Economics, Canberra.

———. 2007. 'Turning isolation to advantage in regional cost-benefit analysis', *Economic Papers* 26(1): 17–28.

———. 2008. 'A century of Australian cost-benefit analysis', peer-reviewed paper prepared for the conference 'Delivering better quality regulatory proposals through better cost-benefit analysis' hosted by the Productivity Commission, 21 November 2007.

Published originally by the Department of Finance and Deregulation as Working Paper WP2008-01. Available at www.dpmc.gov.au/sites/default/files/publications/Working_paper_1_Leo_Dobes.pdf.

——. 2008. 'Getting real about adapting to climate change: using "real options" to address the uncertainties', *Agenda* 15(3): 55-69.

Dobes, L. & Bennett, J. 2009. 'Is multi-criteria analysis "good enough" for government work?', *Agenda: A Journal of Policy Analysis and Reform* 16(3): 7–30.

Dobes, L., Jotzo F. & Stern, D. 2014. 'The economics of global climate change: a historical literature review', *Review of Economics* 65(3): 281–320.

Doessel, D.P. 1979. *Cost-Benefit Analysis and Fluoridation: An Australian Study*. Health Research Project Research Monograph 1. Australian National University Press, Canberra.

Drummond, M.F., O'Brien, B., Stoddart, G.L. & Torrance, G.W. 1997. *Methods for the Economic Evaluation of Health Care Programmes*. 2nd edn. Oxford University Press, UK.

Emerson, C. 2015. 'Doubts over trade deals aren't PC', *Australian Financial Review*, 12 October, p. 46.

Ergas, H. 2009. 'In defence of cost-benefit analysis', *Agenda* 16(3): 31–40.

Ergas, H. & Pincus, J. 2012. *Modelling the Excess Burden of Royalties*. Research Paper 2012-03. University of Adelaide, School of Economics. www.economics.adelaide.edu.au/research/papers/doc/wp2012-03.pdf.

European Commission. 2008. *Guide to Cost-Benefit Analysis of Investment Projects. Structural Funds, Cohesion Fund and Instruments for Pre-Accession*. Directorate General Regional Policy, Brussels.

Evidence Taken at the Bar of the Legislative Council on the Railways Bill in Committee of the Whole Council. Ordered by the Council to Be Printed, 7th November 1871. John Ferres, Government Printer, Melbourne.

Findlay, Christopher C. & Jones, Robert L. 1982. 'The marginal cost of Australian income taxation', *Economic Record* 58(162): 253.

Florida, R. 2003. *The Rise of the Creative Class. And How It's Transforming Work, Leisure, Community and Everyday Life*. Pluto Press Australia, Victoria.

Flyvbjerg, B. 2009. 'Survival of the unfittest: why the worst infrastructure gets built — and what we can do about it', *Oxford Review of Economic Policy* 25(3): 344–67.

Freebairn, J. 1995. 'Reconsidering the marginal welfare cost of taxation', *Economic Record* 71(213): 121–31.

Freeman, M., Groom, B., Panopoulou, E. & Pantelidis, T. 2013. *Declining Discount Rates and the Fisher Effect: Inflated Past, Discounted Future?* Centre for Climate Change Economics and Policy and Grantham Research Institute on Climate Change and the Environment.

Gabbitas, O. & Eldridge, D. 1998. *Directions for State Tax Reform*. Productivity Commission Staff Research Paper, AusInfo, Canberra, May.

Garnaut, R. 2008. *The Garnaut Climate Change Review: Final Report*. Cambridge University Press, Melbourne.

Giles, A. 2015. 'Territory Government explores new rail link'. Media release by the Chief Minister of the Northern Territory. 17 September.

Gittins, R. 2015. 'Economists save us from stupidity', *Canberra Times (Businessday/Opinion)*, 3 August, p. 10.

Goodwin, K. 2012. 'Use of Tablet Technology in the Classroom. Phase I: iPad Trial'. NSW Curriculum and Learning Innovation Centre. NSW Government. Education and Communities.

Government of Victoria. 2014. *Victorian Guide to Regulation. Toolkit 2: Cost-Benefit Analysis*. Department of Treasury and Finance, Melbourne.

Graham, D.J., Gibbons, S. & Martin, R. 2009. *Transport Investment and the Distance Decay of Agglomeration Benefits*. Imperial College, London. personal.lse.ac.uk/gibbons/Papers/Agglomeration%20and%20Distance%20Decay%20Jan%202009.pdf.

Gramlich, E.M. 1981. *Benefit-Cost Analysis of Government Programs*. Prentice-Hall, New Jersey.

Guria, J. 2010. 'Fix flawed values of statistical life and life years to get better policy outcomes', *Insight* 16.

Hanley, N. & Barbier, E.B. 2009. *Pricing Nature. Cost-Benefit Analysis and Environmental Policy*. Edward Elgar.

Harberger, A.C. 1976 (1972). *Project Evaluation. Collected Papers*. The Macmillan Press.

Harding, A., Quoc, N.V., Payne, A. & Percival, R. 2009. 'Trends in Effective Marginal Tax Rates in Australia from 1996–97 to 2006–07', *Economic Record* 85(271): 449–61.

Harrison, M. 2009. 'Assessing the impact of regulatory impact assessments', *Agenda* 16(3): 41–49.

———. 2010. *Valuing the Future: The Social Discount Rate in Cost-Benefit Analysis*. Visiting Researcher Paper. Productivity Commission, Canberra.

Hay, A., Meredith, K. & Vickerman, R. 2004. *The Impact of the Channel Tunnel on Kent and the Relationships with Nord-Pas de Calais*. Final Report to Eurotunnel and Kent County Council. University of Kent Centre for European Regional and Transport Economics, Canterbury.

Hayes, K. & Porter-Hudak, S. 1987. 'Deadweight loss: theoretical size relationships and the precision of measurement', *Journal of Business & Economic Statistics* 5(1): 47.

Hensher, D.A., Ellison, R. & Mulley, C. 2012. *Assessing the Wider Economy and Social Impacts of High Speed Rail in Australia. Report Prepared for the Australasian Railway Association*. Institute of Transport and Logistics Studies, University of Sydney.

HM Treasury. 2003. *The Green Book. Appraisal and Evaluation in Central Government.* The Stationery Office, London.

Howard, P. 2014. *Omitted Damages: What's Missing from the Social Cost of Carbon.* Joint project of the Environmental Defense Fund, the Institute for Policy Integrity, and the Natural Resources Defense Council.

Imber, D., Stevenson, G. & Wilks, L. 1991. *A Contingent Valuation Survey of the Kakadu Conservation Zone.* Research Paper 3. Resource Assessment Commission, Canberra.

Infrastructure Australia. 2013. *Reform and Investment Framework Templates for Use by Proponents.* Templates for Stage 7: Solution evaluation (transport infrastructure). Infrastructure Australia, Sydney.

Jaffe, A.B., Trajtenberg, M. & Henderson, R. 1993. 'Geographic localization of knowledge spillovers as evidenced by patent citations'. *Quarterly Journal of Economics* 108(3): 577–98.

Johnston, J. 2015. 'Is every regulation potentially cost-benefit justified? Methodological pluralism and the estimation of regulatory benefits', session 7 of the annual conference of the US Society for Benefit Cost Analysis, March 2015, Washington, DC. benefitcostanalysis.org/2015-conference-session-7.

Jones, T. 2010. 'Senator Stephen Conroy and Malcolm Turnbull debate the national Broadband Network in the Lateline studio', transcript, Australian Broadcasting Corporation.

Kernohan, D. & Rognlien, L. 2011. *Wider Economic Impacts of Transport Investments in New Zealand.* Research Report 448. New Zealand Transport Agency, Wellington.

Knight, F.H. 2009 (1921). *Risk, Uncertainty, and Profit.* Signalman Publishing, Orlando.

KPMG Econtech. 2010. *CGE Analysis of the Current Australian Tax System: Final Report.*

KPMG. 2012. *Long Run Economic and Land Use Impacts of Major Infrastructure Projects. Peer Review Report Prepared for Victorian Government Department of Transport.*

Krutilla, K. 2005. 'Using the Hicks–Kaldor tableau format for cost-benefit analysis and policy evaluation', *Journal of Policy Analysis and Management* 24(4): 864–75.

Kurukulasuriya, P. & Mendelsohn, R. 2008. 'Crop switching as a strategy for adapting to climate change', *African Journal of Agricultural and Resource Economics* 2(1):105–25.

Laird, J. & Mackie, P. 2010. *Review of Methodologies to Assess Transport's Impacts on the Size of the Economy*. Institute for Transport Studies, University of Leeds.

Lakoff, G. & Johnson, M. 2003. *Metaphors We Live by*. University of Chicago Press.

Leftwich, R.H. 1970. *The Price System and Resource Allocation*. 4th edn. Holt Rinehart & Winston, The Dryden Press.

Leung, J. 2013. *Alcohol Impairment Project: Lowering Blood Alcohol Concentration (BAC), Cost Benefit Analysis*. Safer Journeys strategy. New Zealand Ministry of Transport, Wellington.

Lewis, P., Daly, A. & Fleming, D. 2004. 'Why study economics? The private rate of return to an economics degree', *Economic Papers* 23(3): 234–43.

Lichfield, N., Kettle, P. & Whitbread, M. 1975. *Evaluation in the Planning Process*. Pergamon Press, Oxford.

Little, I.M.D. & Mirrlees, J.A. 1974. *Project Appraisal and Planning for Developing Countries*. Heinemann Educational Books, London.

Lodewijks, J. & Stokes, T. 2014. 'Is academic economics withering in Australia?', *Agenda — a Journal of Policy Analysis and Reform* 21(1): 69–88.

Ludwig, F., Milroy, S.P. & Asseng, S. 2009. 'Impacts of recent climate change on wheat production systems in Western Australia', *Climatic Change* 92(3): 495–517.

Luskin, D., Collins, P. & Ofei-Mensah, A. 1996. *Economic Effects of a Brisbane–Melbourne Inland Railway*. Working Paper 18. Bureau of Transport and Communications Economics, Canberra.

Luskin, D. & Dobes, L. 1999. *Facts and Furphies in Benefit-Cost Analysis: Transport*. Report 100. Bureau of Transport Economics, Canberra.

Mannix, B.F. 2013. 'Employment and human welfare: why does benefit-cost analysis seem blind to job impacts?', in *Does Regulation Kill Jobs?*, C. Coglianese, A.M Finkel & C. Carrigan (eds). University of Pennsylvania Press, Philadelphia.

Marchetti, C. 1994. 'Anthropological invariants in travel behavior'. *Technological Forecasting and Social Change* 47: 75–88.

Mare, D.C. & Graham, D.J. 2009. *Agglomeration Elasticities in New Zealand*. Motu Working Paper 09-06. Motu Economic and Public Policy Research, Wellington.

Maxwell, P. 2003. 'The rise and fall (?) of economics in Australian universities', *Economic Papers* 22(1): 79–92.

McKnight, A. 1982. *The Value of Travel Time Savings in Public Sector Evaluation*. Occasional Paper 51. Bureau of Transport Economics, Canberra.

Miller, P.W. 1985. 'Female labour supply in Australia: Another example of a backward-bending supply curve', *Economic Letters* 19: 287–90.

Miller, T.R. & Guria, J. 1991. *The Value of Statistical Life in New Zealand: Market Research on Road Safety*. Land Transport Division, Ministry of Transport, Wellington, NZ.

Millmow, A. 1995. 'The market for economists in Australia', *Economic Papers* 14(4): 83–96.

Milthorpe, F. 2007. *Consistency in Daily Travel Time — An Empirical Assessment from Sydney Travel Surveys*. 30th Australian Transport Research Forum.

Mishan, E.J. 1988. *Cost Benefit Analysis. An Informal Introduction*. 4th edn. Unwin Hyman, London.

Mishan, E.J. & Quah, E. 2007. *Cost-Benefit Analysis*. 5th edn. Routledge, UK.

Moore, D., Davies, P. & Ehrenberg-Coll, N. 2010. *Commonwealth Games 2018. Feasibility Cost-Benefit Analysis*. LECG, Wellington.

Moss, R., Babiker, M., Brinkman, S., Calvo, E., Carter, T., Edmonds, J., Elgizouli, I., Emori, E., Erda, L., Hibbard, K., Jones, R., Kainuma, M., Kelleher, J., Lamarque, J.F., Manning, M., Matthews, B., Meehl, J., Meyer, L., Mitchell, J., Nakicenovic, N., O'Neill, B., Pichs, R., Riahi, K., Rose, S., Runci, P., Stouffer, R., van Vuuren, D., Weyant, J., Wilbanks, T., van Ypersele, J.P., and Zurek, M. 2008. *Towards New Scenarios for Analysis of Emissions, Climate Change, Impacts, and Response Strategies. Technical Summary.* Intergovernmental Panel on Climate Change, Geneva.

Musgrave, R.A. & Musgrave, P.B. 1976. *Public Finance in Theory and Practice.* 2nd edn. McGraw-Hill Kogakusha Ltd.

Naude, C., Tsolakis, D. Tan, F. & Makwasha, T. 2014. *Social Cost of Road Crashes in Australia: The Case for Willingness to Pay (WTP) Values for Road Safety.* AP-R438-14. Austroads Research Report. Austroads Limited, Sydney.

New South Wales Government. 2013. *New South Wales Evaluation Framework.* Department of Premier and Cabinet, Sydney.

New South Wales Government Department of Infrastructure & Planning. 2012. *Guideline for the Use of Cost Benefit Analysis in Mining and Coal Seam Gas Proposals.* November. Sydney.

New South Wales Government Department of Premier and Cabinet. 2013. *Program Evaluation and Review*, C2013-08. Sydney.

New South Wales Treasury. 2007. *NSW Government Guidelines for Economic Appraisal.* Office of Financial Management Policy Guidelines Paper TPP07-5. The Treasury, Government of New South Wales, Sydney.

New Zealand Transport Agency. 2013. *Economic Evaluation Manual.* Government of New Zealand, Wellington.

New Zealand Treasury. 2005. *Cost Benefit Analysis Primer.* The Treasury, Wellington.

——. 2008, *Public Sector Discount Rates for Cost-Benefit Analysis.* New Zealand Treasury, Wellington.

——. 2015. *Guide to Social Cost Benefit Analysis.* New Zealand Government, Wellington.

Obama, B. 2011. 'Improving regulation and regulatory review. Executive order 13563 of January 18, 2011'. Federal Register, vol. 76, no. 14.

Organisation for Economic Cooperation and Development (OECD). 2007. Use of Discount Rate in the Estimation of Costs of Inaction with Respect to Selected Environmental Concerns. Working group report. Paris.

———. 2015, Incorporating Climate Effects in Transport Appraisal: Valuation of Carbon, Discounting, Risk and Uncertainty. Working group report.

Office of Best Practice Regulation (OBPR). 2014. *Cost-Benefit Analysis. Guidance Note*. Department of the Prime Minister and Cabinet, Canberra. www.dpmc.gov.au/sites/default/files/publications/006_Cost-benefit_analysis.pdf.

Office of the Australian Information Commissioner. 2014. 'Guidelines issued by the Australian Information Commissioner under s. 93A of the *Freedom of Information Act 1982*', Sydney.

O'Flaherty, B. 2005. *City Economics*. Harvard University Press.

Oldfield, S. 2012. 'Tool 4.3: rapid cost-benefit evaluation of climate change impacts and adaptation options', National Institute of Water and Atmospheric Research, www.niwa.co.nz/sites/niwa.co.nz/files/tool_4.3_rapid_cost-benefit_evaluation.pdf.

Pannell, D.J. 1997. 'Sensitivity analysis of normative economic models: theoretical framework and practical strategies', *Agricultural Economics* 16(2): 139–52.

Pearce, D.W., Atkinson, G. & Mourato, S. 2006. *Cost-Benefit Analysis and the Environment: Recent Developments*. OECD, Paris.

Pearce, D.W. & Nash, C.A. 1981. *The Social Appraisal of Projects. A Text in Cost-Benefit Analysis*. Macmillanm, UK.

Perkins, F. 1994. *Practical Cost-Benefit Analysis. Basic Concepts and Applications*. Macmillan, Melbourne.

Pew-MacArthur Results First Initiative. 2013. *States' Use of Cost-Benefit Analysis. Improving Results for Taxpayers*. The Pew Charitable Trusts.

Pigou, A.C. 2005 (1920). *The Economics of Welfare*. Vol. 1. Cosimo Classics, New York.

Pindyck, R.S. 2013. 'Climate change policy: what do the models tell us?', *Journal of Economic Literature* 51(3): 860–72.

Pollitt, C. 2010. 'Simply the best? The international benchmarking of reform and good governance', in *Comparative Administrative Change and Reform*, J. Pierre & P.W. Ingraham (eds). McGill-Queen's University Press, Montreal, pp. 91–112.

Portney, P.R & Weyant, J.P. (eds). 1999. *Discounting and Intergenerational Equity*. Resources for the Future, Washington, D.C.

Prest, A.R & Turvey, R. 1965. 'Cost-benefit analysis: A survey', *The Economic Journal* 75(300): 683–735.

Productivity Commission. 1999. *Australia's Gambling Industries*. Inquiry Report no. 10. Ausinfo, Canberra.

——. 2014. *Public Infrastructure*. 2 vols. Inquiry Report No. 71. Commonwealth of Australia, Melbourne.

Pusey, M. 1991. *Economic Rationalism in Canberra. A Nation Building State Changes Its Mind*. Cambridge University Press, Melbourne.

Queensland Government. 2014. *Program Evaluation Guidelines*. Queensland Treasury and Trade, Brisbane.

Queensland Treasury. 2015. *Project Assessment Framework. Cost-Benefit Analysis*. Queensland Government, Brisbane.

Ramsey, F.P. 1927. 'A contribution to the theory of taxation', *The Economic Journal* 37(1): 47–61.

——. 1928. 'A mathematical theory of saving', *Economic Journal* 38(152): 543–59.

Rattigan, A. 1986. *Industry Assistance: The Inside Story*. Melbourne University Press.

Read Sturgess & Associates. 2000. *Rapid Appraisal of the Economic Benefits and Ccosts of Nutrient Management*. Victorian Department of Natural Resources and Environment, Melbourne.

Resource Assessment Commission. 1992. *Multi-Criteria Analysis as a Resource Assessment Tool*. RAC Research Paper No. 6. Australian Government Publishing Service, Canberra.

Reuss, M. 1992. 'Coping with Uncertainty: Social Scientists, Engineers, and Federal Water Resources Planning', *Natural Resources Journal* 32 (Winter): 102–35.

Reynolds, Q., Lu, W. & Evill, B. 2000. *Brisbane–Melbourne Rail Link: Economic Analysis*. Working Paper 45. Bureau of Transport Economics, Canberra.

Riley, T. 1994. 'The decline of economics in schools', *Policy* 10(4): 43–47.

Rockliffe, N. 1996. 'How road projects affect industry logistics', in *Roads 96. Combined 18th ARRB Transport Research Conference and Transit New Zealand Land Transport Symposium*. Conference Proceedings Part 6: Environment and Economics. ARRB Transport Research Ltd, Victoria.

Rockliffe, N., Patrick, S. & Tsolakis, D. 2012. *Guide to Project Evaluation. Part 2: Project Evaluation Methodology*. Austroads Guide to Project Evaluation 2012 AGPE02-12. Austroads, Sydney.

Rolfe, J. 2006. 'A simple guide to choice modelling and benefit transfer', in *Choice Modelling and the Transfer of Environmental Values. New Horizons in Environmental Economics*, J. Rolfe & J. Bennett (eds). Edward Elgar, UK.

Rothstein, H.R., Sutton, A.J. & Borenstein, M. 2005. 'Publication bias in meta-analysis', in *Publication Bias in Meta-Analysis — Prevention, Assessment and Adjustments*, H.R. Rothstein, A.J. Sutton & M. Borenstein (eds). John Wiley & Sons, UK, pp. 1–7.

Rouwendal, J. 2012. 'Indirect effects in cost-benefit analysis'. *Journal of Benefit-Cost Analysis* 3(1): 25.

Saddler, H., Bennett, J., Reynolds, I. & Smith, B. 1980, *Public Choice in Tasmania: Aspects of the Lower Gordon River Hydro-electric Development Proposal*, Centre for Resource and Environmental Studies, The Australian National University, Canberra.

Sanderson, K., Goodchild, M., Nana, G. & Slack, A. 2007. *The Value of Statistical Life for Fire Regulatory Impact Statements.* New Zealand Fire Service Commission Research Report 79. Business and Economic Research Limited, Wellington.

Scarborough, H. & Bennett, J. 2008. 'Estimating intergenerational distribution preferences', *Ecological Economics* 66(4): 575–583.

Self, P. 1975. *Econocrats and the Policy Process: The Politics and Philosophy of Cost-Benefit Analysis.* Macmillan, London.

SGS Economics & Planning. 2007. *Springvale Level Crossing Grade Separation Project. Preliminary Cost Benefit Analysis.* City of Greater Dandenong, Melbourne.

———. 2012a. *Productivity and Agglomeration Benefits in Australian Capital Cities. Final Report to the COAG Reform Council.* SGS Economics and Planning Pty Ltd.

———. 2012b. *Long Run Economic and Land Use Impacts of Major Infrastructure Projects. Report Prepared for the Victorian Government Department of Transport.* Melbourne.

Shapiro, S. 2013. 'Reforming the regulatory process to consider employment and other macroeconomic factors', in *Does Regulation Kill Jobs?*, C. Coglianese, A.M. Finkel & C. Carrigan (eds). University of Pennsylvania Press.

Sinden, J.A. & Thampapillai, D.J. 1995. *Introduction to Benefit-Cost Analysis.* Longman, Melbourne.

Squire, L. & van der Tak, H.G. 1975. *Economic Analysis of Projects.* World Bank Research Publication. The Johns Hopkins University Press.

Standards Australia and Standards New Zealand. 2009. *Risk Management — Principles and Guidelines AS/NZS ISO 31000:2009.* Standards Australia, Sydney.

Starr, R.K., McQuin, P. & Vincenzi, L. 1984. *Evaluation of Standard Guage Rail Connections to Selected Ports.* Report. Bureau of Transport Economics. Canberra.

Sugden, R. & Williams, A. 1978. *The Principles of Practical Cost-Benefit Analysis*. Oxford University Press.

Tan, F., Lloyd, B. & Evans, C. 2012. *Guide to Project Evaluation. Part 4: Project Evaluation Data*. Austroads Ltd, Sydney.

The Economist. 1999. 'Deep discount', Economics Focus, 26 June.

——. 1999. 'Keeping all options open', Economics Focus, 14 August, p. 62.

——. 2014. 'Grand openings. Changes that will bring scientific discovery more freely into the public domain are happening. About time too', 27 September.

——. 2015. 'Shifting clout. Economists' academic rankings and media influence vary widely', 3 January.

——. 2015. 'Schumpeter. Shredding the rules', 2 May.

Transport for NSW. 2013. *Principles and Guidelines for Economic Appraisal of Transport Investment and Initiatives*. Government of New South Wales, Sydney.

The Treasury. 1978. *Flexibility, Economic Change and Growth. Treasury Submission to the Study Group on Structural Adjustment*. Treasury Economic Paper No. 3. Canberra.

Treager, C.P. 2014 'On option values in environmental and resource economics', *Resource and Energy Economics*, vol. 37: 242–252.

Treasury Board of Canada Secretariat. 1998. *Draft Benefit-Cost Analysis Guide*. Government of Canada. www.tbs-sct.gc.ca/fm-gf/tools-outils/guides/bca2-gaa-eng.asp.

Trigeorgis, L. 1996. *Real options. Managerial flexibility and strategy in resource allocation*, The MIT Press, Cambridge, MA.

Trumbull, W.N. 1990. 'Who has standing in cost-benefit analysis?', *Journal of Policy Analysis and Management* 9(2): 201–18.

Truss, W. 2014. 'Statement of expectations issued to Infrastructure Australia'. Media release WT227/2014, 6 November, by the Minister for Infrastructure and Regional Development, Canberra.

———. 2015. 'Canberra Airport Master Plan Approved'. Media release WT010/2014, 22 January, by the Minister for Infrastructure and Regional Development, Canberra.

Tsolakis, D., Harvey, M. & Miller, J. 1991. *The Future of the Tasmanian Railway System: A Cost-Benefit Assessment of Options*. Report 69. Bureau of Transport and Communications Economics, Australian Government Publishing Service, Canberra.

Tyers, R. 2014. *Service Oligopolies and Australia's Economy-Wide Performance*. Discussion Paper 14.18. Business School, University of Western Australia.

United States Government. 2013. *Technical Update of the Social Cost of Carbon for Regulatory Impact Analysis under Executive Order 12866*. November Interagency Working Group on Social Cost of Carbon.

van Wely, M. 2014. 'The good, the bad and the ugly: meta-analyses', *Human Reproduction* 29(8): 1622–26.

Veldhuizen, L.J.L., Tapsuwan, S. & Burton, M. 2011. 'Adapting to climate change: are people willing to pay or change?' Paper presented at the 19th International Congress and Modelling and Simulation conference, Perth.

Venables, A.J. 2007. 'Evaluating urban transport improvements'. *Journal of Transport Economics and Policy* 41(2): 173–88.

Vickerman, R. 2007a. 'Cost-benefit analysis and large-scale infrastructure projects: state of the art and challenges', *Environment and Planning B: Planning and Design* 34: 598–610.

———. 2007b. *Recent Evolution of Research into the Wider Economic Benefits of Transport Infrastructure Investments*. Discussion Paper 2007-9. Joint Transport Research Centre, University of Kent, Canterbury.

Vincent, K. 2007. 'Uncertainty in adaptive capacity and the importance of scale', *Global Environmental Change* 17:12 24.

Washington State Institute for Public Policy (WSIPP). 2014. *Benefit-Cost Technical Documentation. Washington State Institute for Public Policy Benefit-Cost Model*. Olympia, WA.

Webb, G.R. & McMaster, J.C. (eds). 1975. *Australian Transport Economics. A Reader.* Australia and New Zealand Book Company, Sydney.

Western Australian Program Evaluation Unit. 2015. *Program Evaluation. Evaluation Guide.* Department of Treasury, Government of Western Australia, Perth.

White, B., Doole, G.J., Pannell, D.J. & Florec, V. 2012. 'Optimal environmental policy design for mine rehabilitation and pollutin with a risk of non-compliance owing to firm insolvency', *Australian Journal of Agricultural and Resource Economics* 56(2): 280–301.

Whittington, D. & MacRae, D. 1986. 'The issue of standing in cost-benefit analysis', *Journal of Policy Analysis and Management* 5(4): 665–82.

———. 1990. 'Comment: judgments about who has standing in cost-benefit analysis', *Journal of Policy Analysis and Management* 9(4): 536–47.

Willis, R. 1989. *Implementation of GBE Reforms and Telecommunications Pricing. Statement by the Hon Ralph Willis, MP, Minister for Transport and Communications, 1 June 1989.* Australian Government Publishing Service, Canberra.

Worsley, T. 2011. *The Evolution of London's Crossrail Scheme and the Development of the Department for Transport's Economic Appraisal Methods.* Discussion Paper 2011-27. Institute for Transport Studies, University of Leeds.

Zahavi, Y. 1979. *The 'UMOT' Project.* Prepared for U.S. Department of Transportation and Ministry of Transport, Federal Republic of Germany. www.surveyarchive.org/Zahavi/UMOT_79.pdf.

Zerbe, R.O. 1991. 'Comment: does benefit cost analysis stand alone? Rights and standing', *Journal of Policy Analysis and Management* 10(1): 96–105.

Zhuang, J., Liang, Z., Lin, T. & De Guzman, F. 2007. *Theory and Practice in the Choice of Social Discount Rate for Cost-Benefit Analysis: A Survey.* ERD Working Paper 94. Asian Development Bank, Manila.